# THE STORY OF AFRICA

## BASIL DAVIDSON

## MITCHELL BEAZLEY

Based on the Television Series, AFRICA,
a MITCHELL BEAZLEY TELEVISION – RM ARTS – CHANNEL FOUR TELEVISION
co-production in association with the Nigerian Television Authority

# *Credits*

The Story of AFRICA

**Editor**
James Hughes

**Assistant Editors**
Linda Gamlin
Elizabeth Pichon

**Designer**
Stephen Bull

**Picture Research**
Diana Korchien

**Production**
Peter Phillips

*The Story of Africa* was edited and designed by
Mitchell Beazley International Limited,
Mill House,
87–89 Shaftesbury Avenue,
London W1V 7AD.

ISBN 0 85533 514 9

Typeset by Servis Filmsetting Ltd
Reproduction by Chelmer Litho Reproductions
Printed in the Netherlands by
Royal Smeets Offset B.V., Weert

**The television series AFRICA is a**
**Mitchell Beazley Television – RM Arts –**
**Channel Four Television co-production**
in association with the Nigerian
Television Authority

The television series AFRICA

**Written and presented by**
Basil Davidson

**Executive Producer**
Mick Csaky

**Series Producer**
John Percival

**Series Consultant**
Christopher Ralling

**Directors**
John Percival
Christopher Ralling
Andrew Harries
Mick Csaky

**Production Team**
Gina Hobson
Karla Ehrlich
Julia Richards
Louella Hamer

**Graphics and Animation**
David Raitt
Jim Gibson
Ken Morse

**Picture Research**
Olivia Maxwell

**Research**
Jenny Thompson

**Film Editors**
Graham Shipham
Martin Walsh

**Sound**
Neil Kingsbury

**Photography**
Ivan Strasburg

# Contents

# Foreword

Books are written in solitude but made in companionship, especially if they are books about living history. Thirty-five years of African companionship have gone into the making of this book, years rich in friendship and fruitful in learning, sometimes tough and exacting in their demands on toil and travel, but always leading to memorable destinations and discoveries.

This book is designed as a general guide to everyone who may want to share in these discoveries. Even so, it has been a special case among the books that I have written about the African peoples and their history. This is because I also conceived it as a companion volume to the splendid television series created by Mitchell Beazley Television and RM Arts for Britain's Channel 4 and other national television networks. So it has a history of its own. Many shared in that, for we travelled some 50,000 miles in Africa in order to build our television programmes, forged our way to many far-out places, and found African spokesmen and friends of many vocations: from presidents and professors to peasants and fisherfolk and freedom fighters, from kings to co-operative farmers, and many more besides.

I want to thank them all: our companions of the Nigerian Television Authority; Mick Csaky, executive producer and director; John Percival, producer and director; Christopher Ralling, director and series consultant; director, Andrew Harries; Ivan Strasburg, the chief cameraman; and all the other men and women who combined to make the programmes a success.

These programmes will take their place in the history of Africa. For they have opened new and wide windows on the subject, never available before. I hope that this book, in its different way, may be as useful and enjoyable.

Basil Davidson. 1984

# Chapter 1

# Myths and realities

Africa is a continent but also, in a sense, an island, an enormous landmass linked to western Asia only by a slender neck of land. And yet Africa is as diverse in its climate and vegetation, in its animal and human life, as it is tremendous in size. Countless varieties of natural forms have developed in its plains and hills, its rivers, lakes and inland seas, its shadowed forests and its sunlit spaces.

Mankind was born in Africa, some two million years ago, and overcame there, one by one, the most fundamental problems of survival and growth. It was in Africa that the earliest types of man, the *Homo* genus, evolved and became, through unimaginable millennia, the ancestors of ourselves. Spreading slowly into every habitable region, mankind in Africa has matched the continent's diversities of environment with as many human adaptations. More than a thousand languages are spoken in Africa, and there are as many complex social systems of custom, habit and community life.

Is it reasonable to think of Africa as a single entity of our geophysical world, or of Africans as a single branch of the human species? Oddly enough, it seems that this is what we do, and have always done. Or not so oddly: for Africa is also a continent on its own, placed somehow apart ever since anyone set out to explore and explain it, a tantalizing mystery appearing to belong entirely to itself, and one seemingly without beginning or end.

This seems to be the general consensus among those who have loved Africa, and also among those who have hated the continent (yet often returned to it). Among Africa's admirers, the English princess Marie Louise wrote some 70 years ago: "It is a marvellous country. What is its spell? It lays its hands upon you, and, having once felt its compelling touch, you never can forget it."

And that has been my own experience through more than 30 years of African wanderings and African study: even though there have been times, and not so few, when the whispering sting of ants, mosquitoes or other pests, the blasting breath of lowland heat or the knife-edge chill of the hills at night, not to mention other tribulations, have made me most devoutly wish that I were somewhere else.

It may be, of course, that Marie Louise was a great romantic. But perhaps not, for I myself am no romantic but a questioning wayfarer on the roads of history, of Africa's history, and I think that she was right. There is a large truth in saying that the experience of Africa, and of Africa's peoples, is unique and irreplaceable.

## King Solomon's Mines
Almost ghostly as you approach them through the bush, the walls of Great Zimbabwe remain a challenge to the imagination. They represent the greatest

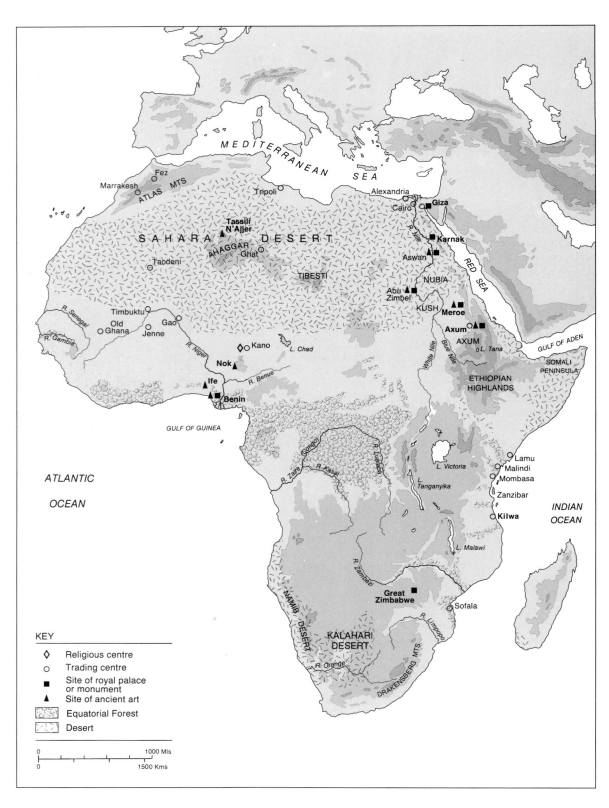

KEY

◇ Religious centre
○ Trading centre
■ Site of royal palace or monument
▲ Site of ancient art
▨ Equatorial Forest
▨ Desert

0 _____ 1000 Mls

0 _____ 1500 Kms

stone structures built in Africa, south of the Equator, before modern times.

Trekking north from the Limpopo river, through country then unknown to Europeans, a youthful German geologist called Carl Mauch was the first to report on them. They marked, he thought, the legendary land of Ophir whence was taken, some thousands of years earlier, the sandalwood for the temple of King Solomon of Israel. Mauch's report was made in 1871. Others followed, and the legend multiplied, being fed and fired by the belief – and to some extent the fact – that treasures of gold were to be found in this country north of the Limpopo. Europeans said that this was the land of King Solomon's mines, or the country of the Queen of Sheba, or the outposts of Phoenician enterprise, or else an ancient colony of some other distant people from beyond the seas. What Great Zimbabwe was *not*, they all agreed, was a product of Africa itself. But we now know that this indeed is what it was: the seat and centre of an African civilization, formed and developed in the country where its walls still stand.

The case of Great Zimbabwe has been a general one. Wherever remarkable things of the past have been found in this continent, Europeans have greatly wished to believe that Africans did not make them, and indeed could not have made them. Africans, it was held by our grandparents and great-grandparents, are nature's children who have invented nothing and developed nothing, and indeed possess no history of their own. Evidence to the contrary, so they believed, must necessarily point to intrusions from outside.

In 1910 Leo Frobenius, a leading European student of Africa and a man of

*The ruins of Great Zimbabwe (left), featuring the so-called Elliptical Building and the solid-masonry Conical Tower, bewildered 19thC Europeans by their size and complexity. Unable to accept the fact that Great Zimbabwe was the work of a 11thC–14thC local African culture, they designated it as the country of the Queen of Sheba. The Elliptical Building kindled romantic fantasies in western minds, as in a Rhodesian Government poster (above) of 1938.*

*A map of Africa, (opposite) shows some of the important prehistoric and pre-colonial civilizations that flourished before the coming of the whites.*

unquestioned erudition, visited Nigeria – though it had still to be given that name as a British colony – and briefly sojourned in the ancient Yoruba city of Ile-Ife. There he managed to acquire seven sculptures in terracotta. They were remarkable for their superb artistic merit, but also because they were lifelike representations of human faces and, in this respect, quite unlike other African carvings. Frobenius took his terracottas back to Europe, where he assured a wide audience that they were the products of a long lost Greek colony on the distant shores of western Africa, or even, possibly, the echoes of the legendary continent of Atlantis.

Frobenius was right off the track of truth, but right inside the style of his times. Yet another case of European refusal to credit African achievement comes from the Somali lands of northeastern Africa. Here, between 1900 and 1920, the Somali leader Muhamad Abdille Hasan carried on a fierce and long resistance to colonial invasion by Britain, Italy and Ethiopia. In 1913, as part of his campaign to form an independent Somali state, Muhamad Hasan brought stonemasons from southern Arabia to build him a series of defensive forts. The strongest of these, a very imposing affair whose ruins still survive, was duly constructed at Tale in what was then, formally at least, British Somaliland. The British found Muhamad Hasan a hard man to beat, and with a reluctant admiration called him the "Mad Mullah" because of his stubborn courage and his habit of writing them letters of scathing irony. They succeeded in defeating him only in 1920, when they sent the Royal Air Force to bomb Tale and other forts.

Photographs of Tale fortress then began to circulate in London, whereupon a learned commentator, writing in a well-known illustrated weekly paper, addressed himself to the problem of Tale's origin: "One feels that the Mullah and his barbarous followers could never have erected such imposing works. In all probability they entrenched themselves among the ruins of a mighty past." For the ramparts of Tale, he went on to speculate, resembled the great Pharaonic forts of the Twelfth Dynasty in Egypt, built soon after 2000BC. But Tale fort, in plain fact, had been built exactly eight years earlier.

## A vast misunderstanding

So legends of this kind multiplied, and, acquiring gritty substance by the sheer passage of the years, they have somehow stuck to Africa's reputation in Europe and America. Essentially, these legends have become the underpinning of the attitudes of modern racism: of the belief that black people are inherently and naturally inferior to white people.

That belief was well established by the 1870s, when Mauch and others hastened to ascribe Great Zimbabwe to the Queen of Sheba, and still just as secure 40 years later, when Frobenius gave unknown Greeks the merit for Ife's sculptured royal heads. European explorers, heralding the high age of imperialism, had greatly fortified it. Returning from travels in the far interior, they assured their audiences back in Europe that Africa's peoples were still living in the dawn of time, and were incapable of progressing on their own.

Captain Richard Burton, one of the most admired of these explorers, wrote the following in 1860, after reaching the shores of Lake Tanganyika:

> The study of the Negro is the study of Man's rudimental mind. He would rather appear a degeneracy from the civilized man than a savage rising to the first step, were it not for his total incapacity for improvement. He seems to belong to one of those childish races which, never rising to Man's estate, fall like worn out links from the great chain of animated nature.

Such ideas were understandably convenient in a period when Europeans were beginning to think – as many were by the 1860s – that Africa was going to be

*The 12thC–14thC head (opposite) of an oni (king) of Ife illustrates the artistic skill and remarkable realism of the ancient Yoruba craftsmen of West Africa. A terracotta head (above) of Olokun, Yoruba god of the sea and wealth, was bought in 1910 by the German ethnographer Frobenius, who thought it was probably the work of Greek colonists.*

their oyster. For if it was wrong to invade and dispossess your equals, it might be morally right to invade and dispossess your natural inferiors, for their benefit as well as for your own. It is easy for us, nowadays, to see this as a vast misunderstanding, or worse, but in those days the misunderstanding had its cultural ancestry.

This ancestry came, partly, from the pseudo-science of that time. Serious men and women were led to believe that humanity was unavoidably ranked in hierarchies one above the other, by scientific if not divine law. The whites were at the top and the blacks at the bottom; and, as it again conveniently appeared, the English and their northern European neighbours were to be found at the top of the highest rank. Popular conceptions regarding the theory of evolution could seem to support this; but so could the arrangement of British society. That too was divided into ranks and hierarchies held to be right and natural, with the capital-owning classes at the top and the newly industrialized proletariat of towns and workshops at the bottom.

But this misunderstanding had a somewhat longer ancestry than this. It derived especially from the Western culture of slavery and the slave trade, a culture that knew black people, for the most part, only as the degraded objects of captive labour: a culture, besides, which required for the "good of society" that black people should remain enslaved. Even so enlightened a man as the Scottish philosopher David Hume, writing in the middle of the eighteenth century, stated:

> [He was] apt to suspect the Negroes to be naturally inferior to the Whites. There scarcely ever was a civilised nation of that complexion, nor even any individual, eminent either in action or speculation. No ingenious manufactures among them, no arts, no sciences . . .

*The Somali patriot Muhamad Hasan, whom the British called the "Mad Mullah" for withstanding their colonial invasion from 1900 to 1920, constructed defensive fortresses that were afterwards believed in Europe to have been the work of ancient Egyptians.*

Others soon went beyond merely being "apt to suspect" a natural black inferiority. Like Hume, the renowned German philosopher Georg Wilhelm Hegel had never set foot in Africa nor, in all likelihood, even set eyes upon an African who was not in some sort of servile condition. Yet in 1831, delivering a series of lectures which rapidly became famous, he felt able to affirm without the shadow of a doubt that the Negro

> . . . exhibits the natural man in his completely wild and untamed state. There is nothing harmonious with humanity in this type of character. At this point we quit Africa, not to mention it again; for Africa is no historical part of the world. What we properly understand by Africa is the unhistorical, undeveloped spirit, still involved in the conditions of mere nature.

It would be easy to multiply such examples. They were the common refrain of European or American thought; and those who struck a different note had little influence, or none at all. Above all, they marched in step with the bustling self-confidence of industrial and mechanical power that seemed the kindly gift of destiny to the peoples who were white, or, at least, to the "better classes" among them. For wasn't this Britain's century, and wasn't Britain the "workshop of the world", shaped and destined to lead the lesser ranks of mankind?

Thackeray gave voice to the reigning mood in his "May Day Ode" of 1851:

*Look yonder where the engines toil:*
*These England's arms of conquest are,*
*The trophies of her bloodless war:*
*    Brave weapons these.*
*Victorious over wave and soil,*
*With these she sails, she weaves, she tills,*
*Pierces the everlasting hills,*
*    And spans the seas.*

The boast was a proud one, even if the bloodless wars, soon enough, gave way to something else. Meanwhile other Europeans might complain at God's dispensation in favouring the English, but they quickly hastened to claim their share in it, and, in sharing it, to absorb the same attitudes of racist hierarchy. What we should now call the racism of nineteenth-century England, the parent of modern racism, became the racism of the rest of the industrialized world: nourished by the same old servitudes, inflamed by the same new ambitions, confirmed by the same ignorance of the "rudimental Negro" and his kind.

### New discoveries

All that, perhaps, is over and done with. Even if the past is also our own country, we have learned to understand it better, and therefore differently. All the same, racism stubbornly remains. Why is that? In this book we are going on a journey of historical discovery, and there will be surprises along the way. Not least, I believe, we shall find some useful answers to this question about racism. We shall find, above all, that racism is a rather new sickness.

Stamped into our cultures by the slave trade, by the hierarchical notions of the nineteenth century and the imperialism of the long colonial period, the prejudice of racism barely existed before the middle decades of the seventeenth century, and scarcely at all in the Middle Ages. Strange ideas about distant peoples, including black peoples, certainly existed then and for long before, no doubt from the beginning of human time. There were always remote peoples "whose heads do grow beneath their shoulders", or whose single eye was implanted in the breast, or whose women delivered five babies at a birth, or whose daily habits were more or less deplorable.

In my own home town of Hereford in western England there stands the great cathedral which Norman bishops began to build in 1106, and here is preserved a rare map of the world composed by a cathedral cleric in 1290. That learned man – and he was very learned for his time and place – drew into his map the beings who were said to live in various regions of a flat earth. What strikes you about his pictures is that the farther they are from home, the more peculiar the creatures become until, very far away, they were not even remotely human.

But none of that had anything to do with racism. The capering oddities of the Hereford Map are only the stay-at-home's stereotyped ideas about unknown beings who inhabit unknown lands. Broadly speaking – and indeed in all cultures – a general rule seems to have governed this making of stereotypes: human deviancy from an accepted norm grows with distance.

Other beliefs could influence that one. In the matter of medieval European attitudes to black people, their outlook could be prejudiced by primeval superstitions connecting blackness with misfortune or (what usually came to the same thing) with witchcraft. The devil, for example, was often imagined in northern Europe as black. How far such attributions were actually made in practice is much less clear. But they belonged, in any case, to a provincial world in which a journey of 100 miles from home, let alone one of a thousand or so, could be expected to take you into very strange company.

Nowadays it is not like that, or not often; we have a different view of deviancy, one that sees it aggravated by social rather than geographical distance. In going on this journey of historical discovery, moreover, we possess advantages never available to previous generations. Thanks to the labour of many hands and scholarly disciplines, the last 30–40 years have taken knowledge deeply along the hidden trails of Africa's development since remote times. We know much more about all that today than was ever known before. If the nineteenth century uncovered the geography of Africa, our own has performed a comparable exploratory task for the continent's history, and in

*A detail from the 13thC World Map in Hereford Cathedral depicts one of the creatures that medieval Europeans believed to inhabit lands beyond the Nile. Deviancy from the norm apparently increases with distance.*

*Captain Richard Burton, the famous 19thC explorer, helped lay the groundwork for modern racist attitudes towards Africans. "The study of the Negro," he wrote, " is the study of Man's rudimental mind."*

still more copious detail. Dispelling myths, this exploration of Africa's past may be numbered among the truly liberating advances of our time.

The white peoples of the industrialized world have long accepted the contribution of peoples from other continents to the growth of civilization. The Chinese and the Indians, we know, created cultures of towering strength and wisdom. America's indigenous peoples raised impressive cities. But Africa has seemed to have no positive part in the human record. Africa, for whatever reasons, has been left out.

Those reasons were in fact based neither in sense or science. So there are two themes in these chapters. One is the unfolding story of Africa's human development, and the other is the changing way in which white peoples have regarded black peoples from ancient times until the present. Both themes invite a journey of discovery. We can begin it with the Greeks of antiquity, and with the Africans they knew and wrote about. It is, for several reasons, a good place to start.

# Chapter 2

# Different but equal

From about 500BC onwards, the Greeks of antiquity not only travelled very widely, but also asked innumerable questions wherever they went and then published what they had learned and believed to be true. None of them did this half so well as Herodotus of Halicarnassus in Asia Minor, a most inquiring Greek historian who, luckily for us, travelled much in Egypt soon after 450BC. His book of study and research is a mine of African information.

The Greeks for whom Herodotus wrote possessed their own ideas about deviancy from the human norm, and how it increased with distance. Applying these ideas to Asia, which they scarcely knew, they came up with the following picture. Going east from Asia Minor, you reached at first a people called the Issedones. These were thought to be pretty much like the Greeks, that is, normal. But beyond the Issedones, Herodotus reminded his readers, "there live the one-eyed Arimaspians", clearly a lot less normal, "and beyond them the griffins who guard the gold", who were not really human at all. The further you went into Asia from the homeland of the Greeks, in short, the less satisfactory did humanity become. The medieval map-maker of Hereford Cathedral would have thoroughly agreed.

But the Greeks had quite different notions about their neighbours across the Mediterranean sea. They trafficked much with Libya and Egypt, since they had trading colonies there. They knew the Egyptians at first hand, and were bound to admire them. For those Egyptians, although their mighty civilization was then well past its peak, were still the leaders of the world in terms of civic order and scientific advance. Built 2,000 years before the Parthenon of Athens, the Pyramids of Gizeh were not only the largest stone buildings ever constructed anywhere; they were also, by their astonishing symmetry, monuments to a mathematical science which the Greeks were only beginning to master.

To the Greeks, moreover, the Egypt of the Pharaohs was the threshold across which innumerable marvels could be glimpsed. Here was the source of spiritual wisdom, because "the names of nearly all the gods", as Herodotus commented to readers who could have found nothing strange about the statement, "came to Greece from Egypt." Yet if Egypt was the source of spiritual wisdom for the Greeks, it was not the origin of that wisdom. This lay farther south.

It lay in lands of the African interior which the Greeks did not know, where dwelt "the long-lived black peoples" who "are said to be the tallest and best-looking people in the world". Here, in other words, deviancy from the norm did not grow with distance. On the contrary, because of the belief in Africa's spiritual primacy, it lessened with distance. Those who read Herodotus would have known this already. Homer's *Iliad* had long prepared them for the information with its tale of how the gods of Greece went every year to "the

# Different but equal

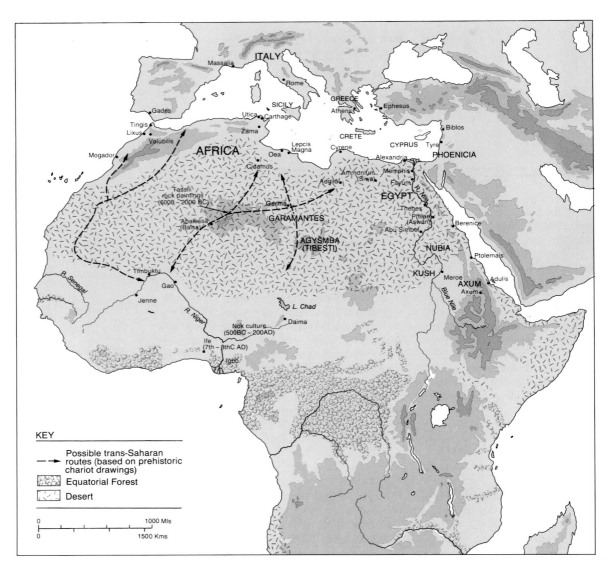

*Africa in classical times. The ancient Greeks and Romans regarded the "Ethiopians" or Black Africans with a respect unaffected by distance, seeing them as "the first of all men" and the founders of the Egyptian civilization.*

Ethiopians" (which we should properly translate as "the black peoples") for an all-god banquet:

*For Zeus had yesterday to Ocean's bounds*
*Set forth to feast with Ethiop's faultless men,*
*And he was followed there by all the gods.*

What was wisest and most ancient came out of Africa. That was the general belief, and it marked the general attitude of the ancient Greeks, the endlessly inquisitive founders of our own civilization. And they set forth this attitude in their many works of art displaying African motifs. Nothing shows it better than a type of two-headed vase, known as *kantheros*, of which several fine examples have survived. For the Greeks of antiquity, the black peoples were different from themselves, but equal to themselves or even, at times, superior.

Herodotus called Egypt "the gift of the Nile", a bountiful land made

20

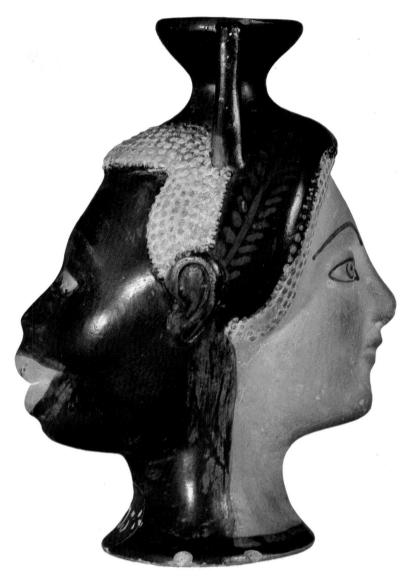

*An ancient Greek* kantheros, *or two-headed vase, shows white and black juxtaposed. For the Greeks, Africans were people of equal if not superior stature to themselves.*

available to man by the flood-laid silt of the famous river, building up its soil year after year. He and his readers also saw the Egyptians as being absolutely African in origin and nature. Here along the Nile, Egyptians had fashioned the highest civilization anywhere, and this civilization, for the Greeks, was African. In support of this they proceeded to add historical explanations to the mythology of the *Iliad*, and some of their explanations reveal an extraordinary prescience.

Writing in about 50BC, the Sicilian Greek historian Diodorus summarized the specialist views of his time. By then the Ptolemies, kings of Greek origin, had been ruling Egypt for almost three centuries, and Greek knowledge of that region of Africa was correspondingly capacious. The black peoples, wrote Diodorus, "were the first of all men, and the proofs of this statement, historians agree, are manifest."

He recorded another agreement among historians. This was that "the Egyptians are colonists sent out by the Ethiopians [the black peoples of the

African interior] and the most part of Egyptian customs are Ethiopian, with the colonists still preserving their ancient manners." Manners and beliefs, that is, concerning the divine appointment of kings, life after death, the value of consulting oracles, or, in more humdrum terms, the customs of everyday life.

Later European attitudes lifted the Egypt of the Pharaohs entirely out of African history, and either added it to the history of western Asia or assigned it to a mysterious isolation. Diodorus and his colleagues, as we have seen, thought just the reverse, and modern science, notably over the past 30 years or so, has gone far to show that Diodorus was right.

### The green Sahara

Far into the middle of the Sahara Desert, a weary southward trail from the shining coastlands of Algeria, bare tides of sand and grit roll to the foot of stark and barren hills. Seen from the air, these rocklands of the Tassili make a landscape of fantastic crags and crumpled gullies. Seen from the ground, they are a sterile wilderness of stone. Nothing of any account lives here; nothing, for countless centuries, ever has.

Late in the 1950s a team of French scientists, led by the Saharan veteran Henri Lhote, made their difficult way into the Tassili. They were looking for evidence of remote human settlement in the time, over 5,000 years ago, when the Sahara was not a desert but a land of flowing rivers and green pastures. They found this evidence, and what they found – an unmatched gallery of superb Stone Age art – added far more than a footnote to the tale of our recovery of Africa's lost history. For the engravings of the Tassili are of a range and splendour all the more remarkable for including scenes of mankind as well as scenes of game and cattle, gods and spirits.

Most of the Tassili pictures are around 6,000 years old or rather less, and what they show confirms the known history of climatic change. The vast Saharan regions began to lose their regular rains, and dry up into desert, after about 2500BC. Here in the Tassili we can see portrayals of the people and animals who flourished there before desiccation set in.

Recent archaeology has filled in some of the background to the Tassili pictures. Here in these wide wadis, marking long dry watercourses and infinitely bleak today, small communities of Stone Age people were making hand-built pottery some time before 5000BC – earlier than any pottery was made in the valley of the Nile. In other words, there were human communities here, developing early forms of settlement and food production. They lived beside broad rivers, and this surprisingly early pottery is found together with fishing tools such as fine harpoons of bone, which indicate a waterside culture with substantial reliance on fishing.

After about 4000BC the Saharan climate became less wet and the rivers fell. The Saharan peoples turned increasingly to the herding of cattle and lesser livestock, while, at the same time, their neighbouring communities in the valley of the Nile, profiting from its high fertility, began to grow cereals.

Much remains to be clarified in a complex story. Yet the balance of evidence, refuting earlier opinions, shows firmly that the earliest Nile Valley communities came originally from the south-west and west. They came, that is, out of the green Sahara. With them they brought their beliefs and technologies, languages, customs and capacity for further development. These wanderers from inner Africa found "the gift of the Nile", and the land of Egypt was born.

This slow infiltration from the Saharan lands provided the principal origins of Egyptian civilization: the "colonists" from the far interior of whom Diodorus the Sicilian wrote 2,000 years ago. And in this great truth we can perhaps now glimpse the beginnings and the spread of that "common fund" of

*Ancient Egyptian veneration for the python, here seen in a painting from the Valley of the Kings (c. 1500BC), is reflected in the cults of African peoples in many parts of the continent. This has suggested a common origin.*

ideas and beliefs, or, as Diodorus put it, of the "manners" of the black peoples, that has seemed most puzzlingly to underlie nearly all the traditional cultures of the continent.

Why should peoples as far apart as the Nile valley and western Africa award magical powers to the python? How could it come about that so many beliefs about the nature of the world's creation, and of the powers of the spirit, should be markedly similar in communities that have apparently known nothing of each other? Or to take a familiar everyday object, what caused wooden head-rest pillows to occur in the far south and north of the continent, as well as in ancient Egypt?

Answers to such questions may well take us back to the great cultural cradle of the Saharan plains, during their many green centuries of long ago. Most of these ancient Saharan peoples, as desiccation set in, were obliged to move elsewhere, carrying their customs and beliefs with them. Some moved eastward into the valley of the Nile, others moved southward into the better-watered grasslands and forests of West Africa; others, again, went north to the fertile shores of the Mediterranean. A few remained to face the encroaching desert, and, like their nomad descendants of today, to forge a way of living in that harshly arid environment.

### The earliest kings

Another point that strikes one about the Tassili pictures is their peacefulness: nobody seems to be hitting anybody, much less killing anybody. Settlement and civilization soon changed that. A small food surplus every year, possible in the Nile valley even with slender technical and organizational means, could gradually build into an accumulation sufficient to support persons who were not food-producers: tool-makers, weavers, priests, law-givers and later law-enforcers who became kings. The history of a labour-divided and power-divided society began. The compensations in more food and comfort were large and many, but so were the consequences in competitive violence. Such problems have remained with us.

Egypt embarked on that necessary but painful and problematic road soon after 3400BC. Two kingdoms had taken shape, one in the delta of the Nile and

# Different but equal

*The barren waste of the Tassili plateau in the Sahara Desert (above) was a fertile country until 5,000 years ago, populated by a number of different cultures. These people recorded their activities and beliefs in a number of graphic and brilliantly coloured rock paintings, before the drying up of the Sahara drove them south and east.*

the other upstream. They warred with each other until the red crown of Upper Egypt had overcome the white crown of the Delta kingdom, and the two powers were joined in a single state around 3200BC. Upon those firm foundations a civilization of unexampled majesty and magnificence then took its rise, and would endure for 3,000 years.

But was this invention of kingship peculiar to northern Egypt? So it has been generally supposed. Those early kings were thought to have drawn their power from control of Nile-side irrigation and a corresponding accumulation of wealth. It has been assumed that both control and wealth came into the hands of a ruling group or class which was then able to boost its power by religious supports and beliefs. These beliefs included "divine kingship", that is, a kingship empowered by God and even identified with God. The great monuments of Pharaonic Egypt are indeed there to show that this is more or less what happened.

But the question still remains as to where the initial move towards kingdoms and kingships occurred. Europeans have commonly supposed that it took place in the Middle East and spread from there into northern Egypt, or else that it was largely an Egyptian invention. Either way, this early Egyptian development did not appear to owe anything of importance to inner Africa, and the "divine kingship" model was supposedly diffused from Egypt into the rest of Africa. Pharaonic Egypt, in other words, could not properly be regarded as an African civilization.

But archaeological exploration of this part of Africa, which seems never to run out of surprises, has uncovered evidence suggesting a different view. The building of the High Dam at Aswan far up the Nile in the 1960s meant that the

*Paintings of horned cattle (opposite), probably dating to before 3,000BC, illustrate the existence of a pastoral society, while the so-called "Monster of Sefar" (above), superimposed on earlier depictions of local wildlife, probably has religious significance.*

upstream lake so formed was going to cover many miles of the Nile valley known to be rich in unexcavated sites. Working in unavoidable haste, teams of archaeologists set out to discover as much as possible before the waters rose to cover those sites for ever.

Furiously pushed for time though they were, the archaeologists made some remarkable discoveries, including one which casts a most interesting light on early kingship. The site for this was an apparently unimportant cemetery near a place called Qustul in ancient Nubia, not far south of the present frontier between Egypt and the Republic of Sudan. The luck of the draw gave this location to the Oriental Institute of the University of Chicago and it looked at first a disappointing one for that prestigious home of Egyptologists. But fortunately the team director, the late Keith Seele, was determined to persevere. What came out of that ancient cemetery seems likely to make history, although Seele himself, sadly, died before the dimensions of the Qustul discoveries could be assessed.

The assessment took time. Quantities of pot fragments and artifacts had to be examined and compared. But when the results began to be published, years later, by Bruce Williams of the Chicago Institute, they promised to overturn all previous assumptions about the purely northern origins of Pharaonic kingship. For here was strong evidence for a succession of 12 kings who had ruled in Nubia – in Ta-Seti, the "Land of the Bow", as it was called then – long before the rise of the first historic Egyptian dynasty. Here was highly recognizable "divine kingship" and a correspondingly advanced political organization, established in the distant south, several generations before it was clearly fashioned in the north.

To summarize these findings about the inner African origins of Pharaonic civilization: the earliest population movements into the valley of the Nile were predominantly from the south and west; the earliest state-forming influence moved in the same direction – not from the north to the south, but the reverse; in modern terms, the Egypt of the Pharaohs was first and foremost the product of black initiative and progress.

### Egypt of the Pharaohs

Once launched, Egypt's speed of development was amazingly rapid. There is no need to go far in Egypt for the evidence of that. Only some seven centuries after the emergence of the Kingdom of the Double Crown, there was enough power and wealth, as well as enough skill and scientific understanding, to build the great Pyramid of Cheops, quickly followed by the almost as imposing Pyramids of Chephren and Mycerinus.

Stand at the foot of the Cheops Pyramid today, and it is still immense, even in terms of the largest modern buildings. It is so enormous that London's Houses of Parliament and St Paul's Cathedral could find space to stand within

*Finds from Qustul in Nubia (below and opposite) have pointed to the existence of a powerful inner African kingdom several generations before the rise of the earliest Egyptian kings. Archaeologists suggest that key aspects of this African civilization were inherited by ancient Egypt, including the notion of sacred kingship. The view of classical Greek historians that much of the ancient Egyptian civilization had an inner-Africa origin thus finds new support*

*Saved from drowning beneath Lake Nasser, created by the Aswan High Dam, giant heads from the temple of Abu Simbel are lifted to safety during the international salvage operation of 1965.*

the area of its base, and still leave room to move around in. Briefly raiding into Egypt in 1799, the French emperor Napoleon ordered his accompanying team of scientists to compute its size. There was enough stone in the Cheops Pyramid, they estimated, to build a wall all round France 3m (10ft) high and 30cm (1ft) wide. A later estimate is that the pyramid consists of over 2,000,000 blocks of well-trimmed limestone, each weighing between 2.5 and 15 tonnes.

Big, yes: but what is still more impressive about these pyramids is their accuracy of construction. By about 2600BC the Egyptians knew enough to build the Cheops Pyramid in such a way that the difference in length between the four sides, at their base, is at most 20cm (8 inches), while its height, rising symmetrically to a top no longer there, reached 146.7m (481ft).

From the standpoint of history, all this is rather disconcerting. History is easier when it grows and develops to an ever greater point of achievement – this is what we expect it to do. But the Egyptians seem to have possessed, almost from the outset of their long imperial story, about as much technical skill and know-how as they were ever to achieve. They spread their empire far and wide,

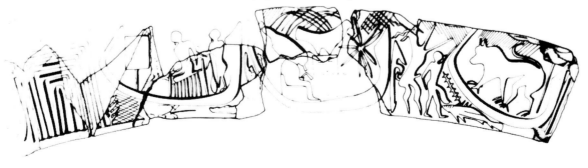

# Different but equal

*The Cheops Pyramid (above), towering over the Sphynx, was built some 4,500 years ago, less than a millennium after the emergence of the Pharaonic kingdom. It indicates a level of scientific and technical skill unsurpassed in all the subsequent development of ancient Egypt.*

deeply across the Sudan, distantly into western Asia; but they remained remarkably the same, or that, at least, is what the evidence seems to show. Having got off to their rapid start, they reached a plateau of development on which they seem to have stayed, apart from upheavals now and then and several remarkable departures from the norm, right down to the decline of Pharaonic power after 1000BC.

That plateau, clearly, was enough for needs and ambitions. These were many and complex, yet the essential keys to our understanding of this memorable civilization in all its splendours, in its pleasures and problems of everyday life, were not to be found and applied until 1822. This was when a 32-year-old Frenchman, Jean-Francois Champollion, crowned years of patient toil with a

*The complex of monuments at Karnak (above) seen across the sacred lake, continue to attract thousands of tourists to the achievements of ancient Egypt. By contrast, wall paintings found in tombs (left) illustrate scenes from everyday life such as harvesting, sowing and reaping.*

*Measuring the harvest. Egyptian wall-paintings illustrate the workings of the ancient kingdom's bureaucracy, providing a background to letters of scribes and officials.*

true decipherment of Egyptian hieroglyphic writing. Thomas Young in England had led the way, and others, above all the German Richard Lepsius, would complete Champollion's work; but it was Champollion who first found and turned the key.

He proved two things. First, that earlier beliefs about the hieroglyphs being symbols or "mysteries" were entirely off the track; secondly, that the signs and pictures which had puzzled men for so long were, in fact, a phonetic script: not exactly an alphabet, but all the same a script capable of being read as an alphabet is read. Once this was understood, Egyptologists could read the hieroglyphs as easily as the script of any other language that could be learned. Pharaonic civilization could be made to yield its secrets from an endless supply of inscriptions on monuments, and writings about many subjects on potsherds and papyrus. Three thousand years of history could be studied.

For a long time, and not surprisingly, the chief effort went into establishing the "dynastic" markers along that march of time: the chronology of the kings of

31 dynasties, and the tale of what they did, how they ruled and whom they conquered. In much the same way, prestige finds were the only ones which really counted, both for what they were and for their value to museums and private collectors.

But more recently Egyptology has moved with the times and shifted from the royal tombs and artifacts to an interest in the details of everyday life. Here again the artistic skills of ancient Egypt, painting everyday scenes and people on the inner walls of tombs of lesser folk, can open many windows on the past. Together with a wider knowledge of the written records, these paintings project a broad vision of the farming year and its festivals, the joys and sorrows of country life, and the celebrations of village gods or spiritual powers.

Contrasting with the mighty monuments, the pillars of Karnak, the majesty of Thebes and all the panoply of royal arrogance, there are texts which bring the reader right down to the village earth. So we find a clerk in high dynastic times, safely behind his desk and duly protected by all the rules and regulations of office, writing in sarcastic vein to a friend who has retired to village life:

I am told that you have abandoned writing and taken to sport, set your face to working in the fields and turned your back on letters? . . . But do you remember the condition of the farmer who is faced with paying his harvest tax when the snake has carried off the corn, and the hippopotamus has eaten the rest? Then the mice abound, the locusts come, cattle devour, the sparrows bring disaster; and what remains on the threshing floor is taken by thieves. And now the clerk lands on the river bank to collect the tax. With him are guards with staves and Nubians with rods of palm, and they say: 'Hand over the corn', though there is no corn. And the farmer is beaten, bound and ducked in the well . . .

Better to be a clerk, my friend, even if you must bow low to the director!

A "people's history" of the ancient Egyptians becomes to some extent possible, but meanwhile the tales and the pride of the dynasties tower above the memories of men. With a few interruptions, the Pharaohs presided over three periods of tremendous territorial and political expansion, respectively in the middle of the third millennium BC, for two or three centuries after 2000BC, and again for some five centuries after about 1600BC.

This was when the ancient trend of influence and initiative, which had previously flowed out of inner Africa northward into Egypt, turned decisively back to the south. Conquering armies enclosed most of the northern part of what is now the Republic of Sudan. Exploring and trading expeditions went to the ends of the Red Sea, penetrated with donkey teams deeply into southern lands, and created trading ties with all the peoples of Libya and the eastern Sahara. Great fortress barriers were built in colonized lands. Plinths and towers were raised to blazon forth the feats of victorious generals and kings. Works of ingenious irrigation, mines of gold, military settlements and all that these implied for civic order and coercion, were developed in distant countries and defended through the years. A library of books could scarcely tell it all.

Decline came later. Sorely priest-ridden, the power of the Pharaohs weakened and was disrupted. Upper Egypt fell to the rule of men from the semi-desert grasslands of Libya, all that was left, now, of a once green Sahara far gone in desiccation. And then, soon after 800BC, there came one more reversal in the tide of influence and power. Kings of the distant southern lands marched north in irresistible conquest, and made themselves the masters of all Egypt for a while.

Who were these kings of the south? One of the treasures of Khartoum Museum depicts them in their power and splendour. It is a huge statue in granite. This was King Taharqa, third king of the 25th or "Ethiopian" Dynasty:

# Different but equal

*A procession of Pharaohs at Karnak. Many of them were of African origin.*

Pharaoh of Egypt from 688 to 663BC, a mighty man of war whom the Israelites, as told in the Second Book of Kings, were glad to have as a protector. His own home kingdom was Kush, in the northern part of the modern Republic of Sudan, and when you contemplate this statue in the Khartoum Museum you know that you are looking at the figure of a man who might be from that country today.

# Chapter 3

# The kingdom of the Lion God

Kush became a kingdom in Nubia around 800BC, ruled all Egypt for a hundred years or so, and then, having withdrawn once more within its own wide southern boundaries, continued to exist and flourish until AD300 or soon after. Its thousand years of Kushite civilization mark another of the high points in Africa's ancient development.

Far up the Nile near modern Egypt's frontier with Sudan, the once sacred island of Elephantine sits rockily in the river opposite the town of Aswan. This island was a revered place of pilgrimage in ancient times, and many visitors came, among them our indispensable guide, Herodotus of Halicarnassus. He came here in search of information about the kingdom of Kush, southward from Elephantine, and its distant capital city of Meroe. The year was around 430BC and Herodotus was catching up with history, for the city of Meroe, then, was less than two centuries old:

> I went as far as Elephantine to see what I could with my own eyes, he wrote, but for the country still further south I had to be content with what I was told in answer to my questions.

The onward road to the south was closed to travellers at the time of his visit, but he learned a lot about it. The whole journey to Meroe took about 57 days, many of which had to be done on donkey-back along the river bank because of the Nile cataracts; but the last part could be sailed by boat, and then you could land almost outside the ramparts of Meroe itself.

We can still do that today. Here at first is the village of Begarawiya whose people can have changed little in appearance since the distant days of Meroe and where we may find, with a little imagination, features very much like King Taharqa's on the granite statue in Khartoum museum. A little beyond there are the tumbled and yet still majestic ruins of the great city itself. Beyond again, on the skyline, a cluster of pyramids show where the Kushites buried their kings and queens. Over to the right, but hard to see until you are close, there is all that still survives of the legendary Temple of the Sun where "the long-lived Ethiopians", as Herodotus was told at Elephantine, made food available to anyone who happened to pass by. Here was a table in a meadow

> situated in the outskirts of the city, where a plentiful supply of boiled meat of all kinds is kept; it is the duty of the magistrates to put the meat there at night, and during the day anybody who wishes may come and eat it.

Nowadays we can easily enough reach the ruins of Meroe from the Sudanese capital of Khartoum, with a short day's travel by road or rail. They are composed of several chief sites within a compass of some 20km ($12\frac{1}{2}$ miles); and each has much to show and tell. Excavated at various times since 1910, and most recently by Peter Shinnie in the 1960s, Meroe itself has revealed a complex of imposing temples and royal dwellings, a wide "occupation field" where

ordinary people lived, and much else besides. The nearby pyramids on the skyline are modest when compared with those of imperial Egypt, but singularly well built and solid, except that several of the best of them have lost their tops. This misfortune seems to have been the result of tomb-robbing, always a growth industry in the valley of the Nile, partly by local enterprise and partly by an Italian called Ferlini who, in 1834, claimed to have found a fine hoard of royal jewels in the top of one of the pyramids.

*Elephantine island (opposite) near the Egyptian frontier with the Sudan was once part of the great Nubian kingdom of Kush. The pyramids of Meroe (above) mark Kushite royal tombs.*

Not far away across the sand-grit plain are other sites of major interest. Here, at Naza and Musawarat as-Safra, one may see how the Kushites, having taken some of their culture from Pharaonic Egypt, nonetheless developed a civilization that became very much their own. Built in good sandstone masonry, finely cut, the temples at these sites show that the Kushites were characteristically African, both in borrowing useful ideas and techniques from whatever outside source they might come in contact with, and in promoting their own ideas and techniques. Here are the effigies of some of the gods of Egypt, but also, much more prominently, those of the gods and rulers of Kush, and notably of their multi-headed lion-god Apedemak, the lord of royal power.

Kush, in sum, can be seen to have been a development of local and original culture together with the assimilation of Egyptian culture and even, by way of trade along the Red Sea and across the Indian Ocean, of influences still more distant. There are godlike effigies that have an Indian air about them; there are metal pots that seem to echo the patterns of China. But Kush also had its own contribution to make.

*An elephant statue (above) at Musawarat, founded c. 500BC, suggests a distinctive African style.*

One of the more practical things it gave to the ancient world, by all the evidence, was an unexampled skill in the training of elephants for war and other purposes. Here at Musawarat, for example, there is a large complex of buildings, a "great enclosure", now known to have been founded in about 500BC and used continuously for centuries after that. Was this a place of Kushite pilgrimage in service of the gods of Kush? Possibly: more probably, however, this complex of buildings was a centre for the domestication of the tough and touchy African elephant. Strong ramps, enclosed by massive walls to form narrow corridors, suggest as much, as do various stone effigies and engravings of elephants, whether in the "great enclosure" itself or on the walls of a nearby temple. These walls had long fallen outward, flat upon the dry preserving sand. Lately restored by a German team under Fritz Hintze, their reliefs are almost as good as new, and show the processions of royal power when the temple was built in about 250BC.

Most of the ruins and artifacts are concerned with those rulers, but a "people's history" can also be partly traced. Broadly, the Kushites were stock-breeders and cultivators who lived along the banks of the Nile, and across the nearby grasslands, in times when these were better watered and wooded than they are today. Their manifest prosperity rested on local food production and on long-distance trade; and they were governed by kings and queens – by a noble caste or class – whose strength was always fortified, as in Egypt, by temple priests teaching that the power of rulers came from the gods.

*Apedemek, the lion-god of Kush.*

They were more innovative than the Egyptians in several interesting ways, and seem to have escaped from the rigid conservatism of the Pharaohs. The Egyptians remained content with bronze for tools and weapons, but the Kushites developed an important iron-smelting industry; heaps of slag at Meroe are still there to show it. The Kushites were also one of the earliest peoples anywhere to develop a purely alphabetic script. And their way of writing, however surprising this may be to those who have imagined that Africans were never able to invent such things, was as effective as the alphabetic script developed by the Greeks.

The wealth and inventiveness of Kush were important in the world of its time. It seems possible, given the political contacts of that period, that Hannibal's war elephants were trained by techniques developed in Kush. Another Meroitic site, not far from Musawarat, links Kush more or less directly with the Christians of the New Testament. There is nothing at this site now except a low earth mound of no apparent interest. But modern archaeology has shown that this mound at Wad ben-Naqa, once a river port of Meroitic trade and travel, was the palace of a famous woman ruler, or Candace, whose name was Amani-Shakhete, and whose portrait, by lucky chance, has survived on a fragment of plaster. Queen Amani-Shakhete ruled Kush from about 41–12BC, and among the queens who succeeded her upon the Kushite throne there was one who found a place in the New Testament. The Acts of the Apostles relate how Philip preached successfully to a high official of the queen of Kush – reigning from this palace at Wad ben-Naqa – as they sat together in the Kushite visitor's chariot "on the road that goeth down from Jerusalem to Gaza".

Whether Philip made a lasting convert of this official on his mission to Jerusalem, or was only the recipient of his courtesy on the dusty trail to Gaza, we do not know, for the Acts of the Apostles say no further. Did this trusted diplomat return to preach the Gospel at Meroe? The evidence is altogether lacking. All the same, Christianity was not long in entering the valley of the Nile, first in Alexandria far to the north. Then, after about AD350, Syrian missionaries brought the message of Christianity to another leading kingdom of those times, Axum, the parent of medieval Abyssinia, which nowadays we know as Ethiopia.

**Ethiopian epic**

Axum took shape in about the first century AD as a powerful trading kingdom in the Tigre region of what is northern Ethiopia today, and flourished through intercourse and commerce with its Arabian neighbours, and by maritime trade

*Fragment of a Meroitic funerary stone shows the distinctive and original alphabetic script invented and used by the scribes of Kush.*

through its Red Sea port of Adulis. By the fourth century its rulers had become rich enough to begin issuing coins of gold; and some of these, struck by a king called Ezana in the middle years of that century (or perhaps a century later: the dates are still contested), began to bear a Christian cross.

This introduction of Christianity, at least to the king and his court, is said on fairly good evidence to have been the work of a Syrian monk called Frumentius. Soon after that time, at all events, the kingdom of Axum began to look to the patriarchs of Alexandria for religious patronage, and we can say, without much risk of error, that the official religion of Ethiopia has been Christian for at least 14 centuries.

What remains of the capital of Axum is sufficiently impressive, Here are giant stelae, shafts of fine-cut stone, that rise to a highest point of nearly 21.3m (70ft); a long-fallen shaft, alongside those that still stand upright, is of even greater length. Below these towering shafts of stone, hidden underground, a maze of catacombs and tomb chambers was surprisingly revealed by Neville Chittick's excavations of 1974. Unsuspected before that time, these chambers bear witness to a royal cemetery of a complexity otherwise unparalleled outside the Nile valley.

There is indeed nothing of Egyptian or even of Kushite influence here. Whatever came from outside derived from the Sabaean civilization of southern Arabia (notably the Axumite adaptation of old Sabaean script into the Ge'ez script which is still used in Ethiopia today), or else, later, from the Christianity of the Byzantine or Eastern Roman Empire. Yet what came from inside this country of rugged plains and distant mountains remained more important. Here was another civilization of inner Africa that took useful ideas from the outside world, but stubbornly remained itself.

Much has still to be understood about Axum: even the reigning order of its kings, who neglected to put dates on their otherwise excellent coins, is still to be agreed. At war with Muslim neighbours after the rise of Islam in the seventh century, the rulers of Axum appear to have abandoned their capital towards the end of the first millennium AD. After 1200, to the muffled tune of distant battles

*A 70ft stela (right) from Axum indicates the achievement of this early Christian trading nation in modern Ethiopia. At Lalibela (below) the successors of Axum carved churches out of the living rock.*

*An Ethiopian "strip painting" (above) tells the story of the Queen of Sheba; the last two rows portray her visit to King Solomon. The castle of Gondar (left) shows the continuing power of the Ethiopian rulers into the 16thC.*

and upheavals, a new seat of power appeared in the mountains of Lasta, farther to the south; and here at Lalibela the rulers and their priests caused massive churches to be hewn from the living rock. Once again, as with the stone shafts of Axum, there are nowhere else any monumental buildings quite like these.

Soon after this, the royal chronicles began to record a new line of kings who trace their origin, by an airy disregard for dates and possibilities, to Solomon the King of Israel many centuries earlier. The popular arts of Ethiopia have long since enshrined the story of the founding of this Solomonic dynasty in "strip paintings" which are still much enjoyed.

Thanks to a merchant called Tamrin, the paintings tell, the Queen of Ethiopia – assimilated conveniently to the Queen of Sheba, or Sabaea, across the Red Sea in Arabia – hears of the wealth and wisdom of Solomon, and decides to visit him. With her – as the Bible also tells – she takes a great train of camels loaded with gold and other goods, but the favour that she finds with Solomon is personal rather than commercial. He falls in love with her beauty and succeeds, by a royal trick, in persuading her to bear a son by him. The queen returns home to Ethiopia and gives birth to Menelik, and Menelik becomes the legendary founder of the Solomonic line of kings.

### Feudal kingdom

Throughout medieval times there were frequent wars between Ethiopia and the Muslims, notably with the sultans of Adel in what is now northern Somalia, while power in Ethiopia shifted from one set of rulers to another and from one region to the next. Soon after 1600 the Emperor Fasilides began to build imposing castles at his capital of Gondar, not far from where the Blue Nile rises in Lake Tana. These castles were built by local craftsmen according to the notions of military architecture then current in the region, though with some clear influences from the monumental building of earlier times. Constructed in brown basalt, they marked a departure from the feudal custom of moving the king's capital from one place to another. Here, for many years, the kings reigned in lavish splendour, as a French doctor, arriving in 1699, was to describe. The throne of the Emperor Iyasu the Great, he reported, was of solid gold, and stood beneath a glittering dome.

A vivid insight into this feudal kingdom and its customs has come down to us from 1774, thanks to the memoirs of James Bruce, a Scottish nobleman who lived at the Ethiopian court for nearly two years, and observed it with an eye for detail that time has shown to have been, for the most part, singularly truthful. At the time, however, he was written off as an inventive romantic.

Getting home to England, Bruce told his story at the court of King George III, and was generally disbelieved. How could there be, in remote Africa, a kingdom with such power and pomp, and a monarch whose infantry numbered 30,000 and whose cavalry wore coats of mail? How could there be an African people whose aristocratic form of government was matched only by their arrogance? Where could African savages have found all that? Bruce went around with his extraordinary tales for a time and then, retiring to Scotland in a huff, sat down to write his book. For the most part, so far as one can see now, he wrote the unvarnished truth.

The Ethiopia that Bruce knew in the 1770s was a kingdom, or group of competitive sub-kingdoms, lying at the heart of present-day Ethiopia. Often severed from outside contact by hostile neighbours and sheer distance, the Ethiopians and their rulers lived much to themselves, conserved their own traditions and variety of Christian belief and, save for times of baronial eruption or foreign attack, were generally able to live well.

They managed to maintain their links with Alexandria, to whose patriarch they continued to look for confirmation of their own patriarch or *abuna*, but otherwise their Christianity, like the rest of their culture, was deeply influenced and shaped by their own regional world of witches, oracles and spirits. Ethiopia has been sometimes thought to be "non-African" because of its religion and its peculiar history of isolation. In truth, Christian Ethiopia has remained as genuinely of its own time and place as have Muslim parts of Africa.

Often challenged from within and without, this ancient polity managed to survive in its embattled mountains, and even, during the colonial scramble for Africa after 1885, considerably to enlarge its frontiers at the expense of its neighbours. Elsewhere, things went variously with Christian polities. Muslim Arabs took control of Egypt – at first, only of northernmost Egypt – in the seventh century AD, but proved tolerant of Egyptian Christians. Their community, known as Coptic (meaning Egyptian), is there to this day, though much reduced in influence since early Muslim times.

Meanwhile the many bishoprics of the old Roman provinces of North Africa, the land that had given Saint Augustine to the Christian world, vanished from the scene; colonies of Greek Christians along the shores of Libya went the same way. As this was happening, however, something quite different began to develop in the Nubian lands of the equally vanished kingdom of Kush, the lands of the lion-god. Missionaries from Byzantium, the capital of Eastern Christianity, set out to preach the Gospel in that little-known country. The results were many. The lands of the lion-god became Christian and remained so for centuries.

**The Christians of the Sudan**

It is not too much to speak of the vivid glow and even brilliance of Christian Nubia, utterly obscured though it afterwards became: so obscured, indeed, that our own world has barely known of its existence.

The Polish archaeologist Michalowski cut through some of this Nubian obscurity during the 1960s, and revealed the truth in its many colours. Literally: for the painted angels, saints and bishops discovered by Michalowski and his team at Faras, not far south of Aswan, were almost as fresh and clear as when the engulfing sand had buried them some six centuries earlier.

Like other teams along the Nile upstream from the high-dam project at Aswan, the Poles had to work against time. They cut down through successive occupation periods at Faras until, nearing bedrock, they came upon the structures of what had been a large church. Here they found wall paintings that were numerous and well preserved, and were able, even as the new lake's waters crawled nearer, to peel them from their walls for conservation in the museums of Khartoum and Warsaw.

Conceived in the styles of Byzantine tradition, these elegant paintings decorated what was quickly recognized as a cathedral, for a list of 25 successive bishops of Faras was another startling Polish find. For several centuries, in other words, this distant African city – now lost for ever beneath Lake Nasser – was the prestigious centre of a Christian civilization in the Sudan. And if its angels and archangels were painted exceedingly white, we may be sure that the congregation was as certainly Nubian black as its bishops. White-skinned angels were simply a Byzantine tradition, although various black Virgins were also worshipped in the lands of Eastern Christianity. We are miles from modern colour prejudice here.

The 22nd bishop in the Faras list died in 1062, according to an inked inscription recovered by Michalowski, and Nubia by then had been Christian, at any rate to some extent, for nearly five centuries. A Syrian chronicler, John of Ephesus, writing in early Christian times, tells us that the first missionary to the

# The kingdom of the lion god

*Christian frescoes (opposite and* above*) from Faras, the distant African city that was once a centre of Christian civilization in the Sudan.*

far south was a priest called Julian. He went on south past Aswan in about 540, and suffered, like many before and since, from Nubia's scorching heat:

> For he used to say that, from nine o'clock till four in the afternoon, he was obliged to take refuge in caverns full of water, where he sat undressed, and girt only in a linen garment like the people of the country wear.

Others followed Julian, but so many of the ancient records of Christian Nubia are lost that we know little more than a broad outline of its history, to which, however, modern archaeology – as in the case of the cathedral at Faras – has added some useful detail. What the early missionaries found were relatively new kingdoms in the lands that had once been Kush. After about AD200 these lands had begun to be infiltrated by nomad peoples from the surrounding plains and, as the power of Kush declined, these nomads founded new kingships.

# The kingdom of the lion god

*Crusader from Christian Nubia.*

At around this point the Meroitic language and culture somehow vanished from the scene, and Nubian language and culture took its place. We do not know how much these newcomers borrowed from their Kushite predecessors, but their kingships, at least, seem to have marked a new departure. Royal crowns and other regalia found in a tomb near Ballana (at about the southern end of modern Lake Nasser) show that they enjoyed a certain splendour, and by the time that the missionaries from the north arrived in what was now Nubia there were three such kingdoms. One of these was in the north, Nobatia with its capital at Faras; a second was south of it, Makuria with its capital at Old Dongola; while the third, southward again, was Alodia with its capital at Soba on the Blue Nile. The missionaries found a sympathetic audience and, officially at least, all three kingdoms became Christian in the years shortly before 600.

But what was won for Christianity in the south was lost, or partly lost, for Christianity in the north. Erupting irresistibly from Arabia, Muslim Arabs broke into Byzantine Egypt in 640, and mastered its capital a year later. So the newly Christian kingdoms in the south had now to settle their relations with a Muslim Egypt. After a rough start they succeeded very well in this. A peace was made that endured for some four centuries, and proved greatly to the commercial gain of both sides. The age was one of tolerance between Christians and Muslims, and in this easy-going acceptance of different faiths an important community of Egyptian Jews also had its share.

Arab travellers have left a few reports of Christian Nubia. They speak of comfort and wealth, but above all of peace. Writing in the tenth century, Ibn Selim al-Aswani says of Soba, the capital of the southernmost kingdom, that it possessed "fine buildings, spacious houses, churches with much gold, and gardens". We know in fact that these Nubians wrote in both Greek and their own Nubian, using an alphabet modified from the Coptic script of Egypt.

Calamity began in the twelfth century, when the long peace with Muslim Egypt finally broke down. By 1323 the northern kingdom of Nobatia-Makuria (joined together some centuries earlier) had passed under Muslim control; and after that an expanding Islam gradually engulfed the whole region, although Christianity seems to have survived in Alodia as late as 1500. Was this another victory for nomad peoples, filtering in from the semi-deserts to west and east, over an urban civilization grown too complacent and comfortable to defend itself? Partly, yes; but there was a more immediate reason why the peace broke down. The reason was the disaster of the Crusades from western Europe.

## Crusades and Holy Wars

The chain-mailed knights of western Europe rode into this complex history on their first Crusade of 1096. They took Jerusalem from the Muslims, heralding seven more Crusades which became, ever more painfully, enterprises in loot and rapine. The year 1204 brought one of its more fearful outrages, when the knights of the fourth Crusade pillaged the early Christian capital of Byzantium, a truly magnificent city of the ancient world. Various Crusades helped in the downfall of the grand Muslim dynasty of the Fatimid kings who had come from Tunisia in the tenth century, and had built El-Kahira, or Cairo, into a city no less splendid than Byzantium itself. In 1168, so desperate was the situation of the last Fatimid ruler, that his government set fire to Cairo rather than allow it to fall into the ruthless hands of the Norman king of Jerusalem, Amalric. The caliph's vizir Shawar is said to have used 20,000 barrels of naphtha and 10,000 torches. The city burned for 54 days.

However motivated, the Crusades fuelled more than the burning of Cairo. They also set a torch to a new hatred as the old religious tolerance vanished. Under their Saracen warrior-leaders, the Muslims replied with holy war, and in

1171 Salah ad-Din, or Saladin as the Christians called him, seized power from the feeble hands of the last Fatimid ruler. In 1187 Saladin retook Jerusalem from the Normans, and his successors remained at war with the Crusaders until these at last desisted.

If the Crusades were useful to Western Europe in opening its provincial cultures to the wealth and learning of the east, they were an unrelieved catastrophe to the lands and peoples they invaded, and Christian Nubia was among the casualties. Facing crusaders from the west, Saladin also found that he had to fight other crusaders from the south. A Nubian army came up past Aswan, where a ruined Christian monastery remains, as a witness to the holy wars of history, and advanced on Cairo. Saladin's brother, Shams ad-Din, met the Nubian cavalry in battle and drove them back across the frontier as far as Faras, which the Muslims also took.

The Muslim advance was never seriously reversed. Gradually, the old monasteries were abandoned. Silence fell upon all that they had known and done. The southernmost kingdom of Alodia held out longest, but in 1525 a Jewish traveller, David Reubeni, found its capital of Soba in ruins and its citizens reduced to living in huts. That is a long story lost in the years. Yet curious echoes can still be heard on the winds of history, and in unexpected places.

## A saint turns black

Around the year 1240, in the then imperial German city of Magdeburg, a famous saint suddenly turned black. More exactly, this is how the saint was depicted in a new statue placed inside the great minster in that year. Always previously, St Maurice had been shown as white; now it was different.

This saint had been revered since late Roman times as a Christian legionary commander, martyred for refusing to slaughter fellow legionaries. Called St Maurice of Thebes (in Egypt) and vaguely thought of as an African, Maurice may not have really existed in the flesh. But he certainly existed in the spirit, and his cult became widely established in western Europe.

Up to the year of this Magdeburg statue, 1240 or thereabouts, Maurice was invariably depicted as truly European in countenance and colour. But then he suddenly becomes black. More, he becomes most obviously and authentically Nubian in face and features. Here in the Minster of Magdeburg, St Maurice is no longer the white saint of Thebes, but the black saint of Nubia, ally and protector from the distant south.

Thinking a little further about this apparently strange transformation, one can see that the worshippers who raised this powerful statue had their good reasons. Not long before, in 1228, the German Emperor Frederick, ruler of the Holy Roman Empire of Germany (among whose largest cities was Magdeburg), had himself embarked upon the sixth Crusade. He did variously well, and there was much fighting. Many went with him, but not all returned. What more natural than that the widows and families who worshipped here should take comfort from this saintly friend in Africa, and revere his stern unbending gaze?

So the transformation is really not so strange. In that Europe of the Middle Ages, in so many ways the inheritor of the civilization of ancient Greece, a black St Maurice could in no way appear out of place. Even so, it seems to me, there is no other monument anywhere that is half so compelling in its confirmation of the common attitude of those times, the mutual attitude of "different, but equal", whereby the generality of peoples, in so far as they could know each other, were joined in a community of mankind across the barriers of distance or superstition.

# The Kingdom of the Lion God

Even three and a half centuries later, the same attitude was still alive. In *Othello* Shakespeare was writing no racist play, nor could he have written one within the culture of his times. He was writing a tragedy of passion, jealousy, the fear of strangers; and if Iago's envy could see Othello as a swarthy ape, to the rulers of proud Venice this arch-stranger was the admired commander of their armies, and one, moreover, who fetched his life and lineage "from men of royal siege". Only in this high perspective can Othello's famous last lines acquire their force:

*Soft you; a word or two before you go.*
*I have done the state some service and they know't:*
*No more of that . . .*
                         *Set you down this:*
*And say, besides, that in Aleppo once*
*Where a malignant and a turbanned Turk*
*Beat a Venetian and traduced the state,*
*I took by th'throat the circumcised dog*
*And smote him thus.*

This was still the world of "different, but equal". Only a later world would tear that community apart.

*Nubian in face and features, the famous medieval statue of St Maurice at Magdeburg.*

# Chapter 4

# Mastering a continent

Pour a libation in West Africa before you embark on any undertaking, and what will you say as the gin – for all good libations should be poured in gin – joins the ground at your feet? You will say, in Twi or whatever language is your own, that you pour a libation "to the ancestors who brought us into the world, who care for us while we are here, and who will receive us when we leave it".

For nothing really dies; and the community of Humankind is not only the people alive in the world, but others, just as much, who have left the world for the land of the spirits, and others again who have yet to enter the world. The ancestors are those who guide and safeguard this threefold community of "the dead, the living, and the yet unborn", because the ancestors in the land of the spirits are the spokesmen of the powers from which all power derives.

"It was the ancestors", say the Shona of Central Africa, "who led us to our country and taught us how to live in it: how to grow food, make iron, and mine for gold." And that has been the underlying tradition in this continent, the means of learning through the oracles, which speak at appointed shrines, what one should do in life and how best to choose one's path. In his poem about a king of his people, the Shona poet H.V. Chitepo has the monarch explain: "I ruled with the power that comes from my forefathers, the power without beginning." It is a belief as old as the ancient world. The tribes of Israel knew it well. "And ye shall divide the land", write the scribes of the Book of Numbers, "for an inheritance among your families: according to the tribes of your fathers ye shall inherit."

It is also a belief or a tradition that helps to explain how ancient Africa was peopled by the forerunners of its present inhabitants, and how those early peoples, long before the time of written records, solved the manifold problems of survival and spread in lands that were often extremely hostile to any human settlement.

## Peopling a Continent

Although Africa was the birthplace of humanity several million years ago, no large or stable populations developed in the immense epochs of the Stone Ages, at least outside the lower valley of the Nile. Until some two or three thousand years ago, all the continent south of the Sahara was populated only by scattered groups of Late Stone Age peoples who lived by trapping game and gathering wild fruits or plants.

There is scarcely any African people anywhere today whose traditions do not speak of their ancestors having "arrived from somewhere else" at some unknown period of the past. Combining these myriad fragments of re-membered history with the systematic work of modern language specialists, and the archaeological evidence of pottery or other artifacts, it becomes clear

*Symbol of the "power without beginning": a wayside shrine in Nigeria.*

that long ago there was a steady movement of people, southwards and eastwards, out of the rainforests of western Africa.

One of the most important strands of evidence for this great migration comes from comparative linguistic studies. The majority of peoples who now inhabit central and southern Africa speak more or less closely related languages that belong to the same large family, known as Bantu. The name comes from a word root found in hundreds of these languages, *ntu*, or humanness, with *muntu*, the singular, meaning person, and *bantu*, the plural, meaning people. Some of these Bantu languages share many features, while others are far apart in structure and vocabulary; yet all of them clearly derive from the same roots. Broadly speaking, those Bantu languages used in the northwest of the continent seem to be older than the southern ones, suggesting that lines of development of all Bantu languages must be traced back to an original source in the northwest: more precisely, to an area that now covers eastern Nigeria and Cameroun.

Putting all the evidence together, the conclusion is that the "ancestral Bantu" began to travel, by a gradual spread of pioneering peoples, out of this area of northwestern Africa about 3,000 years ago. Two areas of secondary dispersal were gradually formed to the south of the rainforests of the Congo basin, and from these, perhaps around 500BC, the spread continued in two directions: southwards into Angola and Zambia, and eastward into East Africa, reaching what is now Kenya by about AD100. From there, "Bantu" culture moved southward through Zimbabwe into South Africa, crossing the Limpopo river in about AD300.

The evidence agrees further that these were the communities which carried various forms of tropical farming and the technology of iron-smelting from one region to another, absorbing or by-passing the Stone Age hunter-gatherers they encountered on their way. But an oversimplified account of successive dispersal, division and new settlement can be misleading: there were no large

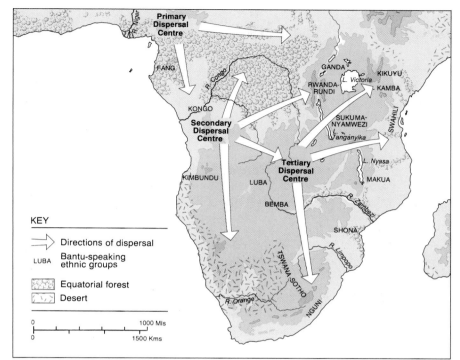

KEY

⟹ Directions of dispersal

LUBA Bantu-speaking ethnic groups

Equatorial forest

Desert

0         1000 Mls

0         1500 Kms

*A pattern of related "Bantu" languages traces the development of peoples south and westward from the rainforests of western Africa, beginning some 3,000 years ago. These communities also brought a knowledge of tropical farming and iron-making to the new regions.*

hordes or masses on the march. Remarkably rapid, perhaps, given the enormous distances and huge natural obstacles involved, the "spread" southward and eastward was extremely slow when measured against the span of a human lifetime. Nevertheless by about 1800, when Europeans began to wander in the inner lands hitherto unknown to them, they found large and stable populations in every habitable region of Africa, numbering perhaps as many as 100 million souls. The ancestors of these peoples had developed ways of mastering environments that were often extremely hostile to human survival, whether through climate or disease. This taming of Africa for the benefit of large and settled populations, we can now see, deserves to be regarded as one of the major achievements of human development.

That is not the way, of course, that Europeans and Americans have generally seen the matter. The brash industrialism of the nineteenth century perceived virtually all Africans as more or less hopeless savages. The British explorer Sir Samuel Baker expressed a common view when, addressing the confident gentlemen of the London Ethnographical Society in 1865, he said that the Dinka peoples he had seen along the uppermost reaches of the Nile were inferior to animals. Their nature was "not even to be compared with the noble character of the dog". He found them altogether deplorable, having "neither gratitude, pity, love or self-denial". Nothing too bad, it seemed to Baker, could be said about them.

There were a few who disagreed with Baker and his kind. They replied that material simplicity was by no means necessarily a proof of spiritual or mental backwardness. "There is more to civilization than railways and telegraphs," the grave Bishop Tozer of Central Africa had objected a few years earlier, and "nothing can be so false as to suppose that the outward circumstances of a people is the measure of its barbarism or its civilization."

But Bishop Tozer could only state the Christian principle of human equality

*Lake Baringo, Kenya, with resident hippos.*

and hope that Christians would believe it. There was far too little reliable information or understanding of African life for any balanced judgement to be sustained or even reached. Nowadays, happily, we are in a very different and infinitely better situation. Thanks to a vast amount of scholarly work, and thanks also to a far better understanding of what is "primitive" and what is not, African life and history can now be judged with more insight and information than possessed by any previous generation.

We see that African peoples succeeded in reaching a viable and even a very successful balance with nature, overcoming a range of environmental obstacles that opposed their survival and development. We see that they did this at a pre-industrial and even pre-mechanical level of material development, but were nonetheless repeatedly inventive and creative.

Much has changed in modern times, but even today one can still find African peoples whose lives and societies point to the way in which this mastering of a continent was achieved. Three such peoples – the Pokot of northern Kenya, the Sukur of eastern Nigeria, and the Dogon of the western Sudan – can teach us much in their different ways – whether political, economic, or religious – about the dramatic and extraordinary background to the continent of today.

**The Pokot**

The Pokot live a short way beyond Lake Baringo, home of fish-eagles and hippopotamuses, where blue waves reflect the clear skies of Kenya and towering hills stretch away to the mountains of Ethiopia. They are one of many cattle-raising peoples in the region, with the Turkana on one side and the Karimojong on the other. Some are settled farmers, but others raise cattle and camels in a country of woodland or thin grazing, and otherwise grow little or no

*Woman of the Pokot: an intensely practical wisdom.*

food of their own. These cattle-herding Pokot live in scattered family units, each with its homestead placed some distance from the next, and although they face many natural difficulties they have long become a stable and self-confident community.

A Pokot family homestead may at first look poor and squalid, and its inhabitants wretchedly primitive and ignorant. Yet anyone who has the patience to live among them will soon find out that appearances are misleading. What the outsider sees as primitive or squalid will become, on better acquaintance, a repeatedly ingenious and inventive adaptation to nature and to nature's possible gifts. Across the years the Pokot have learned an intensely practical wisdom about how best to use the resources of their tough environment.

Cattle are central to their existence. Their beasts are at once the symbol of wealth, respectability, and the means of livelihood. They dislike selling their animals, compose endless songs about them, and generally tend to treat them rather as Westerners treat money in the bank. The fact is that their skills in raising cattle under tropical conditions have enabled them to solve the problems of living in this inhospitable region.

The Pokot way of life relies on other capacities as well. They have developed a capacious knowledge of herbal medicine. To cattle they have added goats and other small livestock, as well as camels introduced in ancient times from the north. But what we are particularly concerned with here are Pokot solutions to the problems of self-government, for in this respect the Pokot are characteristic of a wide range of African communities in historical times.

Here is a people who have no kings, no chiefs, no police force of their own, and really no officials of any kind; and yet they manage to get along perfectly well so long as nobody from outside comes to interfere with them. Their government exists, even if it is hard to see, and consists of a council of elders – the heads of homesteads – who safeguard and enforce the unwritten but always remembered rules of Pokot community life. If someone breaks these rules, the council can call on a kind of informal militia composed of young men belonging to the age-grade of warriors. Age-grades are another aspect of Pokot government: every person belongs to a given age-grade, and goes through life in the same grade along with his or her companions, advancing from junior to senior status as the years unfold. The effect is to bind Pokot society together in spite of the comparative isolation of life in scattered homesteads.

The rules are generally respected, for the Pokot know that they have received – from "the power without beginning", as the poet Chitepo put it – a viable way of life depending on the rules of community survival. Following the same line of thought, their law is little concerned with punishment but much concerned with compensation for loss of life or property, always with the underlying aim of conserving their essential balance with nature.

What does the intrusion of the modern world mean to a people such as this? Now and then a chosen son or even a chosen daughter may be sent for modern education, or depart for the distant towns and their temptations. But the lure of the modern world has not yet appeared to them to offer any superior way of life, and the Pokot, generally, have remained satisfied with what they have. That may look little enough to the outside eye, but to them it represents the peace and companionship that make life worth living.

### Farmers and iron-smelters

Success in raising cattle has been one of the key factors in enabling Africans to settle certain parts of their continent without wrecking their environment or the subtle balance between nature and human needs. But they have also relied on other decisive adaptations and inventions. The Sukur of eastern Nigeria demonstrate two of the most important of these.

The first is of course the ability to cultivate crops for food, something which in Africa began a long time ago. On present evidence the earliest African food crops were developed by peoples of the Sahara before that region began to dessicate after 2500BC, and by the inhabitants of central Ethiopia and the Nile Valley. From those regions the techniques of food-growing were progressively accepted and adapted by peoples living ever further south, and agriculture reached what is now South Africa by about AD300. Bringing large tracts of the African continent under cultivation involved the invention of methods appropriate to sub-tropical and tropical conditions, such as terracing in hill country, irrigation in relatively dry country, and the selection and improvement of food plants borrowed from other climatic zones.

The Sukur of the hills of eastern Nigeria were among many peoples who acquired such techniques and used them to build a strong village economy. But the Sukur also inherited another great technological advance of ancient times, and this again proved crucial to their taming of the environment.

Simple forms of stone tool might be adequate to the needs of early peoples, but when Africans embarked on tropical agriculture they required more elaborate and stronger tools for clearing bush and forest, hoeing, or harvesting. This promoted Africa's interest in the use of metals, and above all of iron. From about 500BC an extensive and increasingly skilled iron technology spread rapidly southward from the grassland borders of the Sahara, very possibly by way of the spread of Bantu culture.

Copper and tin had long been smelted for bronze in northern Africa and Egypt, but one of the oddities of African history is that iron was the first metal to be used in quantity in all the other regions of the continent. With some partial exceptions in the western Sahara grasslands and the southern basin of the Congo river, where copper seems to have been smelted and traded in considerable quantities, Africa moved from the last phase of the Stone Age directly into an Iron Age, and began to do this only a few centuries after the Celts had first brought an Iron Age to western Europe.

Was this another local invention, south of the Sahara, or the adaptation of techniques evolved north of the Sahara? The evidence is inconclusive, and the question is complicated by the fact that knowledge of iron-smelting – a far more difficult process than smelting copper or tin – could have found its way into sub-Saharan Africa by more than one route. This diffusion could have been southward and westward from Meroe (see p. 36), where iron was being smelted around 500BC. An alternative source of this valuable knowledge could have been Celtic Europe, which was linked to West Africa by way of North Africa and the old Saharan trails. Certain types of African smelting furnace suggest that this was indeed the route by which technological diffusion occurred.

The Sukur are among those who always smelted their own iron ore until recent times, and they still do it on rare occasions. Their type of smelting furnace, which is fairly characteristic, relies on inducing a forced draught, or "blast" of air. This encourages the combustion of the charcoal in the furnace so that it reaches the relatively high temperature needed for the extraction of metal from iron ore: a temperature considerably higher than that required for copper or tin. (Gold, of course, occurs in a natural state and calls for no extraction by smelting.)

Loaded with charcoal at the base, the hard-earth furnace was then filled with local ore, which is plentiful in most African regions. "Blast" was applied by bellows inserted at a hole in the base of the furnace, and crude metal was extracted from this hole by forceps as soon as the smelt was ready. Essentially, the operation was the forerunner of modern industrial smelting methods. The metal thus obtained was then repeatedly pounded and reheated so as to produce a form of steel. Though slow and laborious, Sukur iron-making was adequate to local demand for hoe blades, knives or spearheads. There was even enough for the production of strips of iron useful as a trading currency.

## Ritual and belief

With such techniques, locally invented or, more probably, borrowed and developed from overseas sources, Africa's peoples dominated their vast solitudes and made the continent their own. Yet material techniques were only a part of the problem, and perhaps by no means the most important part. The task was to build and impose not only a physical mastery, but a moral and political one as well. Having acquired their techniques, these pioneering peoples had to build them into a viable community life. In other words, they had to embrace them within the ideas and beliefs of what we call religion: they had to ritualize them.

Thus it was that iron-smelting techniques were conceived as the operation of a privileged partnership with the life force that had itself conceived the world. Smiths had to be members of a "mystery" – much as in medieval Europe during another "age of faith" – and were set apart by their services to this "mystery". Smithing could be successful only when approached by way of appropriate rituals, often incorporating a dance, as the Sukur still demonstrate. The gods, or the ancestors who spoke for the gods, had to be invited to approve and apply their occult influence.

In many African societies the work was seen in terms of physical metaphors, an act of creation modelled on the sexuality through which the life force gave

*Sukur ironmakers: members of a mystery as well as of a craft.*

birth to men and women. The bellows represented the male organ, and the furnace was the womb.

It is worth considering just why this ritualizing process was seen as indispensable, because the religions of traditional Africa are the real key to understanding its communities. What we nowadays call religion has often become detached from the concerns and beliefs of everyday life. In the West, religion is apparently no longer considered as an explanation of the world, or even capable of such explanation, and experimental science has taken its place. The religions of traditional Africa, on the other hand, have to be understood as embracing all practical understandings of the world: all the reasons why the world is as it is, and what powers drive it forward or thrust it back. For those who believe in them, these religions not only explain the world but also provide instruction on how to behave in it. From the outside they are best understood as embodying what may be called a science of social control.

Imagine, for a moment, the predicament of those distant peoples who set out to populate and tame their continental wilderness. Any such group would have been small, perhaps only a few hundred souls, hiving off from a parent group and moving into new and unknown territories. Its problems would include not only the physical difficulties of extracting a living from the wilderness, but also, and perhaps still more pressingly, the psychological need to feel at home in the wilderness, to win a mental as well as a physical security, to build and hold together a self-identified community where no such community had existed before.

The solution was found in what we call religion. Each group formed its "charter of survival" from the wisdom of its ancestors, incorporating every new social or material advance into the fabric of its beliefs, and safeguarding the successful operation of those beliefs by appropriate ceremonies or rituals.

Seen from the outside, one can detect how these beliefs in fact upended the process of development. In that long work of taming the wilderness and peopling its solitudes, the saving balance with nature was forged by trial and error, and the necessary rules of community salvation derived from the result. But the community thus formed saw this process the other way round, believing that the ancestral rules and regulations had come first and had produced the balance with nature rather than deriving from it.

Yet what could be more natural, or even inevitable? For the necessary balance with nature, once formed, could not be maintained unless the rules by which the balance had been achieved were kept by succeeding generations. And the rules would not be kept, given the frailties of human nature, unless people recognized strong and pressing reasons for keeping them. The "power without beginning", the power the ancestors derived from God, was also the power to reward or punish, and the life of the community depended upon obedience.

In general, these communities were innately conservative. Even where opportunities for social and economic change were not only present but were seized and exploited, the advice of the elders would still be to hold to the sure and the known. Communities without any such opportunity, such as the Dinka, a pastoral people living in a region of poor, infertile soil, were naturally more conservative than others. For them, any serious departure from the rules of the ancestors would at once threaten their fragile balance with nature. So it was firmly built into the ancient democracy of the Dinka that no family, and certainly no individual, could be allowed to possess more goods than other families possessed. Accordingly Dinka laws, like those of the Pokot, were firmly based on ideas of compensation rather than retribution.

The rules could be broken, and often were: there was nothing in the least superhuman about any of these communities. But if you were greedy, or otherwise offended against the rules, the power of good would assume the power of evil, and then the misfortunes of witchcraft would strike at you. A maxim of the Bemba of Zambia puts this well: "To find one wild bees' nest in the bush is good, and it is better still to find two. But if you find three, that is witchcraft." If you have found two nests, in other words, and still look for and take from a third – threatening someone else's share of honey – then you will suffer for your greed.

Against this force of conservatism there was of course the force of development. The two went hand in hand, or rather sparring with each other. Inequalities appeared, "charters" were revised, rules were changed as communities grew larger in numbers, stronger in their means of survival and wealthier in trade, so that eventually, in some cases, kingships and conquests ensued. By this gradual process, each African people formed its own distinct form of religion: not "ancestor worship", nor "animist" reverence for sticks and stones, or any such clutter of misunderstandings from the speculations of nineteenth-century Europeans, but various ways of reaching and of using "the power without beginning".

Thus the Pokot have forms of belief that underlie and buttress their pastoral lifestyle and its specific forms of economy and self-government, whereas the Sukur, with their agriculture and petty kings, have a quite different religion. We should find the same degree of diversity among other peoples elsewhere. But while these religions of traditional Africa vary enormously with the different histories and lifestyles they support and justify, many of the basic concepts are remarkably similar. If one perseveres a little further, and asks how Africa's ingenious and stubborn thinkers have conceived the great issues of life and death, good and evil, some interesting answers are revealed, particularly among the third people whom I have chosen to visit, the Dogon of the Western Sudan.

The Dogon do not know when they arrived in their present homeland of the Bandiagara hills to the south of the middle course of the Niger river, now a clattering day's motor ride from the river port of Mopti. Some of their traditions say that they used to live along the river itself, but the Dogon have certainly been where they are now for many centuries. Who was living there before them? The Tellem, say the Dogon, were their predecessors, a somewhat ghostly people whose semi-legendary existence gives one a glimpse of the long process whereby Africa's most ancient populations have followed one another down forgotten centuries.

Like some of their neighbours, notably the Bambara, the Dogon have intricate beliefs about the origin of the world and of themselves. The first European to study these beliefs, a Frenchman called Marcel Griaule, began his work among the Dogon some 50 years ago. Griaule made little progress for a long time, but in the end the elders of the Dogon decided that he was worthy of their confidence, so they deputed one of their number, Ogotemmeli, to give Griaule a course in the essentials of Dogon belief. Ogotemmeli's course lasted for 33 days, and the revelations were extraordinary.

What came out was the panorama of a sophisticated and penetrating conception of the meaning of life. From these and further studies one of Griaule's colleagues, Germaine Dieterlen, concluded that the Dogon and their neighbours "have a system of signs which run into thousands, their own system of astronomy and calendrical measurements, methods of calculation and extensive anatomical and physiological knowledge, as well as a systematic pharmacopoeia".

This informed description stands in total contrast to earlier European reactions to the "savage nakedness" of African life, reactions that perhaps still

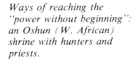

*Ways of reaching the "power without beginning": an Oshun (W. African) shrine with hunters and priests.*

linger in many minds.

Without embarking on a detailed inquiry, modern visitors may learn something of the essence of Dogon belief and culture by watching one of the spectacular festivals with which the Dogon celebrate important events and anniversaries. So let us join the festival known as *dama*.

### The Dance of Life Beyond Death

In a swaying rhythm, one by one, bodies moving to the muted thunder of the drums in the village arena below, the celebrants of *dama* descend from the hills of the ancestors. They will play out the festivals of Life, and of Life beyond Death, that guarantees the peace and onward movement of Dogon society.

The participants are young and handsome men, full of the ardour of their dance and the spirit of its meaning. Each wears on his head one or other of the wooden masks that are the symbols of the Dogon world. As the masked men come into the arena behind elders who lead them at this opening stage, the drums catch up their beat and deepen their tone. The first dancers to enter wear the *kanaga* mask, a two-tiered cross made of light wood with turned-up ends; and in the opening phase of *dama* this is the mask which stands for the power of God the Creator. Other dancers wear masks which represent some part of God's creation, human or animal, threatening or reassuring.

*A Dogon granary door displays most of the elements that make up the Dogon concept of the Creation.*

They come out of the shadow of the hillside, bobbing and swaying between the rocks of the downward path, while the sun of the Western Sudan is still high in the sky. Their skins already gleam with the heat of the day, but they are going to dance for several hours, for the drums will fall silent only when the sun departs. Through these hours they will offer a pageant of the Dogon universe: the people who still inhabit it, the animals they know and live among, and also, still more important, the spirits who preside over it. Last to enter is a man wearing an immensely tall mask, thin and tapering ten feet above his head. This is called "the many-storeyed house", and is also a symbol of the serpent in which the Dogon see the female principle underlying their universe.

Essentially, the *dama* has to do with the survival of the spirits of men and women. The Dogon believe that death need be nothing final, and that with proper attention in this world to behaviour and belief, death can mark the threshold to another world of the ancestors in the land of the spirits. Persons newly dead – and the *dama* is especially concerned with them – are left, as it were, in a state of suspense. As Ogotemmeli explained to Griaule, "the dead lose patience" in this unsatisfactory condition, being neither in this world nor yet in the next, "and cause disorder in the village". It is wise to help them onward into the land of the spirits where they will be at rest.

Along with its portrayal of the pageantry of Dogon life, this is what the *dama* is designed to achieve. The dancers are encouraging the newly dead to quit their "state of suspense" and go forward (or backward, for time in Dogon cosmology has little place) to the ancestors who will award them a due rank as guardians of the people whom they have left behind.

Other mysterious unities of belief await recognition across time and space. In the Biblical story of Genesis, the first people were Adam and Eve who walked with God and shared God's life which does not die. Many African religions tell a story very much the same. They hold that the first people were sent down by God to build the world, and in that remote "time before Time" there was no great separation of people from God. But there came a moment when people offended God by their acts of greed and selfishness, and God decided to withdraw from humankind. In some versions God simply pulled up the ladder or rope which joined heaven with the world, and which the first people could climb up and down as they wished. After this separation came Work, and with

*Overview of a Dogon village* (above). *The* dama *festival of life and death is enacted in the open area in the centre of the village.*

*The dancers (*opposite, above*) descend from their cave above the village in single file, led by one wearing the* kanaga *mask.*

*The* kanaga *dancers (*opposite, left*) celebrate the power of God the Creator. The stilt dancer (*opposite, right*) refers to the Dogon belief that they originated in a country of water herons.*

Work came Death: just as, in the Book of Genesis, Work and Death followed expulsion from the garden of Eden. The *dama* is one of Africa's ceremonies or "services", among the most moving and splendid of them all, whereby people dramatize their "Fall" and seek to rejoin themselves to God by way of God's mercy, which is the wisdom of the ancestors.

Wit and humour help to lighten the essential solemnity of the ceremony, and performers who can reproduce the comic gestures or the prancing movements of the birds or animals they represent are warmly applauded. Others evoke different emotions, for the Dogon universe offers many dangers as well as satisfactions. As the sun goes down the masked dangers begin to weary, and the elders receive their due homage. The mood now is one of reconciliation, celebrating a joyful reassurance in the future. A final display of all the masks, circling the arena, brings the festival to a close.

Tomorrow the Dogon return to their hard reality of toilsome farming in a difficult climate often cursed by drought and pestilence. In an environment that might seem implacably hostile to a less devout people, their ritual has reaffirmed the rightful place of the Dogon in their homeland, and reinforced Dogon convictions and beliefs, especially the belief that mankind should handle life as a gift from God, abusing it as little as human frailty will allow.

If we look at all these matters with the eyes of understanding, and as far beyond sentiment or prejudice as any of us can get, we may begin to find a revelation of the human genius that has known how to tame these lands for habitation and fulfilment. There have been plenty of dark sides to Africa's history: wild moments of social breakdown, violent distortions of belief. There have been many ways in which Africa has needed material development: high infant mortality and the prevalence of disease attest to that. Nothing here was

# The dance of life beyond death

*Dogon symbols of life and afterlife: a granary (above) carries the* kanaga *symbol of creation, while the ancestral home and burial place (right), high in the cliff face above the village, watches over the living.*

any kind of Golden Age. Yet it is easy to forget the other side of the picture, the side which gave attention to the moral imperatives of social and psychological peace. This may be a difficult perception for a modern world in which material development has so far outpaced any moral counterpart as to make that counterpart seem no more than idle superstition or a profitless waste of effort. Yet it is a perception, I think, without which historical Africa cannot be understood.

As the *dama* sways to an end in the gathering night of the Western Sudan, and the last echoes of its drums take flight from the arena, there may be other thoughts along these lines. The truths of the past are elusive, but they exist; and patience can sometimes find and follow them on the wing.

# Chapter 5

# Thrones and rulers

African history begins with the story of how people mastered a continent of tremendous environmental difficulties and in time evolved a wide variety of social and political systems. Notable among these was the magnificence of kingship. The lord of the little kingdom of Sukur might crouch on a dusty stool in a humble courtyard, with three or four perfunctory praise-singers all that he could muster. even when there were visitors to impress. But that was on the fringe of kingly power, and late in time. Great forerunners had amazed the world. Their courts and thrones had glittered with pomp and majesty.

Medieval travellers found the lords of the mighty states of the Western Sudan – Ghana, Mali, Songhay, Bornu – ensconced on carved thrones of blood-red camwood, under domes of saffron silk guarded by great dogs with golden collars and attended by cavaliers in vests of chain mail. The king of the Wolof of Senegal could raise an army of 10,000 horsemen and 100,000 foot soldiers, or so the earliest European visitors went home to report.

Other Europeans found the lord of Kazembe, who ruled in what is now south-western Zaire, surrounded by warriors and officials, and enthroned on skins of leopards and lions, wearing a cloak embroidered with mirrors, so that "when struck by the sun's rays, it was too bright to look upon". The traditions of southern Uganda, even as few as 70 years ago, still spoke with awe about the way that ordinary mortals would not dare to look into the eyes of kings. And the majesty of the kings of Benin, far westward across the continent, was such that no one could publicly come near their presence.

So it is clear that the kingships of Africa form a large and dramatic chapter in our journey through time, even though a majority of African communities, such as those of the Pokot and the Dogon, never found any use for monarchs but much preferred to get along without them. Why and when did African kingdoms come upon the scene?

In searching for the beginning of kingdoms we must go back to the food-cultivation and metal-smithing which had made permanent settlement possible, and marked the transition from nomadic ways of life. Division of labour and craft specialization followed. Chosen elders or priests became chiefs, chiefs became kings with little power, and kings with great power derived from these. Better defences against rival states or communities could be one reason for creating and accepting kingships. The advancement of trade with neighbours, as well as the distribution of the profits of trade, could be another, while personal intrigue and ambition could push the process further once it was set in motion. In all this, of course, Africa's history was substantially no different from that of any other continent.

Kings absorbed the authority of prestigious ancestors, buttressed their dignity with pomp and ceremony, and behaved as though God had always

Os montes claros em africa.

*A medieval map suitably records the civilizations of Western Africa that deeply impressed contemporary Europeans.*

wished them to exploit their subjects. Speaking for "the power without beginning", they became part of the normal order of society for those who had created and accepted them. "Royal authority", remarked the great North African historian, Ibn Khaldun, in about 1400, "is an institution that is natural to mankind". Without kings, he explained, anarchy would rule. The Pokot might be among many who judged this no disadvantage, but to the warring states of North Africa the advantage of having kings appeared an obvious one. They might be an expensive and oppressive nuisance, but were considered, at least by those with access to power and privilege, to be worth the price.

**An ancient legacy**

The earliest African kingships were those of the Nile valley, and seem to have developed before kingships outside Africa. We have already considered their origins and their achievement of powerful governments with elaborate beliefs and ceremonies, deriving from identification of royal authority with the will of the gods. In ways unknown, the same basic ideas about royal power reappeared in other regions across later centuries: westward through the Berber lands of the north, southwestward into the grassland plains and forests of West Africa, and southward again, perhaps carried by what has been termed "the Bantu spread", through the vast regions of the rest of the continent. Small chiefdoms or "proto-kingships" certainly took shape as far south as South Africa by the sixth of seventh century AD.

The Arab historians of medieval times learned a little about this wide diffusion of political ideas and structures. Though their contemporaries seldom visited inland areas, Arab and Berber travellers sometimes came to these distant kingdoms. In the 10th century they knew of strong kingships in the grassland

*A Central African empire, contemporary with the early civilizations of West Africa but unknown to medieval Europe, built the majestic structures (*above *and* left) *of Great Zimbabwe.*

plains beyond the Sahara Desert. A powerful East African kingdom was reported around 945 by the Cairene chronicler and traveller al-Masudi, whose own travels had taken him by ship from the Persian Gulf far down the eastern seaboard. There is no good reason to doubt that, by the tenth century, the more important of such kingships had crystallized into forms of central government as generally effective as any in the Europe of that period.

Later evidence has confirmed the accounts of those historians of the Middle Ages. This evidence is of various kinds, and although little noticed until recent years, has in fact been accumulating for a long time.

### The quest for history

Most of the exploring Europeans of the nineteenth century were after conquests or concessions, but a rare few went exploring for history. One of these, a Hungarian called Emil Torday, penetrated the southern forests of the Congo basin about a century ago. There he found the Bushong, a people of whom nothing was known except that they carved splendidly in wood and were proud of their kings. The elders of the Bushong received Torday with courtesy, and offered him palm wine in one of their distinguished wooden goblets. They were pleased by his interests in the history of their kings.

Torday listened as they went back through reign after reign, but wondered whether this was proper history: where, after all, were the dates? Then came a breakthrough. Torday wrote:

> As the elders were talking of the great events of various reigns, and we came to their 98th king, Bo Kama Bomanchala, they said that nothing remarkable had happened during his reign, except that one day at noon the sun went out, and there was absolute darkness for a short while.

*Bushong wooden headrest with traditional carvings.*

Upon hearing this, Torday leaped to his feet and "lost all self-control: the elders thought that I had been stung by a scorpion". Months later, back in Europe, he looked up at the records of total eclipses of the sun, and found that one of them would have occurred over Bushong country on 30 March 1680. He had found a date for the reign of Bo Kama whose conquests, the elders told him, "were in the field of thought, public prosperity and social progress, and who is remembered in our day by every person in the country". And when had the first Bushong king ruled, 97 reigns before Bo Kama? Nobody knows, but it was possibly in the 13th century.

Torday's experience points to the historical value of African tradition, sometimes called "oral history" because it is transmitted by word of mouth across generations. Among peoples without kingships, such history seldom goes back more than a few generations, but kings made a point of remembering their history and lineage in order to bolster their authority. Sometimes this oral history goes back through many generations, and is fairly reliable, if only because non-literate people attach value to good memory. Occasionally, as with the eclipse of the sun in King Bo Kama's reign, precise dates become possible.

Modern archaeology has greatly extended the number of approximately accurate dates that can be added, thanks largely to the Carbon-14 method of testing organic materials, developed early in the 1950s by Professor Willard Frank Libby of the University of Chicago. We know from this method, for example, that the early bronzes of royal Ife in Nigeria date from around 1300, while those of Igbo-Ukwu, also in Nigeria, may have been made still earlier. The Carbon-14 method has already given us many hundreds of approximate dates for events and monuments of long ago, and is continually adding more.

Other sources of evidence can be correlated with oral histories and Carbon-14 dates. One of them is the occurrence of imported pots, beads, jewellery and other artifacts whose broad date of manufacture is known from their countries

of origin, as with Persian pottery and Chinese porcelain. Another source, increasingly copious after the 1500s, is to be found in the books and reports of early European travellers, and most of all in those of the early Portuguese mariners.

This skillful building of various strands of evidence into a rounded picture of the past is clearly illustrated by the history of the Zimbabwe culture and its imposing ruins.

## Great Zimbabwe

Having rounded the southernmost point of Africa in 1497, five years after Columbus had found the New World, the Portuguese admiral Vasco da Gama and his men followed the coastline northwards and became the first Europeans to see the ports and cities of the East African seaboard. Though they pressed on in their search for India, they were greatly surprised by the wealth and comfort of this coastal civilization, and heard news of an apparently mighty inland country that was another total blank upon their maps. Other Portuguese quickly followed them and took careful notes.

"Beyond that country towards the interior," Duarte Barbosa told a Lisbon audience in 1517, "lies the great kingdom of the Monomotapa". Its kings ruled beyond the inland horizons of what is today southern Mozambique, and they were powerful. Barbosa saw their emissaries at the coastal ports, where they came to buy cottons from India and silks from China. Some of these emissaries, "the most noble ones", wore skins with tassel-tails that trailed on the ground, as tokens of their dignity and status, and carried "swords thrust into wooden scabbards, bound with much gold and other metals, worn on the left side as we wear them." Others carried spears or bows with arrows of finely pointed iron,

*The author stands before the walls of Great Zimbabwe's Elliptical Building. Surmounted by a chevron-patterned frieze, these were once surrounded by many other enclosures and huts. The whole complex was the court and residence of a powerful king of the Shona people.*

for "they are warlike men, as well as great traders".

Getting to this great king's capital, Barbosa heard, called for a three weeks' journey on foot; and there stood the king's palace, "a very large building" constructed, according to another Portuguese report of the same period, "of big and heavy stones within and without, a very curious and well-constructed building in which no cement can be seen." It was known as the great king's *zimbabwe*.

*Zimbabwe* is a Shona word meaning royal court, and we now know that there were about 200 *zimbabwes* and related stone buildings in that inland country, the "seats" of kings, sub-kings and governors. Most were dotted about the grassland plateau now enclosed by the republic of Zimbabwe, but some lay eastward in Mozambique and one at least, at Manikweni, was only 50km (30 miles) from the coast itself. The *zimbabwe* mentioned by Barbosa, clearly the largest of all, was the one we know as Great Zimbabwe.

There it stands now, a truly massive walled enclosure, with other great enclosures built inside it, wall within wall, still reaching at their highest point to 9m (30ft), and built, as the Portuguese reported, of massive stones without cement. Today it seems strangely on its own, mysterious in its solitude, an awesome monster of a building; but the archaeologists have shown that it was once surrounded by lesser stone structures and a dense cluster of mud-and-thatch dwellings.

On the steep small hill nearby, zigzag pathways climb into another maze of ruins until, near their summit, you are standing in a high space ringed by a wall. Here, in the time of the great kings, stood the stone bird-figures of the king's chief oracle, removed by European plunderers nearly a century ago. The bird's name was Shiri ya Mwari, the Bird of God, the eagle whose hoarse cries linked the diviners of the Shona to the wisdom of the ancestors. Lingering here you can catch an echo, more clearly perhaps than anywhere else except at Karnak of the Pharoahs or Meroe of the Lion-King, of a time when gods and kings walked hand in hand.

The expert investigation of these and lesser buildings in the same country began with David Randall-MacIver in 1905, continued with Gertrude Caton-Thompson in 1929, and was again carried forward in the 1950s and later by Kenneth Robinson, Roger Summers and Peter Garlake. With additions and refinements, all the latter specialists agree with the general conclusions of Randall-MacIver and Caton-Thompson. Great Zimbabwe and similar ruins were the work of local Africans, drawing their inspiration from their own traditions. They were medieval in date, Great Zimbabwe itself probably being completed by about AD1300 or soon after. No serious researcher would now question these conclusions.

Yet they were hotly contested at the time, particularly by recent European settlers in Africa and their supporters at home. For obvious reasons these newcomers, who had lately seized the country from its African owners, were extremely eager to ascribe all sign of any former civilization to "some mysterious race who had come from beyond the seas". That was understandable, however mistaken, because once it was conceded that the "natives" of what was to become Southern Rhodesia had comparatively recently built these famous structures, how could it still be affirmed that the descendants of these same "natives" possessed no history, and thus were "barbarous children" without a right to own the land they lived in?

So the settlers invented myths, and these myths were inflated into marvels by the discovery of golden jewellery in the ruins. Soon it was said that this land north of the Limpopo river, so evidently rich in gold, had been the Queen of Sheba's country, some 3,000 years earlier, or, alternatively, the land of King

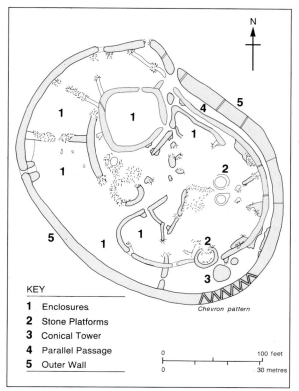

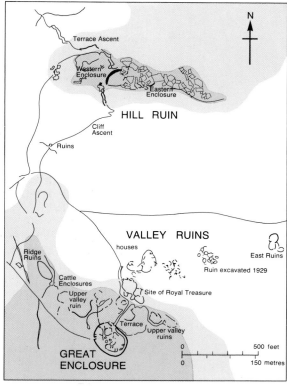

KEY

**1** Enclosures
**2** Stone Platforms
**3** Conical Tower
**4** Parallel Passage
**5** Outer Wall

*Chevron pattern*

Solomon's mines. Such myths might be harmless, but they led to activities which were not. Prospectors drove their ox teams northward and were richly rewarded. An American looter called Burnham, picking over the ruins of the *zimbabwe* at Dhlo Dhlo, collected 18kg (40lb) of "gold inlaid work and gold ornaments", all of which he sent back to South Africa. A little later, in 1895, two British looters, Neal and Johnson, uncovered five burials where the grave goods included 5.9kg (13lb) of gold beads and bangles. They sold these in South Africa for £3,000, and established a looting enterprise called the Rhodesian Ancient Ruins Company. Until halted by enlightened outcry in 1901, the agents of this company took away another 14kg (31lb) of gold pieces. Nearly all these objects from the glory of ancient Zimbabwe were melted down; almost none survived. The damage to history was enormous.

The extent of this damage could be gauged only in the 1930s, when a site of the Zimbabwe Culture in northern Transvaal, on the South African bank of the Limpopo river was examined for the first time. Fine gold objects were sent to Pretoria museum, where the quality of their beaten gold astonished the experts.

Meanwhile, amateur antiquarians were also at work in the area, each of them proceeding on the conviction that local Africans could never have been the builders or even the inhabitants of these palaces and towns. First came an English clergyman, the Reverend Theodore Bent, who arrived by ox team, together with Mrs Bent, in 1891. After clambering round Great Zimbabwe for a month, Bent decided that the ruins could not be ascribed to the Queen of Sheba, much less to King Solomon of Israel, and opted for the Phoenicians of about the same period. This opinion he buttressed with much laying out of compass points and far comparisons. This, though silly, did little damage. Indeed, it inspired a popular novelist, Rider Haggard, to write one of his best stories,

*Site plans of Great Zimbabwe (above) and its "Elliptical Building" (left) show the scale of the complex and the quantity of stonebuilt enclosures. They enhanced the prestige of the kings, but had no military purpose.*

"Elissa, or the Doom of Zimbabwe", in which he told how Great Zimbabwe, "adorned with temples", had been built long long ago "by civilized men in the heart of Africa".

The Reverend Bent may have done relatively little harm, but he was followed by a certain R.N. Hall, who was a real disaster. Hall had absorbed the full mythology, and concluded that, since the Phoenicians had built Zimbabwe in a time when Carthage was a great city, they must have left signs of their presence. Well supplied with money, Hall employed teams of labourers to dig down rapidly through the occupation layers within the great enclosure until, as he believed, they could uncover the signs of Phoenician occupation. No such signs were found, but irreparable harm was done.

Hall and his men excavated down to bedrock, removing as much as 12 feet of the occupation layers of the Shona builders and inhabitants. All this material they threw out into the surrounding bush, and Hall explained that this was necessary in order to remove "the filth and decadence of the Kaffir [local African] occupation". Only in 1904 was Hall's excavation, described by a contemporary archaeologist as "reckless plundering, worse than anything I have ever seen", brought finally to an end. The question then was: did enough evidence remain for expert archaeologists to work on with conclusive results?

### The empire of the Monomotapa

Happily, the answer was yes, as has been amply proved. Archaeologists have found "not one item of evidence", as Gertrude Caton-Thompson reported in 1931, that is "not in accordance with the claim of Bantu origin and medieval date". Clinching evidence has come from three sources.

First, there is the evidence of Carbon-14 dates correlated with that of imported objects, such as Chinese porcelain, whose period of manufacture is securely known. Hall's depradations had clearly lost or destroyed many imported objects as he shoveled out the "Kaffir dirt", but enough remained to confirm the dating sequence. Secondly, there is a great deal of evidence about the Zimbabwe Culture's involvement in the Indian Ocean trade by way of coastal intermediaries, and much of this can be dated. Last but not least, there has come to hand a range of confirmatory evidence from the oral history of local African peoples.

So the whole picture has become remarkably clear. Local African peoples, the ancestors of the present Shona inhabitants, began building in stone around AD1100. Small kingdoms took shape, and the stone builders, using the excellent granite of their country, improved their skills. Prospering by their long-distance trade in the export of gold across the Indian Ocean in return for manufactured goods, notably cotton stuffs, the kings grew stronger and built larger palaces.

The fate of Great Zimbabwe itself remains something of a puzzle, for it was abandoned as a royal court less than a century and a half after its completion, though remaining the seat of an important priesthood. Relatively dense settlement may have exhausted local supplies of timber and soil fertility, since there is no evidence of any military pressure to move. But where did the kings go to? Here Shona oral history comes to our aid. The king who abandoned Great Zimbabwe, Mutota, moved to a new capital in the Mount Darwin area not far south of the Zambezi river. In about 1425, having done this, Mutota set out upon a career of conquest of neighbouring kings. He harassed the people who stood in his way, and some of these gave him the title that stayed with his dynasty right down to the nineteenth century. They called him the Mwana-Mutapha, "the lord of ravaged lands"; and this was the title that the Portuguese misheard as Monomotapa when they sought information about the inland country from the people of the East Coast city ports.

# The empire of the Monomotapa

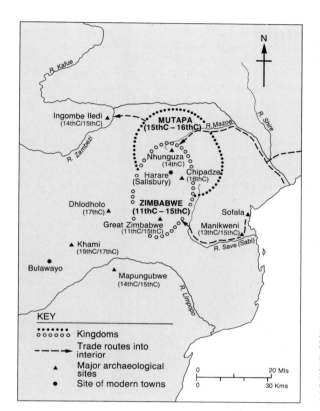

A map of the stone ruins of south Central Africa (left) shows the spread of the Zimbabwe-building culture. The 15thC emperor Mutota (above) greatly extended his territory but abandoned Great Zimbabwe itself.

Mutota's evident intention was to bring all the rulers of the Zimbabwe plateau and of neighbouring Mozambique under his sway. He would then have a single large zone of tax and tribute. This could lead to an increase of wealth and a reduction of local obstacles to the flow of export-import trade. But there is no means now of understanding just what Mutota's immediate motives were in building this large system of political control. All that we know without doubt is that he certainly succeeded, and that by 1480, when Mutota's successor Matope died, the Mwana-Mutapha was recognized as supreme lord of all the lands between the Kalahari and the Indian Ocean, except for the coastal ports which remained in Swahili hands.

This was the "great kingdom" of which Duarte Barbosa took back news to Europe. But by the time Barbosa was on the coast, in the earliest years of the sixteenth century, this territory had in fact undergone a split. The huge system built by Mutota and Matope may have proved too big for its administrative and military structure, for Matope's empire was brief. His death signalled the outbreak of strife between rival Shona kings, and a series of "barons' wars" followed. The empire was divided into the northern lands of the Mwana-Mutapha and a southern kingdom called Urozwi, "the land of the Rozwi", a subdivision of the Shona-speaking group of peoples. At the same time, most of the lesser kings of Mozambique regained their freedom of action.

Great Zimbabwe and other large stone structures of the early building period – up to about 1400 – therefore predate the conquests of Mutota and Matope and the rise of Urozwi. Another group of buildings, dating mostly to 1500–1600, were the work of the Rozwi rulers, and in this group is found the most impressive ruin in the western part of modern Zimbabwe, at Khami near Bulawayo. There the dignity of its divinely empowered ruler was protected in a

*Khami in Matabeleland, near Bulawayo, was one of many Zimbabwes (royal residences) built after the decline of Great Zimbabwe in the 15thC.*

manner as marked as at Great Zimbabwe, though with less architectural magnificence. Other *zimbabwes* on a smaller scale, sometimes housing only a handful of privileged persons, continued to be built for another century or so.

The evidence suggests that the owners and residents of *zimbabwes* belonged to a comparatively small group of ruling families. The most authoritative and qualified of recent specialists consider that no more than 50 *zimbabwes* were in use at any one time. When local timber and pasture were used up, new *zimbabwes* were built and old ones abandoned, or left to the care of a handful of occupants. Furthermore, it is clear that these buildings in stone, large though they were, had no important military function. After the upheavals of the fifteenth century a long peace set in here, and was broken before the nineteenth century only in the north, with the intrusion of the Portuguese into the lands of the Monomotapa.

### Stages of development

Summarizing this complex record, the firm information available today points to a number of broad stages in the political development of Africa's kingships.

If the latest archaeological findings are confirmed, it appears that the earliest kingdoms evolved in the middle valley of the Nile upstream from Aswan, the southern frontier of modern Egypt, nearly 6,000 years ago. They flowered into the royal civilization of the Pharoahs, and reached a strength and sophistication unequalled in the ancient world. This civilization flourished for most of 3,000 years, and was still alive, though under Roman occupation, as late as the beginning of the Christian era.

As new populations took shape and multiplied south of the Sahara, notably with the spread of tropical farming and metal-working after about 500BC, social

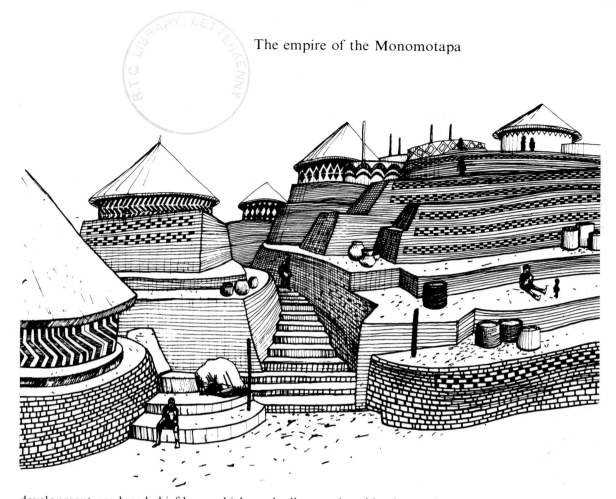

*Reconstruction of Khami.*

development produced chiefdoms which gradually grew into kingdoms wherever circumstances were propitious: in the Western Sudan, for example, where long-distance trade and rivalry for markets were fuelled by a demand for gold, ivory, and other products. So we find that ancient Ghana, in the westerly plains of the Western Sudan, had probably evolved a strong kingship by AD500, or conceivably earlier, and had certainly done so by 700. Neighbouring peoples followed the same line of political development; and by 900 the kings of western Africa were many and magnificent.

Wherever the same kinds of influence were at work in other parts of Africa, they produced much the same results, as farming and metal-working communities multiplied. By about 800 we have good evidence of a strong chiefdom or early kingship in the copper-mining zone of the Katanga (Shaba today), south of the Congo rainforest. A little later the extraction of gold from deposits on the central-southern plateau, mined to a depth of some 24m (80ft) below ground, had reached such proportions that al-Masudi could write in 945 of the large quantity of precious metal exported to the East. And around 1100 we have the foundations of stone-built Great Zimbabwe. All this points to a wide proliferation of early kingships.

By about AD1300, or soon after, the old kingships were replaced or succeeded by others with greater ambitions, and with the military resources and tax-derived revenue to realize their plans. After 1250 the old West African empire of Ghana was succeeded by the larger empire of Mali. The rulers of royal Ife were rich enough, by 1300, to commission fine sculpture in terracotta and bronze, and royal Benin took shape at about the same period. A new range of kingdoms came into being along the hills of the East African Rift Valley and across southern Uganda.

# Thrones and rulers

*Soapstone "Bird of God" from Great Zimbabwe's Eastern Enclosure. These birds may have been symbolic images of the ancestors themselves, sculptured links between earth and sky, man and his origins.*

The lords of the Zimbabwe Culture, as we have seen, similarly enlarged their scope after about 1300. By then, too, the Swahili kings of East African Kilwa were minting their own coins. There is much other evidence to the same effect: the fourteenth century marked an important stage of the development of traditional African kingdoms.

Some of these kingships, in the north and west and east, were much influenced by the coming of Islam with its legal and economic codes. But all of them built on earlier foundations of belief and custom, whose most remote origins seem to have evolved in the valley of the Nile. So there is a real sense in which the peoples of the middle and lower Nile, over distant centuries, had "given back" to inner Africa much that they had developed, in still earlier times, from their ancient African beginnings.

# Chapter 6

# West African brilliance

While Bantu development after about AD1000 was launching states and kingdoms across central and southern Africa almost as far as the Cape of Good Hope, other peoples in the forest zones of western Africa evolved on strikingly parallel lines. They achieved, in due course, a brilliance of their own.

Unlike the Bantu, whose spread through distant regions seems to have begun less than 3,000 years ago, these West Africans, who belonged to language groups other than Bantu, had continuously inhabited their countries since very ancient times. Their remote ancestors had mastered their forest environment to the extent of being able to live by hunting and by gathering fruits and other uncultivated food. Numerous stone tools found scattered in the region testify to a successful and enduring Stone Age population.

Major cultural changes came with the development of farming and the acquisition of metal-working technology, chiefly in iron, which supplemented stone as the material of everyday tools. The techniques of smelting and forging iron were put into practice along the fringes of the West African forest belt soon after 500BC. Among those who made the transition to an early Iron Age were the people of the Nok culture, living astride the lower reaches of the Benue river and across the Jos plateau, in what today is central Nigeria. The Nok culture produced an abundance of small terracotta figures and heads, fine in conception and admirably composed, revealing a detailed and sympathetic observation of the human face. Such clay figures have since been found in many parts of central Nigeria, but the first to come to light were discovered by miners digging for tin on the Jos plateau in the 1940s; Nok, the village where they were found, has given its name to this interesting early culture.

With the gradual diffusion of metal-working technology into the forest lands, there opened a broad sequence of development from very small settlements, to larger ones, from primitive tool-making to skills of considerable ingenuity, and from merely local trade between neighbouring hamlets to complex systems of exchange across wide territories. Social and political forms of self-government that reflected these changes evolved in considerable variety, although they all seem to have originated from simple family systems in antiquity. East of the lower reaches of the Niger river, for example, the increasing complexity of community life led the Igbo and many neighbouring peoples into forms of government by village assembly or by elders who were the heads of lineage groups. Occasionally these elders also became kings. Others, west of the Niger, turned away from the customs of village democracy and evolved distinctive forms of aristocratic and monarchical government. Prominent among these were the Yoruba and some of their close neighbours. In this chapter we will concentrate on two of these peoples west of the Niger, the Yoruba of Ife (pronounced *Ee-fay*) and the Edo of Benin.

The map shows the development of western African forestland peoples, from the Nok iron-age culture originating c. 500BC to the Benin civilization that deeply impressed Portuguese visitors.

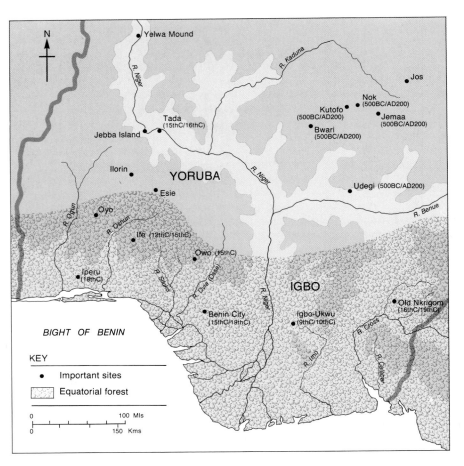

N

Yelwa Mound

Jos

Nok (500BC/AD200)

Kutofo (500BC/AD200)

Jemaa (500BC/AD200)

Bwari (500BC/AD200)

Tada (15thC/16thC)

Jebba Island

Udegi (500BC/AD200)

Ilorin

YORUBA

R. Niger

R. Kaduna

R. Benue

Esie

Oyo

Ife (12thC/16thC)

Owo (15thC)

IGBO

Iperu (18thC)

Old Nkrigom (16thC/19thC)

Benin City (15thC/19thC)

Igbo-Ukwu (9thC/10thC)

BIGHT OF BENIN

KEY

•  Important sites

   Equatorial forest

0          100  Mls

0          150  Kms

### Kingship at Ife

In the beginning, according to the religion of the Yoruba, there was Olodumare, the Spirit of God, majestic in solitude and endless in power. And Olodumare, for reasons that men still dispute, felt the need to create the world. He – or She, for Olodumare is above all such earthly separations – called on lesser spirits, and these created the world in four days, setting aside the fifth for rest and worship: which is why, incidentally, public markets in Yorubaland still occur on every fourth day.

After that, but for reasons that men prefer not to dispute, Olodumare felt the need to create mankind. He (or She) brought people from the sky and set them down at Ile-Ife, the city of Ife; and from Ile-Ife they spread and multiplied across the world.

Ife nowadays is a rather small town in the forest land some 120km (75 miles) from the ocean, but has long been said to have enjoyed a prestigious past. Among other things, Yoruba tradition maintains that Ife was the royal seat of their great founding ancestor, Oduduwa, who despatched his children to launch and govern other Yoruba kingdoms; and this is why Ife remains for the Yoruba their senior and holy city.

The Yoruba consider that these things are true, if also timeless, and have required no material confirmation of the existence of their early kings. But Europeans, insofar as they heard anything at all about such matters, had no such faith in their veracity. Then in 1911, quite suddenly, material confirmation

*A terracotta head from the Nok culture*

of early Yoruba kings took utterly unexpected shape.

It was then, as we have seen, that the German researcher Leo Frobenius visited Ife and obtained a number of terracotta sculptures. These were not only of manifestly great artistic merit; more surprisingly, they were clearly sculptures portraying real people, and were therefore in strong contrast to the abstract styles so generally associated then and since with the arts of Nigeria and other West African lands.

Just because of this, few Europeans of that time were ready to accept the local African origin of these terracottas, and Frobenius himself went so far as to suggest that they might be fragments of the lost civilization of Atlantis, situated on this occasion off the shores of southern Nigeria. But fresh surprises were on the way.

In 1938 Ife yielded still more remarkable finds and, as so often in Africa over the past half century or more, the finds were mere builder's luck. Digging foundations for a house in the middle of Ife, workers came upon 13 bronze heads buried in the soil. A year later at much the same place four more bronze heads were recovered, together with part of a male figure wearing a beaded gown, and some lesser artifacts. One head was bought by the British Museum, which kept it; the American anthropologist W.R. Bascom, who was researching in Ife at the time, acquired two others but later gave them back. All save one of them, today, are in the museum of Ife not far from the palace of the *Oni* or King of Ife, traditional ruler of this Yoruba state.

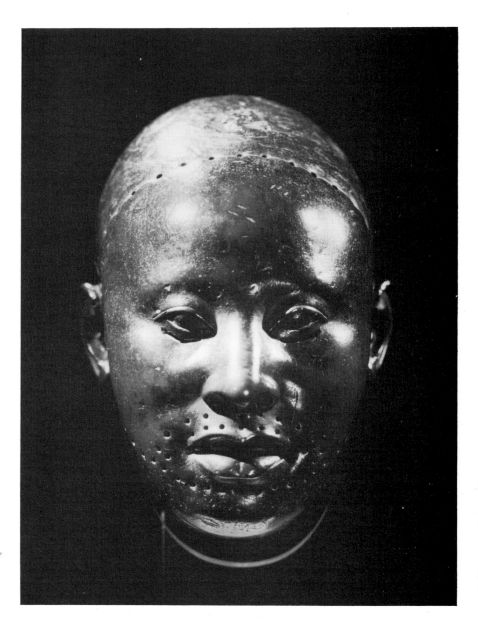

*A lifesize bronze head (13thC–15thC) from the Yoruba city-state of Ife represents a dead king or* oni. *Olodamare the High-God is believed to have created mankind at Ife. The head of the* oni *was used in funeral ceremonies and carried the crown of the dead king.*

These finds were sensational for several reasons. To begin with, they provided a portrait gallery of Ife kings and royal persons that confirmed the earlier evidence of the terracottas. They were conceived and executed to aesthetic conceptions of the highest possible merit. They were cast in bronze by the lost-wax method to a magnificent degree of skill and finish. Nothing could have more splendidly displayed the ancient civilization of Ife and its people.

How ancient? The question was long discussed, but dating by the Carbon-14 method has now enabled archaeological science to place both the bronzes and terracottas found by Frobenius at around 1300, a date that fits very well with other evidence of an historical nature. Yoruba culture by that time had evidently developed within complex systems of aristocratic rule. A flourishing agriculture had long provided a surplus for a non-productive minority which, having gathered power to itself, had embarked on a comfortable urban life of conspicuous consumption. Expanding long-distance trade brought profits to those who could control it, as well as the import of goods and materials not locally available. In the case of the Ife market for fine art, such trade brought copper from Saharan deposits, which smiths could alloy with local tin to make bronze.

Ife and its daughter kingdoms of the Yoruba continued to enjoy independence and prosperity for several centuries, and indeed their descendants are still in place. The *Oni* of Ife presides today in his palace, though without any temporal power, and other Yoruba kings do likewise. Most of these kingdoms were gathered together in the seventeenth century by the Yoruba of Oyo, somewhat to the north of Ife, and an Oyo empire reigned supreme over much of southwestern Nigeria until various disasters laid it low in the nineteenth century.

Yet the famous art of royal Ife was not conserved, and no more sculptured portraits were made to embellish the glory of its kings and princes. The reason for this may simply be that fashions and preferences changed, for certainly there was no deterioration in artistic skill and capacity, at least until colonial times. Generally, the arts of these people and their neighbours have remained at a high level of achievement, and in a variety of styles that range from the abstract to the near-representational.

While the sons of Oduduwa reigned at Ife, another enterprise in Nigerian kingship was adding a different brilliance to this epic of royalty. This was at Benin, about 160km (100 miles) south-east of Ife, and within a day's journey from the shores of the Atlantic. Here, too, sculpture in metal reached heights of excellence, but with the notable difference that some 7,000 Benin works in metal are extant, and that a great deal is clearly known about the history of Benin.

## Royal Benin

Europe first heard about Benin, in any sort of detail, from a Dutchman, Dierick Ruiters, who went there as a merchant some time shortly before 1600. He reported that Benin was a "very big" city, for,

> when you go into it you go into a big broad street, not paved, which seems to be seven or eight times broader than our Warmoes-street in Amsterdam. This street goes along straight without a bend; and where I was lodged, with Matteus Cornelison, it was at least a quarter of an hour's distance from the gate, and yet I could still not see to the other end of the street.

Before entering through the gate Ruiters had noted "a great suburb" outside it. Once within, he saw "many great streets to the right and left. But you cannot see to the end of these, because of their length."

> The houses in this town stand in good order, one close and even with the other, as the houses stand in Holland. Those belonging to men of quality (which are gentlemen) have two or three steps to go up, and in front of each there is a kind of gallery where a man may sit dry. The palace of the king is very large, having within it many square courtyards with galleries around them, where sentries always stand. I myself went through four such courtyards, and wherever I looked I saw gate after gate entering into other places.

Once a year, the king went on "public progress" around the exterior of his palace, "riding a horse adorned with ornaments, with a train of three or four hundred gentlemen, horses and cavalry, and musicians." A Dutchman made a drawing of this progress, and Olfert Dapper years later published it in an Amsterdam collection of 1668.

What were the origins of this impressive city? Here we are on much firmer

*A bronze head (early 16thC) from Benin, the Edo capital. It is believed to represent the mother of Oba (King) Esigie (ruled c. 1550).*

1. Speelders voor den Koning me tamme Ijsers.

ground than with Ife, chiefly thanks to the plenitude of royal traditions at Benin. While kings may have been a great and sometimes pestilential nuisance to ordinary people, they are often useful to historians. Kings in Africa, like kings anywhere else, buttressed their power with pomp and circumstance, and saw to it that they were celebrated in privileged ways, not least with the artistic use of "royal metals", gold wherever available or, as in the Nigerian kingdoms, various alloys of bronze or brass. They also saw to it that their lines of descent and their famous deeds were suitably remembered by persons appointed to remember. This helps us little in the case of Ife, but a great deal in that of Benin, since the Bini or Edo royal traditions of Benin are capacious.

The Benin kingship, which still survives in the person and associated rituals of the reigning *Oba* (an amiable monarch of ceremonial importance), took clear shape around AD 1000 – about the same time as that of Ife and other kingships of the western African forest zones. This approximate date marks a very general transition to mature forms of Iron Age culture in wide areas of Africa, and it was from about this point in time that the foundations of the Zimbabwe kingships also took shape.

Royal traditions retain a little information about Benin's earliest kings, though largely in the form of legend. Firmer local evidence begins to accumulate from about 1400, and then, onwards from 1500, there are many reports by European ambassadors, visitors and traders who were able to reach this city lying near to the edge of the ocean.

The temporal power of Benin and its territorial empire reached a climax about a century before the earliest Europeans arrived. Its kings and governors

*The annual progress of the Oba of Benin, as recorded by a 17thC Dutch artist. The city of Benin extends impressively behind the royal palace.*

79

*Statue of an* oni *(14thC) wearing the traditional regalia, including crown and necklaces with a double bow. He holds a ram's horn in his left hand.*

then controlled a wide band of coastal and near-coastal Nigeria, stretching about 200km (125 miles) from north to south, and as much again westward from the Niger and its delta streams. *Oba* Ewuare, who reigned after about 1440, is especially remembered as an empire-builder, and he is said to have added no fewer than 201 neighbouring towns to those already controlled by his people. He is also said to have made good roads in Benin city, and to have practised as a healer of various kinds of sickness.

As with many other monarchs in Africa, the *Oba* of Benin has been called a "divine king", but the term is misleading. He was neither thought of as divine nor worshipped as a god. Yet his power (and therefore his person) had divine sanction because it embodied the will of ghostly ancestors, who were the spiritual representatives of the Most High.

Divine sanction gave the *Obas* of Benin – as well as the *Onis* of Ife and other rulers of their kind – a prestige that no other person in the community could match or contest; and it surrounded them with awe and mystery. However, the *Obas* of Benin could not be despots, even if a priesthood dependent on their prestige might encourage such an attitude for they had to rule through chiefs and sub-chiefs who were organized in rival groupings so as to complement each others' rights or duties and place limits round the powers of the king. One can draw a rough parallel between the powers of *Oba* Ehengbuda and his English contemporary, Queen Elizabeth I: the scope for action of both these monarchs, no matter how large their renown and royal authority, was essentially much the

*Bronze plaque from the Oba's palace illustrates the ritual acrobatic dance called the* amufi, *recalling a legendary war. Ibises, birds of disaster, perch on the tree.*

same. Ehengbuda, like Elizabeth, might frame a policy and carry it through, or else fly into a diplomatic rage whenever a courtier turned obstructive. To gain his ends, Ehengbuda had to "manage" rival courtiers and flatter or scold. The courtiers, for their part, had to pay attention to the needs of all those who made up public opinion.

The kind of formal admonition that was addressed to the rulers of a much later West African kingdom may reflect the situation at Benin. When chiefs of the Asante state (in the central part of modern Ghana) were "enstooled" with appropriate ceremony and ritual, they were given advice, and expected to follow it on peril of "de-stoolment". The spokesmen of the public said to the enstooling officials:

*Tell him that*
*We do not wish for greediness*
*We do not wish that his ears should be hard of hearing*
*We do not wish that he should call people fools*
*We do not wish that he should act on his own initiative*
*We do not wish that it should ever be said:*
*"I have no time.*
*I have no time."*
*We do not wish personal abuse*
*We do not wish personal violence.*

*Ornate cuffs carved from single blocks of ivory by 18thC Benin craftsmen for the* oba *or king. Half the ivory taken by hunters belonged by custom to the king.*

Visitors from Europe were impressed by Benin's social discipline and civic order, and also by a general stability and self-confidence which they had evidently not expected to find. Much that they saw seemed strange or even shocking: for example, the practice of young unmarried women to walk naked in the streets, or the *Oba's* reputed possession of 1,000 wives; but these visitors also found a welcome and were grateful for it. The citizens of Benin, says another Dutch report of the early seventeenth century,

> are people who have good laws and a well-organized police; who live on good terms with the Dutch and other foreigners who came to trade among them, and who show them a thousand marks of friendship.

Arriving earlier than the Dutch and as keen on missionary enterprise as the Dutch were to be keen on trade, the Portuguese had even received permission to build a church in Benin city and import priests from Portugal. Benin notables began to learn to speak Portuguese, ambassadors were exchanged, and much was discovered about each other's homelands.

All this belonged to a peaceful and constructive period of Afro-European contact along the western seaboard, when the aggression and confrontations of later times were scarcely hinted at. And Benin continued to enjoy independence and prosperity as a great trading city and the capital of a kingdom for a long time after Dierick Ruiters and his friends sojourned in the street whose farther end they could not see.

# Chapter 7

# Caravans of gold

North of the ancient forest kingdoms of Ife and Benin, the dense forests of West Africa thin to spinneys and thickets. Northward again, the thickets give way to open bush and isolated baobab trees, and then at last to bare horizons. These are the plains of the Sahel, the southern "shores" of the Sahara. Far westward they stretch to the coast of the Atlantic, far eastward to the sudden mountains of Darfur. Travelling in the middle reaches of these plains, beyond Liberia and Sierra Leone, one seems to move in an endless silence through a grassland world without limits, frontiers, or shelters from the sun.

Shelters there are, though: ancient cities spread far apart, with villages between, and, in the villages, travellers' inns and wayside caravanserais. For this is a land of trading caravans – strings of donkeys, camels and human wayfarers on foot – that have trailed across these plains for as long as history can remember. And history, here, can remember a long way back.

If you are lucky, as I have been in past years, you may find a teller of history at the inn: perhaps at Kong or Wa, at Ka Ba or Djeliba Koro. I can recall an occasion when the teller, a woman, came into an inn on the trail to Ka Ba at sundown while we were resting, talking quietly, tired from the day's journey. There was a murmur of welcome, for tellers of history in these parts also sing ballads and songs of love and sorrow, comforters to the weary. Graceful in her long white gown, this singer had come to entertain as well as to instruct.

She sang in Malinke, the language of the people of the inn and the country round about, a people of handsome features, ebony black, stoutly built, toughened by hoe labour and hard times. The audience consisted of a dozen men of the region and one or two chance travellers, like us, from far away. But Malinke is a common language of these western plains, and even strangers can be at home with it. The tales, besides, are old and known from generations. Everyone has heard them before, but they are not the less welcome for that. Part of the pleasure is in comparing the skill of different tellers.

The woman chanted her words in clear country fashion, her long fine fingers stretched with the drama of her song and her dark eyes full of meaning. She began with the tale of the coming of Sundiata Keita, also called Mari Diata, who reigned here in the same period that the kings of Ife were commissioning their sculptures, and when Benin was at the beginning of its prestigious story. Sundiata brought peace and honour to the land:

*Sundiata nâ dâ dinyé di ia*
*Mari Diata nâ dâ dinyé di ia. . . .*
*(Sundiata came to rejoice the land Mari Diata came to rejoice the land)*

The tale is long and full of magic and marvels; and the memory is also long, for

# Caravans of gold

*An oasis in the western Sudan, as illustrated by the 19thC German traveller Heinrich Barth.*

Sundiata ruled here 700 years ago. Other tales recall times still more remote, going back even to the *Kaya Magha*, the Lord of the Gold who reigned over ancient Ghana before the Vikings found America or the Normans crossed to England.

Is it all a myth? The audience in the inn did not think so for a moment; but can we, who are strangers, find a trail into those distant years? The caravans of gold are the way to hit upon that trail. They crossed these grassland plains into centuries of history. Though vanished now, they have left their track behind. There is even a map to guide us.

## Wealth-giving trade

Not long after Sundiata ruled in the Western Sudan, a school of map-makers flourished on the Mediterranean island of Majorca. Being Jews, they had access to Muslim and North African sources of information barred to Christians. In 1375 Abraham Cresques completed an atlas that, in its western half, marks a starting point for tracing out the caravans of gold.

These caravan routes crisscross the Sahara on Cresques' map, linking places of power and wealth, and at the focal centre, in the grasslands of the Western Sudan, there sits the crowned king of Mali. His image is painted large on the map, for he was lord of that great trading empire whose early frontiers were

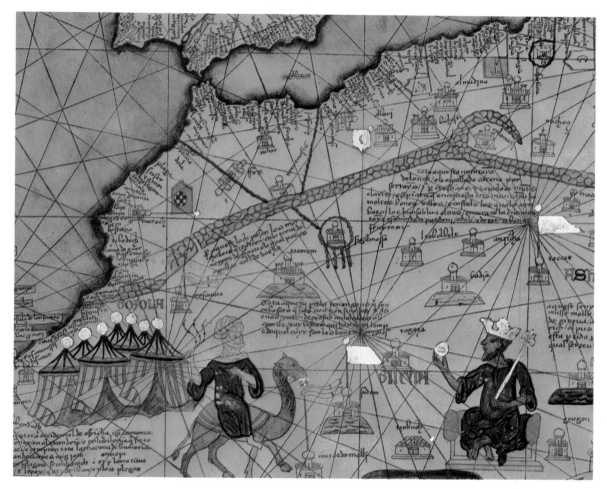

established by Sundiata. The capital of Mali then was probably at Niani in the upper Niger country, nowadays a forgotten hamlet where nothing remains from the past save vestiges of wall. Yet Cresques was right in marking his locality as a focal centre, for it was an entry to the sources of West Africa's gold.

*A 14thC atlas by the Jewish mapmaker Abraham Cresques highlights the emperor of Mali with gold crown, sceptre and orb.*

A chief reason for the strength of Sundiata's realm was the great circulation of interregional and intercontinental commerce that flowed from Asia to Africa and across the Mediterranean to Europe during the Middle Ages. The dynamic heart of this wealth-giving circulation was in West and North Africa, for its basic standard of value was coined and calculated in African gold. It depended on the trading caravans which ran between large and comfortable cities. There might be wars, revolts, and transfers for dynastic power, but the freedom of the trade routes, though blocked from time to time, held firm to the end.

To catch a glimpse of what all this meant, we pick up the caravan trail in the ancient port of Alexandria in Egypt, just over 200 years before Sundiata.

## The Geniza files

In the year AD1000 (or thereabouts) a travel-worn merchant, who had just returned home to Alexandria from a distant business trip, sat down to write to his partner in Cairo:

I have just got back from Almeria [in Spain]. Your business friend at Fez [in

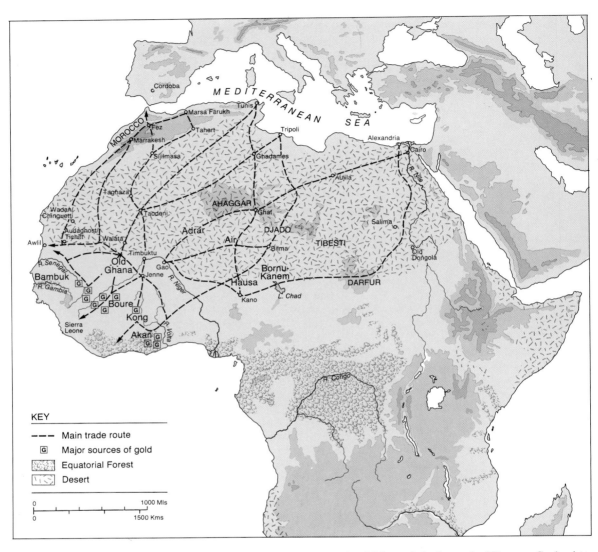

KEY

- - - Main trade route

G Major sources of gold

Equatorial Forest

Desert

0           1000 Mls

0           1500 Kms

*A map shows the long development of trans-Saharan trade between the kingdoms of western Sudan and those of the Arab world.*

Morocco] sent me there a bar of gold [certainly from the Western Sudan] to buy you some Spanish silk. But I didn't think this a good idea, and so I'm forwarding you the gold as it is. On the other hand, a friend of your business friend in Morocco also sent me a certain quantity of ambergris, which I forward you herewith; and he asks you to send me back five flasks of musk equivalent to the price of the ambergris. Please sell the ambergris on getting this letter and buy the musk, for I have to send it off at once.

Ambergris, a waxy substance secreted by sperm whales, is usually found in tropical water, and this consignment probably came from the Atlantic. Musk, like ambergris, is used in making perfumes, and it comes from the scent glands of the musk deer, a species found in the mountain forests of central and eastern Asia. Here in this single transaction we see commerce reaching from one end of the known world to the other. It was, besides, an everyday transaction, one of many dealing in commodities across huge distances. The deal also shows how, although he had West African gold to buy Spanish silk for sale in Egypt, this Alexandrian businessman, attentive to the trend of international markets, saw that bar gold would do better in Egypt than silk. Here we perceive a subtle and far-ranging network of exchange values.

A truly miraculous survival has given us such insights as these. Jews were among the leading promoters of the long-distance trade of the Muslim world in those mutually tolerant times. They suffered no disadvantages because of their religion, and, indeed, sometimes served in high administrative positions in the government of the caliphs of Cairo. Their custom was to preserve any document that mentioned the name of God; and in time this developed into a habit of keeping all their business documents and many private ones besides. The merchants of Cairo stuffed their papers haphazardly into a lumber room, or *geniza*, attached to a Cairo synagogue. And there they remained, safe and sound, until very recent years, when they came into the possession of a number of leading libraries.

The Geniza files – as they may now be called after the research and ordering of many scholars, but above all of Professor S.D. Goitein of the University of California – are a major source of detailed and exact information about the trade of the medieval world. They include about 10,000 items for the period 950–1250, written mostly in Hebrew but using Arabic script, and some 7,000 of these have historical value. Goitein's translations repeatedly confirm a number of basic facts, among which, one of the most important – and in some ways surprising – concerns money.

The gold standard of earlier times had rested on the *denarius aureus*, or gold dinar, of the Eastern Roman Empire. With the rise of Islam, the *denarius aureus* was largely replaced as a monetary standard by the gold *dinar* of the caliphs of Damascus and then of the caliphs of Baghdad; and this new standard spread far and wide. In the 780s, for example, the Anglo-Saxon king Offa of Mercia in remote England, struck some gold coins modelled on the dinar of Islam. But he almost certainly had to melt down existing gold coins to make these new ones, for supplies of gold were virtually at an end in Europe.

In 969 a great change occurred. Powerful Muslim rulers of Tunisia and Algeria, known as the Fatimids through their claim to be descended from Fatima, the Prophet's daughter, took over Egypt from the rival power of the Caliph of Baghdad. In Cairo they built a new city and launched a new dynasty, the Fatimid caliphate, that swung the central zone of Muslim long-distance trade away from Iraq and the Persian Gulf and westward to Egypt and the Mediterranean. In so doing, they enormously reinforced and enlarged the whole great circuit of trade.

The key to this economic success lay in their ability to obtain new supplies of gold from West Africa. Based on this high quality gold, the Fatimid dinar became a uniquely reliable standard of value, the equivalent of the US dollar at the height of modern American prosperity.

Towards 1100, however, the caliphs of Cairo lost control of the production of gold coins to Moroccan rulers known as the Almoravids, the men of the monastery, from their devout origins. From that time the Fatimid dinar was replaced by the Almoravid dinar, or *marabotin*, as it was widely known. But the source was still West African, and thus the origins of the gold standard remained the same.

Now we can reach back to that source, and see how it was made to yield the sinews of trade across the world, from the Atlantic to the Indian Ocean, from Norman England through all Europe to the shores of the Mediterranean. Everything depended on the trans-Saharan caravans between the "ports" on the northern shore of the ocean of rock and sand and the "ports" on the southern shore, or Sahel, in the Western Sudan.

Of the early ports on the northern side of the Sahara, such as Tahert, little

# Caravans of gold

*A 19thC print of the "port" city of Timbuktu (above), where the caravans went northwards across the Sahara. The encroaching desert (right) required skillful navigators.*

has remained, and almost nothing of the greatest of them, Sijilmasa in Morocco. But Marrakesh, founded by the Almoravids in about 1070, still gives some idea of the zest and enterprise of these famous markets and ports of arrival and departure.

*Founded in 1070, Marrakesh became an opulent and busy northern "port" of the Sahara.*

Here the men of the south and the caravan specialists of the great desert, veiled Tuareg and their Berber kind, arrived with their goods and their news after many weeks of travel, and, from here, went back to the Western Sudan in more or less regular convoys. They still do, although nowadays the trade is small, and businessmen go by plane. But in those times, 1,000 years ago, this was not only among the richest trades anywhere, but also, because it fed the gold standard with its metal, by far the most important.

Comparative values are almost impossible to calculate with any accuracy, across so many centuries, but long-range letters of credit between merchants in different cities give some idea of the value of the trade. One such promissory note, dating to 950 (just before the Fatimid period began in Egypt) concerned a trans-Saharan debt of 42,000 dinars. Goitein has calculated that a gold dinar of the Fatimid period, with a weight of 4.233 grams ($\frac{1}{6}$oz), might have had a purchasing power roughly equivalent to about $100 (at 1966 values). So this long-range trading system across the Sahara, and indeed across the seas as well, could certainly tolerate credit facilities running to several million dollars.

# Caravans of gold

## Empires of the West

Though initially modest, the trans-Saharan trade had come into existence long before the Fatimid kings rose to power. Along well-known trails there are Berber caravan markers – roughly sketched carts pulled by donkeys or horses – that were engraved in very ancient times, probably before 500BC. The Phoenicians who founded Carthage obtained gold from West Africa, although the records of how they did this are few. The Greek colonists on the coast of Libya also had contacts with the trans-Saharan south, but again we know almost nothing of their nature.

At a later period, the Romans saw the value of the trade, but left it entirely to nomad intermediaries. A great advance in transportation techniques occurred at this time, around the first century AD, when the Egyptian camel, the one-humped camel of Arabia, came into trans-Saharan use. The "ship of the desert" proved far more useful than horse or donkey, because it could carry more and was built by nature for thirsty latitudes. The Egyptians themselves paid bitterly for being colonized by Rome, but at least that imperial conquest diffused the camel.

The Romans were in general not particularly short of gold, and things went quietly for some centuries. Then the trans-Saharan trade received its second major boost when the Arab conquest of North Africa brought about a Muslim unification that greatly widened the inter-regional trading circuit. Thoroughly aware of the potential of West African gold, the little trading states of Muslim North Africa, notably Tahert and Sijilmasa, sent their agents south in search of business. What they found, after about 750, was the empire of ancient Ghana. It made their fortunes.

Enough hard facts have come down the years, alongside myths and marvels, to give reality and shape to ancient Ghana. In 1068 al-Bakri, a historian of Cordoba, the then magnificent capital of Muslim Spain, published his *Book of the Roads and Kingdoms*. Drawing on first-hand traveller's and trader's reports, he set down what was securely known about West Africa:

> Ghana . . . is a title given to their kings; the name of the region is Awkar, and their present king, who came to the throne in 1063, is *Tunka* Manin. He rules an enormous kingdom, and has great power. . . . When he calls up his army he can put 200,000 men in the field, more than 40,000 of them archers.

The country was rich in gold from a site some eighteen days' journey southward from the capital and the royal metal was prized:

> When the king gives audience, or hears grievances against officials, he sits in a domed pavilion around which stand ten horses covered with gold-embroidered cloths. Behind the kings stand ten pages holding shields and swords decorated with gold; and on his right are the sons of the vassal kings of his country, wearing splendid garments with gold plaited into their hair.
> At the door of the pavilion are dogs of an excellent breed, and these hardly ever leave the place where the king is. Round their necks they wear collars of gold and silver.

Behind this magnificence there lies a long story of West African political and economic development. But this West African enterprise in empire-building was already far advanced by the time that al-Bakri's informants took back news of *Tunka* Manin and his splendour. Ghana, by then, had reached and even passed the zenith of its military and trading power; and the Muslim merchants of Tahert and Sijilmasa, after all, were only following caravan routes opened centuries before by Berber intermediaries of Byzantium and, before that, of the Roman empire and, conceivably, the Phoenicians of Carthage.

Yet the rise of Ghana was more than a mere response to trans-Saharan trading chances. An inner dynamic was at work. We know from al-Bakri that

*Tunka* Manin taxed imports coming into his realm, whether everyday goods like salt, or luxury goods such as fine-tooled Muslim swords, silks and other articles of high living. Likewise he taxed goods going out of the realm, principally gold. But beyond that we can see that he operated a complex and independent network of internal revenue collection.

What we have here, in short, is the political response to all those opportunities for accumulating power and wealth, opportunities that derived from the social and cultural advances which had occurred since West Africa's Iron Age began in about 500BC. It is the same internal dynamic that gave rise, in due course, to the forest kingdoms of Ife, Benin and other West African states.

After AD500 or so, this great region entered a phase of internal development through which new hierarchies of kings and sub-kings were established, together with a type of revenue extraction based, not on feudal landownership as in Europe, but on tribute and taxation. New forms of economic activity, always nourished by expanding trade, went hand-in-hand with new forms of political government.

And the whole process impressively repeated itself down the centuries. Ghana's capital fell to Almoravid invaders from Morocco in 1076. They were Berber nomads and did not stay, but the empire was badly shaken. Decline set in and other West African peoples threw off their obedience to the Soninke rulers of Ghana, and embarked on enterprises of their own. By 1200 the overlordship of the Soninke, maintained through many centuries, was at last on its way out, and in came their major successors, the Mandinka people, southern neighbours of the Soninke.

These systems were not like the empires of modern times. They were sharp at the point of sword or lance, but otherwise easy-going, tolerant of local rights and values, uninfected by racism. Their rulers were seldom concerned to dispossess subject peoples of land or local freedom, much less of their cultural identity. They demanded tax, tribute and ceremonial displays of loyalty. Such demands could be painful and unpopular, yet they were usually indirect and imposed from a distance. And for these demands there could be compensations in the everyday protection of local law and order, and the safeguarding of the caravan route.

When one large system fell apart, another could be built on the same pattern. The Mandinka of the upper Niger country had formed a small kingdom in the eleventh century or earlier; by the thirteenth century they were ready to make their own bid for large-scale power. That was when Sundiata Keita and other heroes rode clamourously into history. They built the empire of Mali, the system that succeeded Ghana. Mali became one of the largest states and one of the richest systems of tax and tribute in the world west of India and China. It enclosed most of the western plains of the Sudan, and, on the reckoning of an experienced traveller, who lived for 35 years in Mali during the first half of the fourteenth century, was "four or more months' journey in length, and as much in width".

Soon after 1450, overall control of the trade routes, and of much the same huge region of tax and tribute, passed from the Mandinka rulers of Mali to the Songhay of the middle Niger country. The Songhay, in their turn, held it until the 1590s, when a sudden invasion from Morocco upset their sovereignty. To the east, meanwhile, in the central Sudan (approximately the north-eastern corner of modern Nigeria and the area around the shores of Lake Chad) another large system developed from about the tenth century under the overlordship of the Kanuri. Its centre of power lay at first in the Lake Chad area, and later transferred to Bornu or north-eastern Nigeria. This empire of Kanem-Bornu drew its trading strength from control of the Saharan routes to

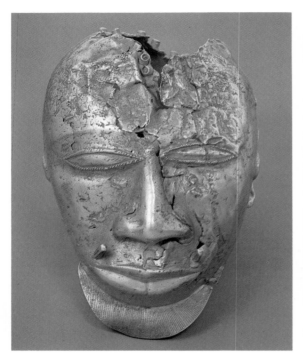

*The splendid crown (above right) and regalia (right) of the Kings of Asante. A gold portrait (or possibly death mask) depicts a ruler (above left).*

the Fezzan and Egypt in the north, and, in the south, from control of the other caravan routes to the forest kingdoms in what is now southern Nigeria.

*The wealth of ancient Ghana in the western Sudan is distantly reflected in the splendid regalia of a King of Asante in the forest country of modern Ghana.*

## A diversity of peoples

Although each of these imposing systems was dominated by a single people or small group of closely related peoples, all of them were very diverse in their composition. They were what is nowadays called "multi-ethnic", making room within their boundaries for all manner of different beliefs and local loyalties. As in other African regions, most of these peoples preferred to have no kings or powerful chiefs of their own, but to regulate their affairs by complex forms of inter-family and inter-clan government.

Things could of course change. Some peoples, like the Bambara (who live in the region of modern Bamako and Ségou on the upper Niger) found in time that kings could after all be useful in fending off other kings or carving out a bigger share of the general wealth. They also found that rivalries for royal power could become a costly nuisance. Others, mainly on the periphery of the big systems, avoided kingships altogether. Among these were the Tallensi (in what is nowadays the northern part of modern Ghana) who evolved a shrewd balance between those endowed with a limited amount of civic authority, and others who were seen as intermediaries of the ancestral spirits of Tallensi country. Having achieved a viable way of life and self-government, the Tallensi saw no point in changing it, and, because they lived on the edge of the big world of the imperial systems, nothing obliged them to change it.

Communities such as these lived within or close to the big systems of overall control, and, generally survived those systems. They, above all, are what has given the cultures of West Africa their characteristic tone and resonance. Yet the big systems possessed their own special brilliance and excitement; and people have remembered them, as we have seen in the case of the ballad singer at the tavern on the road to Ka Ba. Their stories were written, too, in good hard

# Caravans of gold

*Tomb of* Askia *Muhamad, the great 16thC ruler of Songhay.*

text in notable books, such as the *Tarikh as-Sudan* and the *Tarikh al-Fattash*, composed by scholars at Timbuktu in the seventeenth century.

Each of the great West African dynasties produced its heroes: the *Mansa* Kankan Musa, who built Mali to the full extent of its power early in the fourteenth century, and who found his own sensational entry to a wider history (see p. 110); the *Sunni* Ali who forged the Songhay empire in years of undefeated battle and hard diplomacy; and the greatest of the Songhay rulers, *Askia* Muhamad, whose sixteenth-century tomb at Gao is there to this day.

These hero kings played out their various roles, none of which could have been simple to perform. While balancing the pressures against and around their royal power, they had to provide for the development of two constant themes: the caravans of gold with all the long-distance trade, and the power of West African Islam. The product of these two forces was political change.

# Chapter 8

# The impact of Islam

Several of the old "port" cities on the southern shore of the Sahara have survived into modern times, but none survives as solidly as Kano in the Hausa country of northern Nigeria. Kano today is a bustling centre of new business and industry, schools and colleges, departments of local and state government. Yet it remains a place where the links between present development and past history are easy to find. Most obviously, they exist in the gated walls that surround the oldest part of the city.

These walls are centuries old. As early as 1500 a North African traveller, whose book has come down to us, described Kano as "encircled by a wall made of beams of wood and baked clay; and its houses are built of the same materials." Yet even in 1500, Kano's walls and enterprises were far from new.

The same traveller noted that Kano's inhabitants were "civilized handicraft workers and rich merchants", and this was a prosperity that endured. Three hundred years later Heinrich Barth, the German explorer, estimated a city population of some 30,000 people, and was greatly impressed by its production of cotton cloth in cottage workshops around the neighbourhood of the city. Coming from a Europe of "satanic mills" and other horrors of the industrial revolution, he found a very different situation:

. . . If we consider that this industry is not carried on here, as in Europe, in immense establishments, degrading man to the meanest condition of life, but that it gives employment and support to families without compelling them to sacrifice their domestic habits, we must presume that Kano ought to be one of the happiest countries in the world.

Only the government of the day, he thought, left much to be desired. But by the 1850s, when Barth visited the city, the political life of Kano had gone through many phases.

Founded in about 1000, the city had grown into the capital of one of the Hausa kingdoms of northern Nigeria. By 1400, Hausa government had developed a subtle system of checks and balances on the use of political strength, and the king of Kano, far from wielding despotic power, had become, in a real sense, a constitutional monarch. Trade and production for trade – whether of foodstuffs or of manufactured goods – provided the economic base, and in Kano production for trade was on the grand scale. As this type of economy expanded, so also did its trading range, and local trade merged with the long-distance networks connecting forest communities in the south with trans-Saharan communities far in the north. The question then arose as to who should control these expanding networks.

The early answer, in terms of governing organization, was to operate a "family system". The operation of this system in such Hausa states as Kano will not have been much different from its workings in ancient Ghana and Mali,

*Part of the ancient wall of Kano, described in 1500 as "made of beams of wood and baked clay".*

where we know that ruling families divided and subdivided power between their members – mostly men, but sometimes women as well. The outcome of this method was that the king himself (or, more rarely, the reigning queen) was little more than the "first among equals". This functioned well enough for a time but, with continued expansion of the system, kings found that uncles, brothers or nephews tended to carve out territories of their own, and make a bid for independence. Tax and tribute then failed to arrive in due quantity, being retained at source, and the kings began to lack revenue for the gifts and payments that could alone ensure their continued authority.

The solution to this problem owed much to the legal and administrative codes of Islam, the religion of the Prophet Mohammed, which was then growing in popularity among rulers and urban populations south of the Sahara. It consisted essentially in undermining the family system of government by appointing as governors, treasurers, generals and other officials, men who belonged to no ruling family. Ideally, it was found, such officials should be drawn from humble families, preferably of servile conditions, whose whole careers and livelihood would then depend upon the will and favour of the king, their master. These "king's men" could then be played off against the hereditary nobles.

The change was not made easily. Some kings who tried it were quickly cast down by indignant nobles, but shrewd kings succeeded and the change took root. Gradually, each system came to rely on a public service of appointed men as well as on hereditary nobles. That was broadly how the Kano system operated when our North African traveller admired its gates and walls around

*The town of Kano in the 1850s, as portrayed by the German explorer Heinrich Barth.*

the year 1500.

What is called "defence" is always a priority where kingships are concerned, and in West Africa the first important innovation of the empire-building period was stirruped cavalry: stirruped because, just as in Europe or Asia, mounted soldiers without strong foot supports were easily tumbled by lance or mace in the shock of battle. But stirruped cavalry, well trained and in sufficient number, could just as surely win any battle they were sent into. It is no exaggeration to say that all these major systems, at least after about 1350, were built and maintained – or eventually overthrown – by tough troops of long-service cavalry. These troops quelled revolts, safeguarded the caravan routes, embarked on useful conquests, and looked after the safety of kings.

But they had to be regulars. Only professional soldiers could be well enough trained in cavalry warfare, and only professionals could always be available. Besides, no king could safely allow amateurs to get their hands on expensive mounts and all the gear that went with stirruped cavalry – chain mail, quilted horse armour, good weapons – and carry these off for private and possibly subversive purposes. So the kings raised troops of professionals – usually from men of servile condition, captured in war or otherwise without civic rights – and kept their armouries under lock and key for whenever weapons were needed.

The system worked in Africa as it worked elsewhere. And it had the extra value, much prized by monarchs and courtiers, of permitting splendid ceremonial displays. A local Kanuri writer has left us an eyewitness description of one such occasion in the 1560s, when his master the king of Kanem-Bornu (in north-eastern Nigeria) *Mai* Idris Alooma, received ambassadors from the

*The stirruped cavalry of the old Hausa kings is recalled in the dress and equipment of a contemporary royal ceremonial.*

# The impact of Islam

*The emir's bodyguard in traditional dress during a festival at Katsina, Northern Nigeria, recall the "king's men" of earlier times.*

mighty Sultan of the Ottoman empire. With the *Mai* rode troops of quilt-armoured cavalry – considerably more colourful than the motorcycle escorts of today:

> All the soldiers mounted their horses after equipping themselves and their horses with armour, with breastplates, shields, and their best clothing.
>
> When we had ridden a short way we met the messengers of the Sultan. The troops of our lord were drawn up on the west side in rank after rank, leaving space between their ranks for the wheeling of any restive horse.
>
> Then our troops charged [in ceremonial homage], and the ambassadors galloped their horses towards us. This continued for a long while, until the infantry were tired of standing still.
>
> O, my wise friends and counsellors, have you ever seen a king who is the equal of our lord at such a moment?

Firearms were the next military innovation, and they too called for professional handling. Very few guns appeared in the Western Sudan, or any part of West Africa, before the 1500s. Then small troops of musketeers began to be raised, armed with the muzzle-loading weapons of the day, usually imported from Ottoman sources in North Africa and Egypt. But the military value of these weapons consisted of little more than the noise they made and the reputation they earned. Killing power came later.

## Islam in West Africa

For all their military innovations and impressive displays of strength, these vast West African empires brought long periods of peace and prosperity to their territories. The fourteenth-century writer, Ibn Battuta of Tangier, spent some time in Mali during 1352 and recorded his impressions of life there. His was the life of a wandering scholar, common in those times throughout the lands of Islam, just as in Christian Europe. Ibn Battuta's travels from one Muslim community to another had already taken him as far as China, and by the time he reached Mali he could make many comparisons. On the whole, he was impressed by what he found. Of Mali's peoples he observed:

> One of their good features is their lack of oppression. They are the farthest removed of people from it; and their sultan [the emperor of Mali] does not permit anyone to practise it.
>
> Another [of their good features] is the security embracing the whole country, so that neither traveller there nor dweller has anything to fear from thief or from usurper.

He found them honest and devout, "always dressing in fine white clothes on Friday", the Muslim day of rest; and if on that day "a man does not go early to the mosque he will not find anywhere to pray because of the press of people." Much importance was attached to memorizing the Koran, and failures were penalized: "They clap fetters on the children if there is any failure on their part in this memorizing, and the fetters are not removed till the memorizing is done." Ibn Battuta's North African conservatism found this worthy of approval, just as he was repeatedly shocked by the relative freedom enjoyed by West African women.

Islam had come to West Africa over 500 years earlier, with the caravan merchants of the eighth or ninth century, but it had been slow to take root. Not until the eleventh century did West African kings and courts begin to find it useful to accept Islam as one of their faiths, while conserving their respect for the ancestral shrines and the beliefs of the peoples over whom they ruled. For many years after that – well into the eighteenth century in most parts of West Africa – Islam remained a religion only of the towns, while country folk worshipped their own gods as before.

But Islam proved increasingly attractive to rulers beset by new problems of development. And it was all the easier to accept because, unlike Christianity later on, Islam could accommodate a wide variety of local loyalties and religious customs, provided that its adherents confessed the oneness of God and the uniqueness of the Prophet Mohammed.

The attraction of Islam for these rulers was that it linked their courts to the wider world of the Muslim *umma*, the "family" of Islam, and thus rescued them from provincial isolation. The pilgrimage to Mecca became a great affair for anyone able to afford it. Beyond this, Islam could provide a unifying cement of belief and companionship across ethnic and other traditional divisions.

In these ways, as in the influence of its legal and administrative codes, Islam worked in those times as a persistently modernizing faith. One of its major innovations was its insistence on the importance of literacy and the value of book-learning. While little children had to recite the Koran by heart, their elders studied various branches of Muslim scholarship, whether civilian or religious. The great cities of the Western Sudan became distinguished centres of learning that were recognized as such across the whole Muslim world.

Communities of the learned gathered in the cities, sending off their own wandering scholars, and, in return, welcoming the visits of scholars from afar: North Africa, Egypt, Muslim Spain and other places still further afield. Libraries were assembled, and greatly prized. Books were written and published in manuscript copies: histories such as the *tarikhs* or Chronicles, written in Timbuktu, as well as a wide variety of works of secular or religious commentary, such as those by the famous Ahmed Baba (a few of which are still in circulation to this day). According to a sixteenth-century report, the trade in books in the region was more profitable than any other.

Kings consulted prominent jurists and demanded their advice: What should a Muslim ruler do about the nudity of girls and unmarried young women? How should markets best be regulated? Who should have the final decision in matters such as standardization of weights and measures, credit facilities, or the

*Old Timbuktu was a centre of religious and secular literacy, and famous for its scholarship in all the lands of Islam.*

payment of debts? In which ways should Islamic law, the *sharia*, take precedence over local customs? Little by little, as the systems grew more complex, the contribution of Islam became woven into the cultural and economic life of the great West African empires.

### The old "ports" of the south

Trade was the life blood of these empires, as we have seen, and the city "ports" of the Saharan "shore", provisioning the caravans on their northward route to the Sahara wastelands and welcoming them on their return, were vital. None was more important, after about 1300, than Jenne in the middle region of what is today the modern republic of Mali. Thanks to its strong defensive position within the inland delta of the river Niger, with broad arms of the river providing barriers on either side, Jenne could long defend its independence; unlike Timbuktu, it was never an imperial city.

Today it rests within its ochre-brown walls of beaten earth, as though nothing had changed save the road that leads to it. Here history can materialize in the noonday heat with a string of camels or a stir of merchants – and there are plenty of both. They gather and crowd in the famous marketplace that stretches from the threshold of Jenne's noble and imposing mosque.

"It is because of this blessed city," wrote the chronicler of Timbuktu, Abderrahman as-Sadi, in the 1650s, "that the caravans flow in to Timbuktu from all points of the horizon." By then the prosperity of the great systems was long past its height, but this Soninke historian could still affirm that "Jenne is a great city, flourishing and wealthy, one of the grand markets of the Muslim

*Jenne mosque (above) still presides over a busy marketplace that was described in the 1650s as "one of the grand markets of the Muslim world". The* harmattan *dust storms (left) were only one of the hazards facing travellers before they reached port.*

world," where merchants of salt came from the far north and merchants of gold from the south. Besides these there were many learned men, scholars of the Western Sudan, "who are jurisconsults, theologians, persons both devout and virtuous." It is a picture drawn by a local patriot, but a true picture all the same.

Nowadays a small provincial centre of the modern republic of Mali, with its Niger neighbour Mopti gaining more importance, Jenne is still a place of many echoes. The merchants of the *dyula* or Mandinka caravans may no longer crowd its gates, but this was the way they came, northward from the mines and panning stations of Asante by way of Bigho on the forest verge, and Bobodyulasso in the plains. And this was the way the return imports came, with Saharan salt their biggest item.

Luxury goods also came south across the desert, and in fact were always a staple of the long-distance caravan trade, since substantial profits were best yielded by goods of small weight and great value. Even stray luxury goods from England found a place in this trans-world trade. When an invading British force sacked the Kumasi palace of the king of Asante in 1896, they found a fine metal pitcher of English make among the loot taken from the palace. The pitcher bears a marking that dates it to the reign of King Richard II, shortly before the year 1400. Someone must have brought it down through Jenne.

That nameless merchant of long ago will have surely come south by way of Timbuktu, the major southern terminal at the desert's edge after about 1300. Of marvellous reputation, Timbuktu remains an enchanting city of markets and memories, of comfortable dwellings hidden behind the silent face of dust-laden walls, and of enterprising traders still dreaming of fortunes to be made upon the highways of the desert.

*This metal ewer, made in England during Richard II's reign, is one of a pair looted by British troops in the palace of the King of Asante (modern Ghana) in 1896. The Trans-Saharan trade will have taken it there.*

From Timbuktu, the northbound caravans had to face the challenge of the desert in weeks of bitter plodding to the "ports" on the northern shore. The Sahara then was a little less enormous in its size, but crossing it by foot or camel was just as painful as today.

The caravans went northward through the centuries. For at least 700 years they fuelled the great circuits of interregional and intercontinental trade that underlay the glory of the Muslim Middle Ages and saw the development of Christian Europe. And throughout that same momentous cycle of history the peoples of West Africa, whether in their grassland plains or in their forest country near the coast, evolved and diversified. Their organization of wealth and government developed from simple systems, weak in political articulation and primitive in their command of economic growth, into strong and complex systems. This was the multi-cultural civilization, built through those centuries, that forms the background of the West Africa we know today.

### Across the great desert

As we head northward from Jenne and Timbuktu, Ibn Battuta can be our guide. The Moroccan writer recorded with particular feeling his last crossing of the Sahara, in 1352, and his story of the journey is still very readable. For the first part of the journey he travelled with a Berber caravan as far as Takadda, a big centre of desert salt mining, and from there, changing caravans, he went on northwestward to Sijilmasa and so home to Fez by gradual stages. Although he travelled with a large group, he still made good time. A modern Saharan caravan is expected to average about 34km (21 miles) a day, if nothing goes wrong; Ibn Battuta's, over the toughest stretch of the crossing, actually did some 27km (17 miles) a day.

At first the dangers seemed more apparent than real, but not for long. Of his earlier southward crossing of the desert, Ibn Battuta recalled:

In those days we used to go ahead of the caravan, and whenever we found a place suitable for grazing we pastured our beasts there. This we continued to do till a man named Ibn Ziri became lost in the desert. After that we neither went ahead nor lagged behind.

The man was searched for in the wilderness of waterless sand, but was not found. After that, a few days later:

We met a caravan on our way, and they told us that some men had become separated from them. We found one of them dead, with his clothes on him and a whip in his hand, under a little tree of the kind that grows in the sand. There was water a mile or so away from him.

Crucial to survival was the *takshif* or guide, always a Berber, born and bred in the desert. Approaching the oasis of Walata, the *takshif* would be sent ahead of his caravan to provide for its reception there. But:

Sometimes the *takshif* perishes in that wilderness, so that the people of Walata do not know about the caravan, and all or many of its people (with their water skins exhausted) perish (before help comes).

In that wilderness there were many demons of thirst and heat:

If the *takshif* is alone, they play with him and seduce him so that he becomes diverted from his purpose and perishes because there is no clear road or track. There is nothing but sand blown about by the wind, so that you see mountains of sand in one place, and then you see them transported to another.

A reliable *takshif*, says Ibn Battuta, is one who has done the journey many times. "I thought it remarkable that our own guide was blind in one eye and diseased in the other, and yet he knew the way better than anyone." He took them safely through to Walata, and was thought to have thoroughly earned his pay of 100 *mitcals* of gold (about 420 grams).

Ibn Battuta liked Walata, and stayed there for 50 days. Its people, he found, had "strange and remarkable ways", not least because of the freedom enjoyed by their women and the absence of jealousy felt by their men. Visiting the chief judge of Walata, he was introduced by that dignitary to "a young and remarkably beautiful woman":

When I saw her I hesitated and wished to withdraw, but she laughed at me and experienced no shyness. The judge said to me: "Why are you turning back? She is my friend." I was amazed at their behaviour, for he was a scholar and a pilgrim.

The same judge, he learned, was even intending to take his lady friend on another pilgrimage next year. Still worse for Ibn Battuta was the absence of male jealousy:

One day I visited Abu Muhamad Yandakan al-Masufi, in whose company we had come, and found him sitting on a carpet. In the courtyard of his house there was a canopied couch with a woman on it conversing with a man seated. I said to Abu Muhamad: "Who is this woman?" He said: "She is my wife."

"What connection has that man with her?"

"He is her friend."

"Do you agree to this, when you have lived in our country, and know the teachings of the *sharia*?"

Abu Muhamad replied to me: "The association of women with men is agreeable to us and a part of good conduct, to which no suspicion attaches. They are not like the women of your country."

I was astonished at his laxity, I left him, and did not return thereafter. He invited me several times but I did not accept.

Many unexpected things awaited Ibn Battuta as he crossed the desert, but all went well and he suffered no damage except to his feelings about what was right

# The impact of Islam

*The city of Fez: journey's end for the notable 14thC traveller and writer, Ibn Battuta.*

and proper. At the end of December 1353 he left the desert behind him and climbed into the snow-laden mountains of the Atlas, finding this a more difficult road than "any I have seen in Bukhara, Samarkand, Khurasan and the land of the Turks". Then, at last, he came to his destination in the fountained gardens of Fez. There he was welcomed home by the Sultan of Morocco, "the Commander of the Faithful, may God support him, and kissed his noble hand, and deemed myself fortunate to see his blessed face".

# Chapter 9

# Africa and Europe: a medieval partnership

Looking northward from Tangier, birthplace of Ibn Battuta, you can see the cliffs of Africa-in-Europe across the sea. Even today the haunting rhythms of southern Spain remind the visitor that this was once al-Andalus, the land of milk and honey developed by Arabs and Berbers, and a centre of Moorish civilization throughout the Middle Ages. At the heart of modern Cordoba there still stands (though long converted to Christian use) the great mosque of the caliphs of al-Andalus, one of the most elegant religious buildings anywhere. Seville and Granada, also, retain splendid fragments of their Muslim past.

Arab generals had crossed into Spain at the head of Berber armies in 710, and Gibraltar, or Jebel Tariq, still bears the name of one of those generals. They were followed by many other settlers from Africa, mostly of Berber origin. Much of Spain, including its fertile southland, became an integral part of the civilization of Islam, and in some ways its most brilliant part. It remained so for more than 500 years, at first under Arab princes until the eleventh century, and then under Berber rulers from Morocco. Here there evolved one of the most advanced and tolerant societies of the medieval world.

All this was a repetition, if a singularly splendid one, of the pattern that tended to occur whenever nomad warriors discovered the superiority of settled, urban life over what they had known before. Here in al-Andalus, life became comfortable. Great works of irrigation were built to water fertile valleys, and soldiers became country gentlemen in peaceful manor houses. Kings built palaces and laid out gardens of leisure. Cordoba alone had several hundred *hammams* or public baths. High living flourished in fine clothing and footwear, good conversation, decorative arts. Trade and learning crossed all frontiers.

And who did the work? North African herdsmen brought their pastoral skills to the upland country. Others from North Africa settled in the plains and married local girls from populations that had lived here from Roman times and long before. They formed a new community of farmers, Muslim and Arabic-speaking for the most part, but soon native to the land.

Rural prosperity brought wealth to the towns, and the towns flourished on their trade with places near and far, as well as on a wide variety of skilled crafts that ranged from metal-working to the building of stone bridges. All this meant work for free men and women; but it also meant work for slaves. Just as in England and France of that period, the culture of al-Andalus relied on the work of persons who were not free men and women. But what was the experience and status of these medieval slaves?

## A different slavery

The condition of slavery existed everywhere in the world, and the slave trade was a great European speciality. Christian raiders in eastern Europe sold non-

# Africa and Europe: a medieval partnership

Christian captives to the Franks, and the Franks employed them at home, and also sold them again to the Muslim prince of North Africa and Spain. The Italian city states did much the same – the Genoese, operating from the Black Sea, were even excommunicated by the Pope for selling Christian as well as non-Christian Europeans into slavery in Africa. Cordoba in the tenth century had more than 3,000 of these East European *esclavons*, mostly in royal service.

Africa sold slaves as well as buying them, sending captives north into enslavement with the trans-Saharan caravans. Ibn Battuta's caravan from Takadda included no fewer than 600 girls who were being taken to North African markets, and the trans-Saharan trade as a whole must have taken many thousands of West Africans into North African and European service. Every king or potentate had his quota of "disposable persons" for local use or sale abroad. Most of these were captives taken in raids on neighbouring peoples, or in wars between states, or else were convicts sentenced by courts of law to the loss of their civic rights.

What happened to the slaves? With rare exceptions untypical of the economies of those times, there was no large-scale use for them. Above all, there were no plantations. Slaves were used predominantly as domestic servants, or as concubines if they were women. However, a number of slaves became skilled workers, trusted clerks, officials, eunuchs in harems, or warriors in royal guards.

The life of a slave could be painful and oppressive, with more than its share of cruelty and sorrow. Yet it was often the case that this medieval slavery could be a very bearable plight, once the misery of homesickness and the perils of the journey were past. Here again the invaluable Geniza files tell an interesting tale. Goitein has concluded from them that medieval slavery, more often than not, "was a personal service in the widest sense of the word, which, when the master served was of high rank and wealthy, carried with it great advantage as well as social prestige. In or out of bondage, the slave was a member of the family."

It would of course be quite misleading to suggest that medieval slavery was an enviable condition. Yet, apart from the armies and the naval galleys, it was a servitude that was individual, not collective, and therefore at least capable of being humanized. Sometimes it was more, for, writes Goitein, "the acquisition of a male slave was a great affair [in medieval Egypt] on which a man was congratulated almost as if a son had been born to him. No wonder, for a slave fulfilled tasks similar to those of a son."

That is what the West African evidence can also confirm. There is an old Asante saying, *Akoa a onim som di ne wura ade* – a slave who knows how to serve succeeds to his master's property. The slavery of those centuries, in short, was a form of wageless labour in economies not yet adapted to wage-paid employment. Taken into the family as bonded servants, slaves could work themselves free, marry their masters' sisters or daughters, acquire wealth on their own account, and even climb on to thrones.

New careers for slaves began with the rise of the "king's men" in the great political systems of West Africa. In the politics of those times, whether in Africa or elsewhere, a shrewd ruler's first concern was to appoint his own royal guards, and keep them loyal to himself alone. Usually these guards were recruited from imported captives and, although regarded legally as of slave status, were then treated as privileged and well-rewarded retainers.

The military coups of those times were the work of such loyal guards, who seized power in times of stress, when nobody else could challenge their weaponry, training and tight organization. Slave kings of African origin ruled states in medieval India. The Mamluks, strong rulers of late medieval Egypt after 1200, were all slave guards by origin, mostly from western Asia, and under their rule no man might win succession to the throne unless he too was of slave status. One of the most successful rulers of the Mali empire in the Western Sudan was a slave usurper.

From a marketing standpoint, slaves were valued for their beauty if they were women, or for their strength if they were men, but they were also valued, men and women alike, according to their skills. Once in safe employment, slaves tended to live better, and sometimes far better, than non-slaves, so that medieval slavery was by no means the worst fate open to working people.

Much later, in colonial times, there were administrators who said the same. Complaining of the harshness of forced labour during the 1930s by otherwise "free" peasants or herdsmen in Italian Somalia, a colonial official wrote that this coercion had become "a good deal worse than slavery". A slave cost money, and would be cared for by his owner "as a carter cares for his donkey"; and if the slave should die, the owner must then buy another. "But when a Somali native dies after being assigned to his [colonial Italian] employer, or becomes unfit for work, it is merely a matter of his employer's asking the government to provide another one for nothing." This situation, in fact, was to become general in all colonies employing large-scale forced labour; and there were to be many such colonies.

An important point about medieval slavery is that slaves worth having – those with skills of one kind or another – were expensive both to buy and to maintain. The Geniza files show that the average price of a slave in Fatimid Egypt (*c.* 970–1100) ran at about 20 gold dinars, or nearly one year's income for a family of modest means. Slaves were rich men's goods. Al-Bakri in the 1060s

*The mosque of al-Azhar, one of the glories of old Cairo, famed as the "metropolis of the universe".*

commented on the excellent female cooks to be bought in Awdaghost, where caravan merchants stayed to rest and refit after coming south across the Sahara, but reported that you would have to pay 100 dinars for any one of them. Earlier Andalusian records list the price of a black slave in Cordoba at 160 mitcals, or about 150 dinars; and that, for comparison, was also the price of a small house in the same list. The Andalusian dinar varied in weight, but was generally a little less than the Fatimid or Almoravid dinar – approximately four grams of fine gold. How many persons could afford a slave at 600 grams of gold, not counting upkeep? Even in that wealthy community of southern Spain, how many could afford several slaves?

The medieval world knew many servitudes and inequalities, and the oppressions of slavery were among them. But in the development of slavery we need to see these as they really were, something usually very different from the far worse servitudes that came later in transatlantic plantations or elsewhere.

### To the Bab al-Zuwaila

From the city ports of the north Saharan shore, the caravans for Cairo went overland through Tunisia or sometimes by sea. Many headed towards Cairo which, in the words of the great fifteenth-century North African historian Ibn Khaldun, had become:

> the metropolis of the universe, the garden of the world, the throne of royalty embellished with castles and palaces and adorned with monasteries and colleges lit by the moons and the stars of erudition.

This was the new city, al-Kahira, built by the Tunisian conquerors after the 960s, and later embellished still further by the "building sultans" of the Mamluk period of late medieval times. Several of its architectural masterpieces are still intact: the mosque and university of al-Azhar, the mosque of al-Hakim with its minarets and ramparts, the mausoleum of Sultan Qala'un, and others.

*A minaret of the mausoleum of Sultan Qala'un (above, left) and the courtyard of the university of al-Azhar (above, right), "lit by the moons and stars of erudition", evoked the admiration of visitors to medieval Cairo. But it was through the 10thC Bab al-Zuwaila (left) that the caravans of gold reached the city from West Africa.*

*Gold insignia from West Africa, worn by senior officials of the king.*

The gateway to these marvels for travellers from the west and south, whether then or later, was by way of the Bab al-Zuwaila, built in the 980s. Its bulky strength speaks still for the power of the caliphs of Cairo, but its name is evocative of the old caravan trade. For this was the *bab* or gateway to and from Zuwaila, one of the key trading states of North Africa through which there came and went a large part of the commerce of that world, based on the golden coins struck from West African metal.

Through this crowded gateway there came traders, soldiers, men of learning on visits to the "metropolis of the universe", and even kings. In 1326 Ibn Battuta passed through on his first pilgrimage to Mecca, but two years earlier a far more prestigious pilgrim had preceded him. This was the emperor of Mali, *Mansa* Kankan Musa, many weeks away from his West African capital at Niani, on a journey that would be long remembered.

### The pilgrimage of *Mansa* Musa

Legendary tales were told of it for centuries. Three hundred years later, compiling his *Tarikh al-Fattash*, or "Chronicle of the Seeker", the Soninke historian Mahmud Kati of Timbuktu described the emperor's caravan of many thousand courtiers and much gold, and the loving care that he took of his favourite wife, Inari Konte, during the traverse of the desert.

Queen Inari complained of being unable to sleep because of the dust and dirt of the journey. She longed for a bath. Suitably solicitous, the emperor called for the commander of his slaves, Farba, and explained the problem:

> My good Farba, ever since I married her, my wife has never once asked me for something, for anything, that I could not give her. Until now, tonight, when she asks me for a river in this void of nothingness. God alone could do it: it's beyond my power.

Farba put his slaves to digging a long trench, walling it with stones and grit, and plastering the wall with an oily material. Once fired, this provided a surface "as smooth as glazed pottery". The bath was filled with well water from pots, and at sunrise the queen and her ladies took their bath, "radiant and rejoicing".

In due course the emperor and his numerous train of camels, courtiers and servants arrived at the Bab al-Zuwaila and entered the famous city. We can now leave legend behind, for we have a detailed account of the Mali ruler's visit from the pen of a Syrian writer resident in Cairo, Ibn Fadl al-Umari. He completed his history in 1342, but drew first-hand on the memoirs of an Amir Hajib, who was the Mali emperor's particular guide and "conducting officer" during the Cairo visit.

The Amir's first job was one of delicate diplomacy because the powerful Mamluk ruler of Egypt naturally expected a visit in due form from the royal pilgrim. But this posed difficulties. *Mansa* Musa objected that he had travelled only for the pilgrimage, and did "not wish to mix in anything else". The Amir Hajib quickly saw that the visitor's real objection to calling on the Sultan was imperial pride, "because he would be obliged to kiss the ground and the Sultan's hand". What emperor would want to do that? Amir Hajib wrote:

> He continued to make excuses, but the Sultan's protocol demanded that I should bring the emperor Musa into the royal presence, so I kept on at him till he agreed. When we came into the presence of the Sultan, we said to the Mali emperor: "Kiss the ground!" But he refused outright, saying "How may this be?"

Tact managed it. "An intelligent man who was with him whispered to him something we could not understand, and he said: 'I make obeisance to God who created me!' Then he prostrated himself and went forward to the Sultan." Face was saved all round, and the two great men sat down together. Immense hospitalities were organized.

Not to be outdone in giving gifts, the visiting emperor unloaded a vast amount of the gold brought from Mali. The Amir Hajib told al-Umari:

> This man flooded Cairo with his benefactions. He left no courtier nor holder of a royal office without the gift of a load of gold. The Cairenes made incalculable profits out of him and his suite in buying and selling and giving and taking. They exchanged gold until they depressed its value in Egypt, and caused its price to fall.

Even 12 years after, according to al-Umari, the price of gold on the Cairo market had still to recover from the Mali visit. Remembering it, merchants boasted to the same writer of the provincial simplicity of the visitors, who "believed anything they were told", and "might buy a shirt or a cloak or other garment for five dinars when it was not worth one."

But in the end the laugh was on the other side. For the visitors saw that they had been taken for a ride, and, like other tourists before and after, began to contemplate revenge. After a while they

> formed the very poorest opinion of the Egyptians, because of the obvious falseness of everything said by them, and of their outrageous behaviour in fixing the prices of the provisions and other goods they sold.

Returning homeward after visiting Mecca, the emperor and his train took care to borrow large sums of money for the needs of their journey, promising to repay after they had reached Mali once again. But repayment was long in coming, or did not come at all.

## Atlantic voyage

The Amir Hajib told al-Umari of another intriguing conversation. He had asked the emperor how he had come to his throne, and the talk, it seems, had turned to the size of the Mali domains, which reached to the westward as far as

# Africa and Europe: a medieval partnership

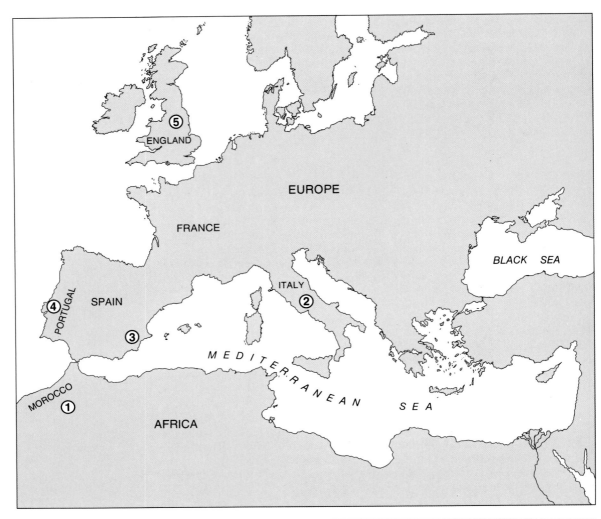

The map shows how West African gold provided the basis for the medieval gold currencies of Europe, by way of the Almoravid dinar (1). Florence minted a gold "florin" (2) in 1252, to be followed by many other states such as Spain (3) and Portugal (4). England also minted African gold, as acknowledged by the elephant on a 17thC "guinea" (5). This influx of gold was crucial to the economic developments of Europe that gave rise to the glories of the Renaissance.

the shores of the Atlantic, in what is nowadays Senegal. The emperor recalled for the Amir Hajib:

> The king who was my predecessor did not believe that it was impossible to discover the furthest limit of the Western Ocean, and he wished vehemently to do so.

So he equipped 200 ships with men and the same number with gold, water, and provisions enough to last them for years, and he said to the man appointed to command the expedition:

> "Do not return until you reach the end of it, or your food and water give out." They departed, and a long time passed before anyone came back.

> Then one ship returned, and we asked the captain what news he had brought. He said: "Yes, O Sultan, we travelled for a long time until there appeared in the open sea what seemed a river with a powerful current. Mine was the last of those ships. The other ships went on ahead, but when they reached that place they did not return; and no more was seen of them, and we do not know what became of them. As for me, I went about at once and did not enter that river.

But the emperor did not believe the returning captain's story. He resolved to try again, and do it himself. The emperor Musa told the Amir Hajib:

> Then that Sultan got ready 2,000 ships, 1,000 for himself and the men whom he took with him and 1,000 for water and food. He left me to deputize for him, and he embarked on the Atlantic Ocean with his men.

> That was the last we saw of him, and so I became king.

Truth, exaggeration, or a tall story told to astonish the Cairenes? There was in fact no great reason why intrepid voyagers should not have sailed west from Senegal, and, by using the westward-prevailing winds and currents of those latitudes, have reached the Gulf of Mexico. Given enough food and water, the only real problem would have been to say afloat. There is even some interesting though inconclusive evidence, largely from works of art, that some Africans did indeed manage to reach Central America before any Europeans.

But coming back again was quite another thing, as the emperor's story indicates – how the one ship managed to return no one knows. For it meant facing winds and currents from the east, and there was still no sailing rig, west of the Indian Ocean, which could enable a ship to do that. There, the Chinese had long developed what they called "boring-into-the-wind" sailing rigs, and the Arabs had borrowed from them. But no kind of regular transatlantic communication or colonization would be possible until "boring-into-the-wind" rigs arrived by way of the Mediterranean. When that happened, a century later, it would herald the era of European maritime discovery.

## Africa's impact on Europe

Meanwhile Europeans had to be content with a place on the sidelines of the great trading circuit based on a monetary standard provided by West African gold: a gold standard which Europe did not have. Moreover, after the assaults of the Crusades and the Muslim response, no Europeans went through the Bab al-Zuwaila or any other gateway to the wealth and science of the Muslim world, except by special trading arrangement.

Such arrangements existed for the European export of slaves to Africa, but otherwise were few until the thirteenth century. This was when the chief economic systems of western Europe began to develop a new power of export of manufactures to African states, and a corresponding power to import African gold in payment for such exports. Then at last, after an interval that had lasted since Roman times, Europe could once more obtain enough gold to mint gold currencies, and so tie itself into the wider commerce of Africa and Asia.

*Detail of a painting (c. 1510) by the German artist Grünewald (right) shows St Erasmus and St Maurice, whose features clearly reflect the influence of the Magdeburg statue (see p. 46). The depiction of a black attendant in Gozzoli's Journey of the Magi (1459–61) (opposite) illustrates the medieval acceptance of Africans as "different but equal".*

The Italian city states of Genoa and Florence took this crucial step in 1252, followed by Perugia in 1258 and Lucca in 1273. Soon afterwards the gold *fiorentino* or "florin" of Florence became a model for new gold currencies in the rich principalities of the Low Countries – Flanders, Brabant, Hainault and neighbours – as well as in France and England, where the first gold currency was issued as late as 1344.

The point here is that the gold resources of Europe had long been exhausted. Silver there was in plenty, and afterwards there would be still more, with the arrival of Spanish silver galleons from the Americas. But it was not until Europe received imports of West African gold, by way of North Africa, that commercial "take off" occurred in the High Middle Ages. So there is a real sense in which the foundation of the European Renaissance and its splendours, in and after the fifteenth century, depended on the miners, merchants and political leaders of Africa.

Direct contact with the ultimate sources of African gold, beyond the Sahara, was prevented by the "Muslim barrier", and all attempts to sail round the barrier proved vain until the 1430s. Such failures were epitomized by a sketch drawn into the great atlas of Abraham Cresques in 1375. Far down in the left-hand corner of the atlas there is a little sailing galley off the wide western bulge of Africa. Alongside it is a note by the map-maker explaining that this was the galley of Don Jaime Ferrer, who set forth in 1345 from a north Mediterranean port to sail to the "River of Gold", but who never returned. He too, like the sailors of the Mali emperor, lacked the necessary sailing rig.

Stray records show that a good many Africans from beyond the Sahara did in fact reach Europe, either as ambassadors from states such as Benin and Kongo, or as inquiring visitors, or as captives taken by Portuguese slaving ships. They were accepted, in those pre-racist times, just like other strangers: that is, according to their status and not their colour.

# Africa and Europe: a medieval partnership

Black Girl, *a sympathetic portrait by the Dutch painter Flinck.*

As late as 1507 the Scottish King James IV appointed a black lady, recently landed from a Scottish ship, as Queen of Beauty at a splendid tournament of the Scottish court. The whole affair was as broad in its fun as the temper of the times. It was duly celebrated by the Scots poet Dunbar in 1509:

*Long have I sung of ladies white*
*Now of a black I will indite*
*That landed out of the last ships*
*Who fain would I describe perfect*
*My lady with the muckle lips. . . .*

However light-hearted, the occasion offers for us a useful commentary upon the attitudes of those times, when strangers might be unusual in appearance but were accepted and cared for. This had been the attitude of the Middle Ages; it continued to hold firm through the sixteenth century.

This acceptance of Africans as being "different, but equal" – continuing the older attitudes of Classical times – is evident in the paintings of the period. Whether they portrayed black peoples as princes, merchants or mere servants, the masters of the Renaissance painted them all as equal human beings. Travellers' tales might speak of Africans who had no heads, as Richard Eden wrote in 1555, but "have their eyes and mouth in their breasts"; and such images might arouse wonder or dismay among all who were told of them. But when it came to Africans who lived alongside Europeans, and were seen in the flesh, Velasquez and Rembrandt and their like drew them as persons in every way comparable with Europeans, whether rich or poor, humble or proud. And were not these Africans, in any case, citizens of the land of the caravans of gold, and even subjects of the black Lord of Mali, long made famous by the atlas of Abraham Cresques?

# Chapter 10

# Cities of coral stone

Coming out of the East African interior, down long trails through easy smiling uplands, or across dry dull plains with little water and less comfort, the inland traders of old East Africa journeyed to the coastland of the Swahili.

This coastland was a market of major importance for them as well as a place of rest before they once more assembled their caravans of carriers and set their faces westward to their homelands in the interior. Here along the coral shelf of this Indian Ocean seaboard they found the buzz and business of city life, as well as contact with the wide Eastern world: northward with the lands of the Arabs, eastward with India and Sri Lanka, Malaysia, Indonesia and even China. They could stand on the quayside of Swahili ports, and watch the ships come in from all those distant countries, and meet their crews and passengers, and barter their inland goods for the wares of India and Cathay.

This ancient traffic, as valuable to the East as was the West African circuit to the West, is known from a pile of written evidence, remembered chronicles, tales and songs, and the witness of long-abandoned walls and coral ruins along the glittering seaboard. Nowadays the traffic barely exists, yet it can still tell much about East Africa's history.

## *Swahili*: The people of the coastland

Lamu is one of a cluster of inshore islands, each with its town and harbour, within some hundred yards of the coast of northern Kenya. The old dhow fleets of the long-range ocean trade are little more now than a memory, but occasionally a big *jahazi* of the coastal trade may swing by, its single gull-like sail billowing above the forward-leaning mast. Then another may come sliding to the quayside with a sudden shivering rattle as the broad sail comes down, followed by shouting in Swahili as the news of its arrival is relayed; it has been happening in much the same way for centuries.

Eighteen hundred years have passed since the earliest detailed account of the East African trade was compiled for fellow mariners by a Greek captain of Roman Egypt. He wrote of the harbours along this coast, of their exports and imports, their hospitality, habits, interests and skills. Many followed that unknown mariner. Yet it was the Arabs of Islam, and chiefly the Arabs of southern Arabia and the Persian Gulf, from ports such as Muscat and Siráf, whose partnership with coastal Africans first linked Lamu and its sister ports into a network of maritime trade across the Indian Ocean.

After about 700 this coast witnessed the steady rise of trading middlemen. Though African in its people and nature, this civilization became increasingly Muslim in its religion and in much of its local culture. Because of this, it took the name that we still know it by today: Swahili.

Zanj was the name used by medieval Arabs for East African peoples, but the

# Cities of coral stone

*Lamu on the East African coast was in medieval times part of a maritime trading network which extended across the Indian Ocean and as far as China.*

name itself was evidently much older. Something like it appears in that earliest account by the Greek captain of Roman Egypt, for he wrote of the East African coast as the "seaboard of Azania". The name survives today in that the island of Zanzibar, or *Zanj-bahr*, "coast of the Zanj". Yet medieval Arabs also knew this coastland as the *swahil* or shore – a variant of the same Arabic word, *sahel*, used for the West African "shores" or the Saharan ocean of rock and sand. Joining themselves to the culture of Islam, the people in ancient ports like Lamu went on speaking their own Bantu language, but also borrowed useful words from their Arab visitors. They began to call themselves "Swahili": the people of the coastland.

Here along the seaboard were city ports that played the same role as Jenne and Timbuktu on the other side of Africa: they linked buyers and suppliers in two great zones of production and purchase. From the first zone, inland, came African caravans with gold, ivory and other goods for sale abroad. From the second, across the Indian Ocean, came ships from many countries with cotton stuffs and luxury goods for the kingdoms and peoples of Africa. In between, organizing the exchange with a shrewd eye to their own profit, were the Swahili.

Just as in West Africa, the leading men and merchants of the "intermediary ports" accepted Islam, thus linking themselves to the wider civilization of the outside world. They evolved a Muslim culture without losing their African nature and identity, just as the many Muslims of western Africa retained theirs; or, later, Christian Africans became Christians without ceasing to be Africans. The study of Swahili history is thus seen to be very relevant to an understanding of Africa's overall development.

The most southerly of these trading harbours, known to the Greeks of Roman Egypt as Rhapta, probably stood near the delta of the Rufiji river in the southern part of modern Tanzania, but its exact site is still unknown. In 1967 the British archaeologist Neville Chittick showed that the oldest harbour of Muslim times was on Manda island, close by Lamu, where a local trading settlement appears to have taken shape early in the ninth century.

Many other trading settlements developed in the wake of Manda, from Mogadishu and Brava in modern Somalia to ports more than 3,000km (1,870 miles) to the south – a distance greater than that from Maine to Florida. Some grew into city states of power and wealth, such as Malindi and Mombasa in the north, and Kilwa in the south. Others, like Manda and Mafia, were island harbours of less importance. But all were well known along the coast and across the ocean, just as the more important of them were well known to the kingdom and communities of the African interior.

*The East African dhow was designed to sail against the wind many years before the technique was developed in Atlantic waters.*

Their reputation was enhanced by many travellers' stories, not least by those fabulous and popular tales of old Baghdad, *The Thousand and One Nights*. An Arabic account of the ninth century tells how Sindbad the Sailor voyaged far to the south and found marvels there:

Blessed by a favouring wind, we sped upon the foamy highways of the sea, trading from port to port and from island to island, selling and bartering our goods, and haggling with merchants and officials wherever we cast anchor.

## Swahili civilization

Medieval Arab literature contains many books about "the roads and kingdoms". Al-Masudi, one of the first and best of medieval Arab geographers, retired to Fustat (the old city of Cairo) just before the Fatimid conquest in the tenth century, and summarized what he had learned and seen at the end of a long and adventurous life. With an eye to a catchy title, he called his book *The Meadows of Gold and Mines of Precious Stones*. It is still very readable today.

Writing about his voyages in East African waters, "in the seas of the Zanj", al-Masudi recalled his last voyage home to Arabia from "Kanbalu" (possibly Pemba or Zanzibar) in the year 304 (or 916 of the Christian calendar), when he travelled with a shipowner of Oman who was later lost at sea with his ship:

For there the seas are like mountains which the sailors call "blind waves" because they fall away into deep valleys and yet never break into foam. I have travelled much on the seas: on those of China, of the Mediterranean,

# Cities of coral stone

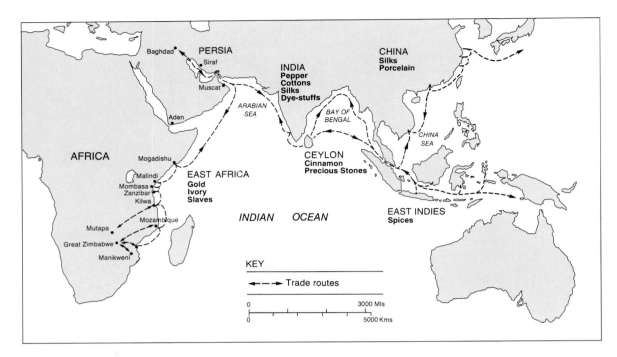

The map shows the far-ranging area of East African trade before the coming of the Europeans.

Caspian and Red Sea – but none of them, I saw, was as dangerous as those seas of the coast of the Zanj.

It was on this voyage, it seems, that he learned about a "king of the Zanj" who ruled an inland territory reaching all the way southward to what is now Mozambique. His kingdom produced gold and ivory that flowed to all the cities of the East. Most of the ivory went to India and China for a variety of decorative or courtly uses, "and if it were not for this great export there would be plenty of ivory in our Muslim lands".

Who was this East African "lord of the gold and ivory"? Al-Masudi's earlier and evidently more detailed writings are lost, but the general shape of the answer is not in doubt. He was one of the kings of the inland country, developing later into the Zimbabwe Culture, who organized a long-distance trade in early times (earlier, indeed, than we should have known if it were not for al-Masudi's passing reference). This was a trade that began in a small way and grew in size and importance, especially after the twelfth century. Al-Masudi also tells us that a principal place of gold export was Sofala, which we know was located not far south of modern Beira in southern Mozambique.

In 1976 a remarkable discovery confirmed the general run of al-Masudi's narrative. In that year a British archaeologist succeeded in showing beyond doubt that a stone ruin close to the coast south of Sofala, at a place called Manikweni, belonged to the Zimbabwe Culture. This, the first ruin of its kind to to be found near the coast, was built in the characteristic style and shape of those on the high plateau of the interior, although using limestone blocks instead of granite; Manikweni was a big stonewalled *zimbabwe* or royal dwelling.

Its inhabitants had been skilled metal workers of the later Iron Age of the region, and were involved, as the artifacts found on the site also showed, in long-distance trade with sea merchants of the Indian Ocean. Clearly a coastal outlier of the inland kingdoms of the Shona group of peoples, Manikweni's earliest walls were begun in about 1170, or little more than 50 years after the earliest stone walls had been raised at Great Zimbabwe itself.

Not surprisingly, this ancient relay station of inner African trade and politics near the coast of Mozambique acquired its own "Phoenician myth" among Westerners, just like its companion sites of the interior. As late as 1961, a Portuguese "authority" described Manikweni as a monument to remote Portuguese history. Those who built these long-fallen walls, he said, were "prehistoric Portuguese who had come from Atlantis and had manned Hiram's ships on their voyages to Ophir".

In fact, like Great Zimbabwe, Manikweni was African in origin and medieval in date. The recent lifting of this particular veil has brought us another proof of the old and enduring partnership in trade which joined the enterprise of the inland Shona and their coastal neighbours to the skills and commerce of the Arabs and other Indian Ocean peoples. This was the partnership that gave rise to the seaboard civilization of the Swahili.

The word "civilization" is justified here, even in its narrowest sense of "city life". For the Swahili built cities, and became, in medieval terms, a distinctly urban people. They built in the coral stone of their seaboard, rough grey "rag" from the shore of the Indian Ocean, runneled, very hard when dry, and entirely appropriate to architecture in this place. In its style, too, this architecture was distinctive: though increasingly Muslim in inspiration after the tenth century, it nevertheless remained true to non-Muslim traditions. Among the coral ruins of old Swahili towns on the middle stretch of their coastland, the mosques display embellishments of entirely local origin. Their handsome *mihrabs* point faithfully to Mecca (practically due north) but alongside them are tombs marked by stone pillars of a type found nowhere else. And with these, again, we meet a characteristically African openness to new ideas and fashions from elsewhere. The pillar tombs were decorated with inset plates of Chinese porcelain or fine pottery from the Persian Gulf, some of which can still be seen in place. Mosques and houses displayed the same mode of decoration.

*Reconstruction of an early 15thC Chinese ocean-going vessel. A fleet of such ships visited East Africa in 1417.*

The Swahili citizens of these towns developed a rich oral literature in songs and epics and, at least since the eighteenth century, an equally distinctive Swahili literature written in an Arabic script. Their verse conventions may often have followed Arabian models, but the content and meaning of their poetry remained markedly their own.

All this reflected the Swahili role as market middlemen, linking the caravans of the interior with the ships from overseas. Their own entrepreneurs travelled far in both directions, sharing in the caravan trade with the kingdoms of the Zimbabwe Culture, and also sharing in the maritime skills of the region. Like the Arabs and Indians, the Swahili had the sailing and navigating expertise – learned initially from the Chinese – to voyage out of sight of land for long distances; and they possessed these skills many years before such things were learned in Atlantic waters. It was done by a combination of lateen-rigged sails – capable at least to some extent of "boring into the wind" – and the use of the magnetic compass, together with position-fixing by reference to the Pole Star and its "guards".

Though largely forgotten later, the city ports of the Swahili enjoyed a wide repute in the medieval world. Writing in Sicily in the twelfth century, the Arab historian al-Idrisi said that they exported iron "to all the lands of India". A Chinese commissioner of foreign trade in Fukien province of southern China recorded in 1226 that the East African cities imported "white cotton cloth, porcelain, copper, and red cottons" by way of ships that came every year from the maritime states of western India. Even the Italian Marco Polo, though his Far Eastern travels never took him to East Africa, had something to say about "the coast of the Zanj" in his travel book of 1295.

*Delicate porcelain imported from China embellishes a typical "pillar-tomb" of the Swahili civilization on the East African coast.*

Swahili kings exchanged ambassadors with distant monarchs, and sent ambitious gifts. In 1414 the city of Malindi even managed to present a giraffe to the emperor or China, notwithstanding the enormous problems of transporting such an elongated creature and keeping it alive on the long sea journey. This particular feat of diplomacy also had an interesting sequel. In 1417 the Chinese high-seas admiral Cheng Ho began a series of western voyages that took him as far as Malindi in that year, and, on a second occasion some years later, to other Swahili harbours. It must have been an impressive visit for, in the words of a Chinese commentary:

> The ships that sail the southern seas are like houses. When their sails are spread they are like great clouds in the sky. Their rudders are several tens of feet long. A single ship carries several hundred men, and stores a year's supply of grain. There is no account of the dead and living, no going back to the mainland, when once they have entered the dark blue sea.

Gold and ivory went eastward, together with rhinoceros horn (much valued for its supposed aid to virility) and a trickle of slaves. Captives were sent from the coast or from the great island of Madagascar, but they were few. Though outrageous enough in the sufferings it imposed, this medieval Indian Ocean slave trade was a minor affair, never depopulating whole communities. The slaves it carried were used almost exclusively for domestic labour and military service, just as was the case in Europe during the same period.

### The "Queen of the South"

These coral cities continued to flourish until early in the sixteenth century, when disaster struck; but the earliest Portuguese visitors had time to describe this wealth and comfort before it disappeared. The kings of Mafia, Zanzibar and Pemba, wrote Duarte Barbosa,

> . . . live in great luxury. They wear fine silk and cotton garments bought in Mombasa from the Cambay (Indian) merchants. Their women, too, go bravely dressed, and wear jewels of fine Sofala gold, of silver in plenty, with earrings, necklaces, bangles, bracelets; and their clothing, too, is of fine silk.

# The "Queen of the South"

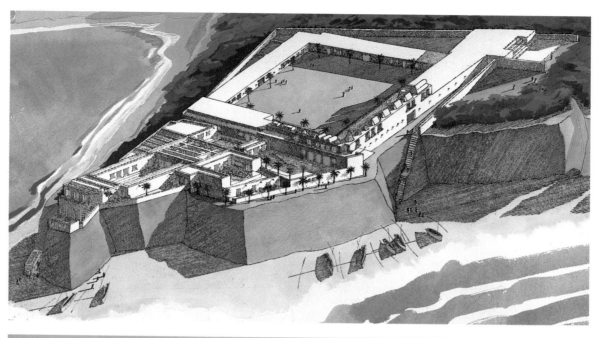

Kilwa: palace of Husuni Kubwa as it appears today (below left), and as it looked in the days of its wealth and power (above). A decorated doorway from nearby Lamu (below) suggests something of the elaborate art of Swahili culture.

*Remains of the octagonal bath (above) at Kilwa palace, built in 1300.*

The larger cities had many-storeyed houses, rising tier upon tier as the ground sloped up from the beaches. Mombasa, according to Duarte

> . . . is a very fair place, with lofty stone and mortar houses, well aligned in streets. It is a place of much trade, and has a good harbour where craft of many kinds are always moored, and great ships ply between Mombasa and Sofala, and others with the great kingdom of Cambay.

Mombasa vied with Kilwa, the "Queen of the South"; but Kilwa probably had the edge. Long abandoned and in ruins, the city stood upon an island – Kilwa Kisiwani, "Kilwa of the Island" – within a majestic bay protected on almost all sides from the ocean (a bay that was big enough, it would be said by British sailors of the nineteenth century, to shelter half the Royal Navy). From this favoured position, the kings of Kilwa rose to power and wealth after about 1100, largely because Kilwa enterprise enabled them to corner the export trade in gold and ivory from the inland kingdoms of Zimbabwe.

Growing rich through trade and high taxation of the imports and exports that passed through their hands, the Kilwa kings and merchants enjoyed high living. Enough is left of their city to show that lavish displays of wealth became the fashion, and were indulged in for at least three centuries. Nothing shows this better than the splendid palace built by one of its kings early in the fourteenth century. Much ruined now, it remains impressive.

### The palace of Husuni Kubwa

A small fee nowadays will take us by *ki-dhow* – a modest boat with creaking sail and occasional paddle – across the solitude of Kilwa Bay to this palace of Husuni Kubwa, Great Husuni. Approaching the shore, we push through mangroves to a little beach, and we have to wade ashore. Here steps led down to the sea, and they are still just about climbable. Along the clifftop are the ruins of the palace together with a large octagonal bath for the king and his ladies on the edge of the sunlit cliff. Alongside dozens of private rooms and audience halls there were warehouses and adjacent buildings, making a complex that was

# The palace of Husani Kubwa

*The great mosque at Kilwa, completed in 1450.*

inhabited and used for about 150 years. It was undoubtedly a great affair, and was among the buildings of Kilwa singled out for mention by Ibn Battuta, who came here in 1332 on his way to India. Dictating his memoirs many years later, he remembered Kilwa as one of the most impressive of all the cities he had seen. "The whole of it," he wrote, "is elegantly built."

The Great Mosque nearby was also there in Ibn Battuta's time, but it was improved and enlarged with additional domes and arches 100 years later, when more dwellings were added for the devout and learned men who lived or sojourned there. Far out on the rim of the fifteenth-century Muslim world, here was another proof of civic grandeur and ambition. Duarte Barbosa, who also came this way soon after 1500, found Kilwa "a town with many fair houses of stone and mortar, with many windows after our fashion, very well arranged in streets, with many flat roofs." A Portuguese artist, at about the same time, made a drawing of it that was clearly far from fanciful.

Barbosa noted the carved doors that may still be seen today. And, though hard to imagine now, he reported that "orchards and fruit gardens" lay around the town, well irrigated by fresh water. Here again was a "land full of food", for it was part of Kilwa's business to supply fruit and vegetables to land caravans and ships that arrived here after long, hungry travels.

A castle guarded the town, but its purpose was of chiefly local significance. Neither the land caravans nor the ocean fleets had aggressive intentions here, though this would change in later times. Indians and Chinese both had the strength and technology to embark on overseas invasions, but, at least in East Africa, they seem to have had no wish to do so. A Chinese philosopher, Chian Hsieh, set the general tone in a text of 1618 that was evidently applicable to earlier years. He advised mariners and merchants who made contact with "barbarian peoples" to have no fears of their hostility. "The only things that one should be really anxious about," he wrote, "are the means of mastery of the waves of the sea – and, worst of all dangers, the minds of those avid for profit and greedy for gain."

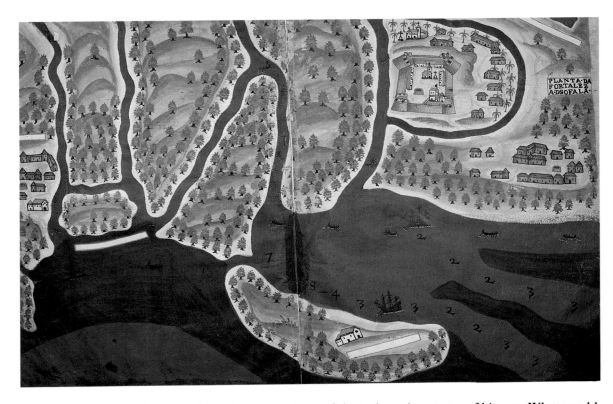

*A 16thC Portuguese map of Sofala shows an early European trading post on the "coast of Zanj", the East African seaboard.*

At this point we meet one of the truly curious turns of history. What would have happened if the Chinese had followed up Cheng Ho's pioneering voyages of the early fifteenth century with a regular development of their own Indian Ocean trade? At the least, one may reasonably think, they would have secured a leading position and influence in those waters. Yet the Chinese did nothing of the kind. On the contrary, the years after Cheng Ho's voyages saw the "sea-going party" at China's imperial court utterly defeated by an "inland party". The latter held that foreign trade was damaging to China, since the country's indifference to exports meant that foreign imports must be paid for in hard cash.

By 1500, with the "inland party" winning all along the line, China's great shipyards were closed down, and the building of an ocean-going ship had become a crime that carried the death sentence. The long-haul crews were dispersed and the captains pensioned off. Nothing remained of Chinese ocean enterprise.

Yet in those same years another maritime enterprise crept eastward out of the Atlantic round the southernmost tip of Africa, and this was an enterprise that was to change everything. The Chinese philosopher's description – "avid for profit and greedy for gain" – could have fitted few people as accurately as these adventurers from the West. Centuries of generally peaceful trade now came to an end, and very brief was the warning.

# Chapter 11

# Disaster from the West

"In the year of the Prophet 903 [AD1498]," a near-contemporary Kilwa historian wrote, "there came news from the land of Mozambique that men had arrived from the land of the Franks [that is, from Europe]."

These men had three ships, "and the name of their captain was al-Mirati [Admiral Vasco da Gama]." After a few days there came word that the ships had passed Kilwa – they were, in fact, carried northward on the tide past Kilwa bay – "and had gone on to Mafia. The lords of Mafia rejoiced, for they thought there that the Franks were good and honest men. But those who knew the truth confirmed that the Franks were corrupt and dishonest persons who had come only to spy out the land in order to seize it."

It must be said that da Gama and those who followed him from Europe did their best to prove the rightness of this judgment. In thus discovering "the Franks", the Swahili and their Indian Ocean partners also discovered a piracy that went beyond anything they had known before. Not only did the Portuguese wreck and loot cities; much worse in the long run, they seized control of the Indian Ocean trade and eventually ruined it.

Da Gama's first voyage did little more than forecast what was going to happen. After a brush at Mombasa, where he was received with suspicion, he went on to Malindi. There he got hold of an unlucky pilot, probably an Arab, who steered his little fleet on the south-westerly monsoon to Calicut in India. Arriving there, da Gama followed his usual practice of sending ashore one of the convicts he had taken on board in Portugal for this purpose. Under sentence of death at home, such men were regarded as expendable "first contacts".

The encounter was prophetic. As noted in the flagship's logbook, the convict at once met a "Moor of Tunis" on the quayside. This man understood Spanish or Portuguese, and clearly had his wits about him. "May the Devil take you," he replied to the newcomer, "What brought you here?"

Plunder rather than trade was the answer. Da Gama's homeward cargoes were said to have brought a profit 60 times the amount of the king of Portugal's investment in the voyage. At last the "Muslim barrier" was fully rounded, and the king now conceived ambitious plans for the future. "We hope with the help of God," he informed the king of Spain, "that the great trade which now enriches the Moors of those regions [the Swahili and their Indian Ocean partners] will now be diverted to the men and ships of our own kingdom." The trading galleys of Venice, he told the Venetian ambassador, had better stop going to Egypt for cargoes from the Golden East, and come instead to Lisbon.

What the Portuguese could not take on sea they took on land, and other Europeans were going to do the same. "There is here a power which I may call irresistible," the missionary saint, Francis Xavier, was noting sadly in 1545, "to thrust men headlong into the abyss, where besides the seductions of gain and

*Vasco da Gama (above) sailed with three ships (right) along the East African coast in 1498. The Portuguese mariners were quite rightly suspected as "corrupt and dishonest persons who had come only to spy out the land in order to seize it".*

the easy opportunities of plunder, there is a torrent of bad example and evil habit to sweep them away."

The Swahili cities suffered even before those of India. On his second voyage, da Gama told the king of Kilwa that he would burn the city to the ground unless homage and tribute were paid to the king of Portugal. Ravasio followed suit at Zanzibar. Saldanha stormed Berbera, Soares wrecked Zeila, d'Acunha assaulted Brava where, in Barbosa's contemporary report, the Portuguese "slew many people and took great spoil in gold and silver". But none of the coral cities suffered as sorely as Kilwa and Mombasa, the richest on the coast.

In 1505 Francisco d'Almeida brought eight ships to anchor off Kilwa city, and stormed the town. Hans Mayr, a German aboard d'Almeida's flagship, wrote down what happened:

First to land was the Admiral; others followed him. They went straight to the royal palace, and granted their lives only to those Moors who did not resist.

A man leaned from a palace window waving a Portuguese flag, but he refused to open the gates. They broke them down, and finding the place deserted, rushed through the rest of the town "with its many strong houses of stone and mortar and plastered with various designs". They then called for their priests:

The vicar-general and some of the Franciscan fathers came ashore carrying two crosses in procession and singing the *Te Deum*. These went to the palace, where they set up a cross and the Admiral prayed. Then everyone started to plunder the town of all its merchandise and provisions.

It was the same at Mombasa to the north. Here the raiders met with stiff resistance, and cannonades were exchanged. D'Almeida fired the town with burning arrows shot into the thatch roofs, following with an assault in force. When the town was taken, according to Hans Mayr,

the Admiral ordered that Mombasa should be sacked, and that each man should carry off to his ship whatever he found, so that at the end there would

be a division of the spoil. Then everyone started to plunder the town and search the houses, forcing doors with axes and bars.
Much Sofala cloth was taken, and
a large quantity of rich silk and gold-embroidered garments, and carpets also. One of these, without equal for its beauty, was sent to the king of Portugal with other valuables. A day later they plundered the town again.
Writing afterwards to his neighbour of Malindi, the king of Mombasa claimed that his people, on returning to their city after the raiders' departure, found "no living thing in it, neither man nor woman, young nor old, nor child however small. All who had failed to escape had been killed and burned."

The northerly Swahili cities eventually recovered, and Swahili culture rose to new achievements, but the splendid past remained only a memory. A poem of 1815, the popular *Utendi wa Inkishafi* of a poet of Lamu, tells of departed glories and the vanities of ambition: of "rich men with their silver and gold" who walked "with heads held proudly and eyes closed in scorn". They dwelt in "lighted houses aglow with lamps of crystal and brass [where] the nights are as the day"; only, in the end, to come to dust and ashes. The essence of that lament of Lamu is expressed in two of its lines:

*Madaka ya nymba ya zisahani*
*Sasa walalilye wana na nyuni. . . .*
(Where once the porcelain stood in the wall niches
Now wild birds nestle their fledglings)

*Francisco d'Almeida, who plundered Kilwa in 1505.*

That, exactly, was Kilwa's fate. In 1817 two British officers of the *Nisus* frigate landed on Kilwa Island. Pushing their way from the beach through tangled bushes, they were astonished to find many ruins overgrown by vegetation, and wondered to each other what forgotten people could possibly have built them.

### A meeting of equals
How were matters proceeding, meanwhile, on the other side of Africa?

West Africans had first met the "Franks" some 60 years before d'Almeida's sack of Kilwa, and at first the experience of sudden assault was much the same. Portuguese chroniclers of the time tell of raiding expeditions mounted against Berber herdsmen of the far Western Sahara:
And so it chanced that in the night, they came to where the natives lay scattered in two camps. And when our men came close, they attacked these natives very lustily, shouting "Portugal" and "Sant'Iago", causing much alarm. And so in the confusion the natives began to flee, though there were men who defended themselves with spears, especially one who fought face to face with Nuno Tristão, defending himself to the death.

Three other natives were killed, and ten prisoners taken who were men, women and boys. And our men would have slain and taken many more if only they had all attacked together at the first onslaught.
That was in the 1440s, but further down the Atlantic coast, beyond the estuary of the Senegal river, strong kingdoms dealt firmly with this raiding from the sea. Either the visitors came and stayed for peaceful trade, or they were refused all contact. According to a Portuguese account of 1506:
At the mouth of the Senegal river you find the first black peoples, and that is the beginning of the kingdom of Jolof. Its king can put 10,000 cavalry and 100,000 infantry into the field.
An exaggeration, no doubt; but the strength of the Jolof (Wolof) kingdom, as other evidence shows, was no laughing matter. Offering peaceful trade with these unexpected visitors from the sea, this kingdom and its neighbours found

the offer rapidly accepted.

There were other reasons why the peace was generally kept, and why early West African experience of Europe was in contrast with events along the Swahili coast. Here in West Africa no rich cities stood upon the seaboard, inviting piracy, because until now this had always been an empty ocean, a sea frontier beyond which there seemed to be nothing and nobody. The Indian Ocean trading circuit and community had no counterparts here. Along the seaboard there were only minor chiefs ruling unimportant fishing villages and hamlets, all of which looked to the inland country for trade and opportunity.

Whenever strong kingdoms reached to the coast – having an interest in important salt or dried fish – they nonetheless had their backs to the ocean. The Yoruba of south-western Nigeria still celebrate their goddess of the sea, Yemanja, as they did then, but they were never a sea-going people. Ambition, profit and enterprise led inland, and that was where the rich cities lay. "Far away in the interior", said the same Portuguese report of 1506, "there is a kingdom called Timbuktu":

> It is a great city. And there, too, is the city of Jenne, inhabited by black people and surrounded by a wall of pounded earth. Brass and copper are highly valued, red and blue cottons, salt, much else . . .

But there was no getting there save possibly by peaceful means. Even the large and comfortable city of Benin, though no more than a day's travel from an anchorage in the estuary of the Benin river, could be entered only with permission.

Royal alliance and trading partnership therefore had in general to take the place of the piracy practised in the Indian Ocean. Africans could usually impose their own terms on these arrivals at the empty frontier of the Atlantic, which they now discovered with much interest to be a possible frontier of commerce. Needing land bases on what became known as the Gold Coast, where endless ocean surf made the long-term anchoring of trading "hulks" impossible, Europeans built castles on the sea shore. But the castles were built on land belonging to local owners, and an annual payment of rent was made to them.

*Sir John Hawkins, raiding the West African seaboard for slaves in 1567, assisted two African kings in a local conflict. His reward was a present of over 300 prisoners of war.*

### Meeting the whites

African memories of first encounters with white men have come down in a variety of tales and songs. These earliest whites were sometimes mistaken for reincarnations of saintly ancestors, but this was an error that was rapidly corrected. More often, reversing the European stereotype that equated blackness with the Devil, Africans saw white arrivals as a portent of harm or danger. But this tended to be the village reaction; sophisticated kings and chiefs generally took a different view. In 1567 the English mariner John Hawkins, raiding for slaves along the western seaboard, had reached Sierra Leone and, having acquired 150 captives, was ready to sail with them for the West Indies. But while getting ready to sail, as his logbook records,

> there was a Negro sent as an Ambassador to our General from a king of the Negroes who was oppressed by neighbouring kings. He desired our General to grant him succour and aid against his enemies, and this our General granted him.

Hawkins took 200 Englishmen ashore and joined two local kings against two other kings. A big fight ensued, which Hawkins and his two royal allies won, and Hawkins was rewarded for his aid with a gift of more than 300 captives.

The king of Benin also took Portuguese soldiers into his service, or at least welcomed them at court. The same occurred elsewhere. Such rulers were already familiar with the notion of distant lands and peoples, for they were linked in one way or another to the overland trading circuit, and news came from afar. Now that the empty ocean had become a frontier of business opportunity, they set about exploiting the change. They welcomed visitors for whatever they could bring in profit or social diversion, and moved to secure good information about the lands from which these visitors had come.

In 1486 the king of Benin sent his first ambassador to Portugal, because, in the words of the Lisbon records, this king "desired to learn more about these lands [of Europe], the arrival of people from them in his country being regarded as an unusual novelty":

> This ambassador was a man of good speech and natural wisdom. Great feasts were held in his honour, and he was shown many of the good things of these kingdoms [of Portugal and Spain]. He went home in a ship of [our] king's, who, at his departure, gave [this ambassador] a gift of rich clothing for himself and his wife; and, through him, [our king] also sent a rich present to the king of Benin.

Catholic missionaries were also sent and, in due course, a Portuguese ambassador. Acting as the latter in 1516, Duarte Pires wrote to Lisbon that the king of Benin "accords us high honour, and sets us at table to dine with his son; and no part of his court is hidden from us, but all doors are open."

Such exchanges were not rare. A son of the Angolan king of Kongo was invited to Portugal and trained for the priesthood. In 1518, this prince travelled to Rome and was made a bishop by the Pope before being sent home again. "Royal brothers" in Europe and Africa hastened to make alliance with each other, and whatever misunderstanding there may have been as to the real intentions on either side, diplomatic correspondence was exchanged in words of careful courtesy. This situation endured for many years. A Dutch print, made in Amsterdam as late as the 1640s, shows the ambassadors of Holland kneeling to the king of Kongo at a reception.

Some of the sculptural arts add their own commentary to these early encounters. The bronze plaques designed and cast for embellishment of the pillars of the king of Benin's palace frequently depicted scenes of everyday life, and these included Portuguese knights and soldiers, accepted as "an unusual novelty" at court. Local carvers turned their skill to the portrayal of these sea-going visitors, or of their distant kings and nobles. Some of these fine carvings have survived in the form of decorative salt cellars or the like, and they throw a vivid light on the attitudes linking these widely separated peoples between whom, as yet, no lasting hostilities had commenced.

*A Benin sculpture of a Portuguese soldier, possibly a mercenary in the service of the Benin oba.*

## How backward was Africa?

It is worth considering here the real differences in levels of development that then lay between the civilizations of Europe and Africa. How wide was the effective "power gap", the gap in technological capacity, between the more advanced peoples on the two sides?

Between the kingdom of Portugal and the kingdoms of the Wolof of Benin, not to speak of the inland empires of Mali, Songhay, or Bornu, the gap was evidently narrow. True, the Portuguese – and other Europeans who came after them – could mount cannon on ocean-going ships and use them to good effect. They had more small firearms, and usually better ones, than any available in Africa. They also possessed a ruthlessness in warfare, very much the product of their European history, that was generally absent in Africa then. These advantages could break open the doors to the Golden East, but certainly not the doors to West Africa.

The Europeans had literacy, although proportionately little more than the countries of African Islam. They had metal-working skills, but these were not much superior to African skills of the same kind. They had far greater mechanical capacity, but as yet applied it rather seldom in practice. They made excellent cotton cloth, but in certain respects, such as the fast-dyeing of cottons, their skills were inferior to those then practised in Africa. They had ship-building and navigating skills that were unknown in western Africa but were commonplace within the Indian Ocean community, including the Swahili. In all such ways, the effective gap in power and technology was still a small one. Often, in practice, the greater strength lay on the African side.

In political skills the Portuguese had no superiority at all, and this applied in quite large measure to the Spanish, French and English as well, although not, a little later, to the Dutch. The Europeans tended to come from rigidly authoritarian kingdoms emerging from, or still plunged in, feudal wars; and they discovered African kingdoms often far more stable and even popular in their forms of government than anything within their own experience. They may have found these African forms of government hard to understand, but few among them could reasonably claim any European superiority.

The Portuguese court, true enough, tried to assume a superior role, if only to support its new claims to overlordship in Africa. This led to some confusion. Portuguese nobles easily mistook for hierarchies of feudalism, structures of social ranking that were in fact altogether different. Early in the sixteenth century the Portuguese king, intending to "improve" what he took to be the feudal system of the kingdom of Kongo in Angola, sent out a *regimento* or royal briefing to his royal brother of Kongo, advising him to adopt titles of nobility such as "princes, dukes, marquises" and so on. It was scarcely a success.

Otherwise they sent out missionaries with orders to build churches, if they could get permission, and make converts to Christianity. Again the superiority can be said to have lain on the African side, for whereas African rulers had little difficulty in admitting the Christian faith to their pantheon of respectable belief, the Portuguese, like other Europeans later, could see in African faiths nothing but blind and brutish superstition. And the same was true in a wider perspective of social life. African music, dancing, mime and spectacle seemed to these Europeans only a wild and vicious indulgence in the sins of the flesh. To Africans, such a view of the matter could only appear as intolerant foolishness or a sad incapacity for enjoyment. There is much in the records to show this.

The *potential* power gap, of course, was already wide. Western Europe now had behind it a long period of mechanical invention and technological ingenuity, built on economic need and on the science inherited and developed from classical times. This was the age when Copernicus, Bruno and Galileo would begin the scientific explanation of the universe.

Yet potentiality is not the same as actual achievement. Inventions become effective only when they are socially applied, and their application depends not on inventiveness but on economic growth. The European watermill, for instance, had been a Roman development of a Greek invention elaborated in Egypt. The first known watermill in Europe seems to have been built in Roman France sometime shortly before AD300. Yet this most useful invention spread at the speed of the snail. The first watermill recorded in Britain dates only from 838. The reason for this slow application was not, one may accept, that the invention remained unknown. It was that milling by human or horse power could continue to meet the demand for flour until economic expansion developed in the Middle Ages.

Cultural change was correspondingly slow. Bruno was burnt at the stake and Galileo was silenced by the Holy Inquisition and its threat of torture; what Everyman knew or believed was still what the canons of the Church had taught. Landing at the mouth of the Congo river on his first great pioneering voyage, Diogo Cão set up a cross or *padrão* to claim the land for Christ and his temporal

*An ivory salt cellar, carved by a Benin craftsman to a Portuguese commission, represents two Portuguese dignitaries with their attendants, surmounted by a ship.*

king. His inscription stated that this was done "in the year 1681 since the Creation of the World, or 1482 since the birth of Christ", and any suggestion that the first date must be totally absurd would have seemed outrageous. Western Europe might now stand on the threshold of tremendous intellectual advance, but very few people there had the faintest inkling of any such revolution.

*Dutch ambassadors kneeling to a 17thC king of Kongo. An earlier Kongo king vainly expressed a wish that "in these kingdoms there should not be any trade in slaves or any outlet for them".*

What people thought about each other corresponded to this state of affairs, and all the evidence suggests that their attitudes were still very much of the "different, but equal" kind. The wealth and splendour of the Golden East might dazzle these Europeans and drive them to frenzies of theft and violence: but what they wanted and what they took, very clearly, was what they could not produce at home. It is unlikely that anybody in d'Almeida's ships – inwardly at least – can have believed they were bringing with them the fruits and proof of a more advanced and peaceful civilization. None of the early Europeans to reach Benin, or the other well-ordered polities of western Africa, would have thought they were visiting their natural inferiors. On the contrary, they looked for an even-handed partnership, and were happy when they found it.

## A partnership in trade

In West Africa the partnership prospered. The new frontier of trade along the ocean seaboard soon widened with the arrival of ships from European lands other than Portugal. They brought goods that were liked: European cottons and woollens went well in the local markets, as did brass basins and luxury curios such as imitation pearls, swords of exotic design, the occasional firearm, and even braided jackets and cocked hats. "Manillas" or bracelets of European copper could usefully supplement copper imports from the Saharan trade.

Most of these imports were fed through royal treasuries and warehouses. West African kings, like those in Europe, retained a strict hold over their foreign trade, simply extending the controls developed for overland trade to cover the overseas traffic. It was found that European imports were easily paid for. What the Europeans most wanted was gold and, after that, ivory, pepper and fast-dyed cottons, as well as a trickle of slaves for domestic use in Europe. None of these exports called for any great productive effort.

This, of course, was bad news for the overland traders. At first they were greatly puzzled by the reduction in gold deliveries to the north. Then, investigating, they found themselves competing with sea-borne rivals whom they could neither fend off nor over-reach. It was during this early period of coastal partnership with Europeans that the old caravan routes began their irreversible decline. Trans-Saharan caravans would retain commercial import-ance until well into the eighteenth century, and the salt caravans are still flourishing down to this day. But the high days of trans-Saharan trade, and the political developments sustained by it, were passing into history.

Warrior-kings in the northern territory of modern Ghana still bear witness to those times. The present ruler of Gonja is the 32nd of his line, and his oldest ancestor on the Gonja "skin" or throne is remembered as a warrior among warriors. This man, one of a unit of cavalry riding south from Bambara country on the middle reaches of the river Niger, was originally in the service of an emperor of Songhay, the *Askia* Dawud. Shortly before 1575, the *Askia* sent cavalry south to find out what had gone wrong with his gold supplies from the mines and rivers of Asante. The riders got as far as the fringes of the great tropical forest but there, being mounted, they had to stop. Deciding to stay permanently, they launched seven little kingdoms, and Gonja, in the course of time, became the first among them. What the ruler of the far-flung Songhay empire thought about this is not recorded, but in any case he soon had other things on his mind. Songhay was invaded by gold-seeking Moroccans in 1591, and shortly afterwards fell apart.

The bad news for the overland traders was good news in Europe. For some 30 years or more the Portuguese reaped handsome returns with little rivalry from other nations. Their "gold caravels" from West Africa could even outdo in value the great Spanish "silver galleons" from the Americas. In 1540 the English got into the act with an initial voyage that took back pepper and ivory. Then, in 1553, Captain Windham carried home no less than 68kg (150lb) of gold, though he died before reaching England. A year later Captain Lok returned with 182kg (400lb) of gold, and a few years after that Captain Towerson pillaged 23kg (50lb) of gold from a French ship on the coast. He reported that, much to his annoyance, other French ships had escaped with 318kg (700lb) of gold. As we see, Europeans on the coast were already treating each other as fair game, with the English setting the pace.

These were fabulous gains for a Europe acutely short of precious metal. West African voyages might be expensive to mount, and were sometimes attended by catastrophe, but the fortunate ones were exceptionally profitable. European merchants found to their delight that a copper or brass basin could be sold on the African coast for the equivalent, in gold, of some £30 sterling in the values of the 1550s. Furthermore, pepper and ivory could command high prices on European markets, lending an additional profit to each voyage. Lok's voyage of 1554 is thought to have realized an overall profit about ten times larger than the capital outlay.

And the slave trade? Pursuing good relations with their African partners, in rivalry with the Portuguese, the English and the French kept off it altogether for a long time, and, save for a few raiding expeditions, this state of affairs continued until well into the seventeenth century. The Portuguese, as we have seen, had taken back captives almost from their first probing voyages down the western coast. They continued to do this by agreement with the Senegalese and other coastal kings or chiefs, who were happy to find a market for their stock of "disposable persons". Although amounting to some 700 a year by the 1460s, and more later, this was still just a trickle compared with what came later. In Portugal and Spain, demand for slaves from Africa was small, since domestic slaves from eastern Europe were still cheaper. And the risks were less: apart from other dangers of the sea, Portuguese or Spanish merchantmen were always liable to seizure by northern raiders or "privateers".

Being expensive, however, black slaves became fashionable, and, being fashionable, were better treated than other slaves. The Portuguese royal chronicler Eannes de Zurara, writing in 1453, was among those who remarked on this:

> Yes, and certain widows of good family who had bought some of these female slaves [from Africa], either adopted them or left them a portion of their estates by will; so that in future they married right well, and were treated as free.

> Suffice it to say that I never saw any of these [black] slaves put into irons like other captives, and scarcely one that did not turn Christian and was ungently treated. And I have been invited by their lords [owners] to the marriages and baptisms of such; at which they made no less solemnity about their former slaves than if these had been their children or relatives.

The condition of African slaves in medieval Europe seems remarkably similar to that of black slaves in Fatimid Cairo centuries earlier, as recorded by the documents in the Geniza files.

*A Benin carving shows two Portuguese fighting. But European rivalries only helped to swell the Atlantic slave trade into a flood.*

But a worm was already in the fruit of this humanity and tolerance: the Portuguese had found another and different use for African slaves. Sugar plantations worked by slaves from eastern Europe or Turkey already existed on the Mediterranean island of Cyprus. Now the Portuguese discovered that they could reproduce much the same economy on Atlantic islands such as São Tomé off the equatorial coast. For this purpose they applied to the nearby kingdoms of Angola for the necessary slave labour. This was forthcoming, but soon the supply of "disposable persons" who had lost their civic rights proved too small.

Raiding and kidnapping quickly followed; and in 1525 we find the king of Kongo complaining to his royal brother of Portugal:

> The demand is so great that we cannot count its size, since Portuguese traders are every day taking our people, sons of the land and sons of our noblemen and vassals and our relatives, because [local] thieves and men of evil conscience seize them, wishing to have the things and goods of your kingdom. They seize them and sell them, and, Sire, so great is the corruption and licentiousness that our country is being completely depopulated.

> Therefore we beg Your Highness to help and assist us in this matter, commanding your agents that they send here neither traders nor goods, because it is *our will that in these kingdoms there should not be any trade in slaves or outlet for them.*

The Kongo king's scribe underlined those words, but the emphasis was useless. The trickle was growing to a flood, and nothing now would stop it.

São Tomé was to remain a slave island until well into the twentieth century, and other Atlantic islands, such as those of the Cape Verde archipelago, would also take their share of forced plantation labour. Even so, these were small islands, incapable of absorbing a great many slaves. But then, in 1492, there fell upon Africa the curse of Christopher Columbus, and a mighty curse it proved to be.

Columbus discovered the Caribbean for Spain, and other adventurers quickly discovered more. They dug mines and established plantations, but none was of any use without labour. The Spanish accordingly went for slave labour, and with both hands. "It has been said of the Spanish conquistadors," recalled the Trinidadian historian Eric Williams, "that first they fell on their knees and then they fell on the aborigines." In a few terrible years the Spanish ran through the Carib populations of the West Indian islands, as well as multitudes on the adjoining mainland. Then they turned to Africa.

# Chapter 12

# The curse of Columbus

A pleasant ferry conveys you nowadays from the modern port of Dakar, capital of the republic of Senegal, to the little island of Gorée, not far out in the blue Atlantic. There is nowhere better for a weekend picnic. Here are quiet alleyways between rose and ochre-plastered buildings of the seventeenth century, as well as a popular tourist attraction in the shape of a "slave house": but the old devils of the place are long since exorcized.

With cells for about 20 captives at a time, the house dates from the period when the trickle of slaves had yet to become a flood. Approached from the landward side, it is a little mansion that seems to hold no great terrors even from its earliest memories. But approach it from the sea, and the aspect is rather different.

Boats from the slaving ships came to anchorage, as we can today, on stones beneath a blank wall. Set in this wall is a rectangular opening as tall as a man. From this place small groups of captives walked along a plank to the waiting boats. The boats rowed them out to a ship, and the ship transported them to the Americas.

Change the scene from the island of Gorée to a frowning fortress on the Gold Coast of modern Ghana. The Swedes first built it in 1655; the Dutch took it from them, and then in 1664 the English took it from the Dutch. This is Cape Coast Castle, centre of English maritime power in West Africa for some 200 years of sorrow.

Like other castles along the Gold Coast – and in the end there were more than 40 of them – Cape Coast was built and maintained to accommodate the flood of slaves that poured across the Atlantic after the 1650s. Gorée might have held a score of captives, but Cape Coast eventually had room for 1,500 at a time. The moral attitudes of those days are revealed in the actual structure of the building: below there are slave cells and, exactly above, there is the chapel for their Christian captors. The massive iron cannon are still there as well, facing seaward, for the possible enemies were rival Europeans. There was little threat from inland, since these were castles built for the most part with the full agreement of the local owners of the land. They were the embodiment of a new partnership.

How did the trickle become a flood? In 1505 the king of Spain, responding to "developments" in the Caribbean, sent a ship from Seville to the Americas with 17 black slaves and some mining equipment. Meanwhile, a Portuguese fleet bound for the Indian Ocean was blown off course and made a landfall at what is now Brazil. Soon afterwards the same process of exploitation and depopulation was set in motion there, as it had been in the Caribbean. In 1510 the first consignment of black slaves, carried from Spain or Portugal, was sold in the West Indies, and by 1515 there came back to Europe the first Spanish import of

The North-West Prospect of Cape-Coast Castle.

CAPE-COAST is y'Largest,Strongest,& most beautifull Castle belonging to the Royal. Afr.ª Compªon of y' Coast of Guinea.Here is y' Residence of y' Gen.ªl Who presides over Eight other Forts,besides Several Factories.It lyes in y'Latitude of 5.ª North,which (tho'very near y'Equinoctial Line) yet is it accounted y'most wholsome air in Guinea.Under Shelter of y' Guns, is built a Large Populous Negro Town.The People are of a Warlike Sort. Their Religion is altogether Pagan,their Fitish day,or Sabbath,is on Tuesday.Their Chief provision is Fish,& Canky (further described in plate 14) Nevertheless y' Castle is indifferently Stored with Mutton,Goats,Hogs,& Fowles,from y'Inland Country,also some Venison,but at a very dear Rate

*Cape Coast Castle, seized from the Dutch by the English in 1664, became the centre of English trading power in West Africa.*

slave-grown Caribbean sugar. As the demand for labour increased, Spain began to convey black captives directly across the ocean from Africa to the Americas, with the first shipment setting sail in 1518. But the plantation slave trade remained comparatively small in numbers all through the sixteenth century. As late as 1592, the biggest slaving contract proposed by the king of Spain provided for the delivery from Africa of only some 38,000 captives over a period of nine years, or about 4,250 a year. Of these, the contract stipulated that no more than 3,500 each year must be landed alive. The king was moving cautiously, if only because black slave revolts in the Caribbean had already cost the planters dear.

Portuguese deliveries of captives to Brazil were considerable by 1660, and other nations now took a hand. In 1603 the English began their own colonization in the Caribbean, followed by the French in 1626, with the Dutch and others hard behind. At the same time there came the colonization of the eastern seaboard of North America, with the Pilgrim Fathers landing from the *Mayflower* in 1620, and many more soon after them. With the consolidation of Mexico and other Spanish possessions, the whole seaboard was now a destiny for captives from Africa.

The word "captives" is significant, for until this time the great majority of Africans shipped across the Atlantic had already been slaves when sold to European traders: that is, they were "disposable persons", captured in war or found guilty of crimes by courts of law. This was the way that the old slave trade had been conducted from immemorial times. But now it was different. The reign of King Sugar and King Cotton had begun across the Atlantic, and it called for millions of slaves, with the dead continually replaced by the living. This set in motion a process of forced migration larger than any other in history. It laid the foundations of American development. It nourished the English and French economic growth that led on to great technological and scientific progress. The human record knows no combination more grimly contradictory: the piling up of wealth on one side, but the misery of mass enslavement on the other.

For Western Europeans the trade became "everyone's honeypot". Extraordinary fortunes were made. To take one example: an English labourer called William Miles, who signed on as ship's carpenter in Bristol for a voyage to Jamaica, had £15 – enough to buy a cask or two of Jamaican sugar for sale in

England. Spending his profit on English manufactures for export to West Africa, he exchanged these goods for captives who were carried to the West Indies for sale against sugar; he then brought back the sugar thus purchased for sale in Europe. The Miles estate grew hugely, and in less than two generations was worth more than £500,000, enormous wealth in the values of that time.

Retiring with their fortunes to the English shires, the West Indian planters and traders outshone all other businessmen in their lavish mansions and prestigious spending. Great cities scrambled into wealth: Nantes in France, Bristol and Liverpool in England, others elsewhere. "What the building of ships for the transport of slaves did for eighteenth-century Liverpool", Eric Williams has commented, "the manufacture of cotton goods for the purchase of slaves did for Manchester." And Manchester was now to be the focus of England's industrial revolution.

From about 1650 onwards, these were the burgeoning fruits of a three-sided enterprise in profit: first, from the export of cottons and other goods to West Africa; secondly, from the sale of captives into American and Caribbean enslavement; and thirdly, from the sale in Europe of slave-grown produce. The relative size of these profits obviously varied with time and chance. Probably the third "side" was far more profitable than the actual sale of captives, but the latter could also yield financial gains. It is in any case true that the "triangular trade", of which the slave trade was an essential element, may be said to have done much to lay the financial groundwork for English and French industrialism.

This triangular trade and its profits could never have been fuelled by the limited supply of "disposable persons" from Africa. Few of the new victims had

*A 17thC "slave house" on Goree Island, off Senegal. African captives passed through the narrow opening between the flights of stairs, and walked along a plank to the ship that would take them to the Americas.*

*The slave fortress of Elmina, one of more than 40 located along the Gold Coast (modern Ghana).*

the status of slaves before they were sent aboard the ships. This new slavery of the plantations involved the capture and degradation of free men and women. That is why the slave trade required a new partnership.

### A business of kings

African kings and chiefs along the coast entered this new partnership without any enthusiasm, but found themselves drawn from one concession to the next. Once their available pool of "disposable persons" had become too small for the European demand, they faced a difficult choice: either they must obtain more captives by war or purchase, or they must turn down the chance of European imports.

Generally, the second choice was seen as worse than the first, for it meant shutting the door on this new frontier of trade – a development which would, in turn, undermine the chiefs' own positions. For these positions depended partly on the chiefs' ability to bring in desirable imports and distribute them among their people. That was why they monopolized foreign trade: then, as later, political and economic power marched together. "None but kings and great men trade here," affirmed a famous king of Asante, "the same as myself." Earlier, a French slaving captain had confirmed as a general truth that "the trade in slaves is the business of kings, rich men, and prime merchants".

No doubt an alliance of coastal rulers could have insisted that the Europeans should sell their goods only for gold and ivory and pepper, as in the days of the older partnership; but no such alliance ever proved possible. So the supply of captives for export became an irresistible road to violence, gradually thrusting aside all refusals and hesitations. Yet at the outset there were many of both.

King Agaja's case is worth remembering here. In 1708 Agaja assumed the kingship of the Fon of inland Dahomey (nowadays the republic of Benin, though many hundreds of kilometres from the ancient Benin empire). At that time the Fon people were suffering from raids for captives carried out by little

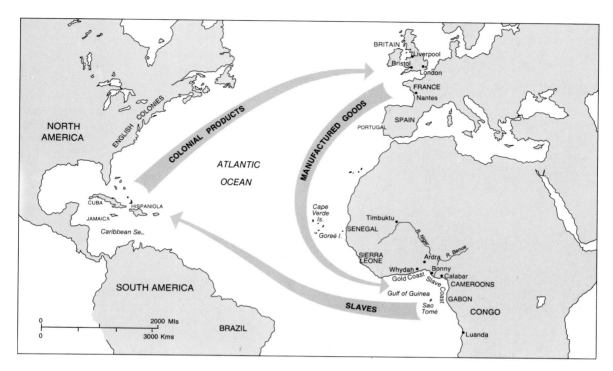

states along the seaboard. These states not only harmed the Fon with their raids, but also acted as a barrier between the Fon and the European sea-merchants. Badgered by their Yoruba neighbours, the Fon also needed guns and gunpowder for their own protection, but found it hard to get them because of the coastal barrier.

Agaja removed this barrier. In 1725–28 he conquered all the small coastal states and brought them within his kingdom – Ardra, Whydah, Jakin and others – so that King Agaja and his trade commissioners were now in direct contact with the pursers of European ships at anchorage. The Fon king realized and accepted that Europeans would sell guns and gunpowder only if captives formed part of the purchase price. He now proposed a new kind of contract, using as his intermediary an Englishman, Captain Bullfinch Lamb, whom he had captured during his conquest of the coastal towns. Agaja sent Lamb back to England with a present of 320lb of gold and 80 captives for the English king, together with a plan that would put an end at least to the *export* of slaves. Agaja's proposal, as reported by Lamb, was that "the Natives would sell themselves to us, on condition of not being carried off".

As an attempt at economic progress, this was far ahead of its time. The establishing of plantations in West Africa itself only became interesting to the English some 150 years later; in Agaja's day they merely wanted to enlarge their plantations in the West Indies. In any case, Lamb failed to keep his promise to Agaja that he would return to West Africa with a report on his mission. And Agaja, for his part, gave up his attempt to prevent the export of slaves.

Thus the Fon coast remained the Slave Coast, and the little seaboard state of Whydah became a rendezvous for the slaving ships of many nations. A contemporary account of the place comes from John Atkins, a ship's surgeon who became ship's purser after coastal fevers had killed off almost everybody else in the crew. Writing in 1737, Atkins stated that Whydah was then the greatest slaving point along the whole coast, selling off as many slaves, as all

*Map of the "triangular trade" shows how Europe, West Africa and the Caribbean were connected in a commercial network very lucrative for Europe but ruinous for Africa.*

the rest together, 40 or 50 sail (French, English, Portuguese and the Dutch) freighting thence every year.

He recorded that King Agaja bought captives for export from his neigh-bours, but "if he cannot obtain a sufficient number of slaves that way, he marches an army and depopulates".

This export trade of Agaja's, incidentally, was the means of transferring to Haiti (then the French island colony of St Dominique) the famous "voodoo" or python cult. Voodoo was initially a local religion of the little seaboard states such as Whydah, and tactful inquiry at Whydah even now will reveal python shrines that still survive. When King Agaja's Fon armies swept into Whydah and its neighbouring states, the local priests led resistance to the invasion. Like other "politicals", they were put aboard ships for permanent exile and landed, as slaves, in Haiti. They took their cult with them.

In the trading partnership's fateful chain of cause and effect, guns and gunpowder became ever more necessary to rulers such as Agaja, either to raid for captives or else for defence against neighbours with the same ambition. There developed, increasingly, an equation between the supply of captives by one side and the supply of guns by the other. Of course there were many other items in the trade – other European exports, and other African exports – but the guns-for-captives contract remained essential.

Gun-makers in Europe were pleased enough. The rising English city of Birmingham was said to be exporting guns to West Africa at a rate exceeding 100,000 a year by about 1750: the overall totals were in any case enormous. European governors and agents on the West African coast were less delighted by this arms trade. As the Dutch governor of Elmina Castle on the Gold Coast put it in a letter of 1700, wholesale European supply of firearms "gives them [the Africans] a knife to cut our throats".

But the European supply of guns had become as unavoidable as the African supply of captives, and for the same reason. In the words of the governor:

we are forced to it, for if we would not [sell guns], the English, Danes and Brandenburghers would sell them. And even if we [governors] could all agree to refuse, the interlopers [private sea-merchants not controlled by royal companies] would abundantly furnish them. And since guns and gunpowder have for some time been our most saleable merchandise, we should do poorly without our share in it.

So the bloody partnership between "kings, rich men and prime merchants" on either side continued, adding one new violence and degradation to another.

*Olaudah Equiano, an Igbo sold to slavers in 1756 at the age of nine, gained his liberty in England and took an active part in the campaign to end the slave trade.*

### Different and inferior

The days when black visitors to Europe could be met with respect, and even honour, were passing rapidly away. And yet they were not quite over. A handful of blacks even received higher education in Europe. A young man from the Gold Coast (modern Ghana) entered the German university of Halle in that same year of 1727 when King Agaja was trying, fruitlessly, to stop the export of captives. Receiving a doctorate of philosophy at Wittenberg in 1733, Anton Wilhelm Amo was praised by the rector as a man of high gifts and civilization.

Olaudah Equiano, 50 years later, made much the same impact. Captured and sold in Igboland (eastern Nigeria) in 1756 when nine years old, Equiano eventually gained his liberty in England and became an ocean sailor. In 1788 he took an active part in the English campaign to abolish the slave trade, and published a book on the subject that gained a considerable influence. He later married a Miss Cullen of Cambridge and became a respected local figure.

But generally, by now, black visitors found respect only if they were members of the partnership. It was the custom, then as later, to invite king's

sons to Europe as a means of strengthening a trading advantage against rivals. As top people, they were easily welcomed by other top people. "There are two black princes of Annomabu [Gold Coast] here," wrote Horace Walpole in his London diary of 1749, "who are in fashion at all assemblies: of whom I scarce know any particulars (of their story), though the women all know it and ten times more than belongs to it." They were duly received by King George II, and accorded due honour in exchange for their homage. Visiting a play at Covent Garden, they were greeted by polite society with "a loud clap of applause", and doubtless had much to say about their social success when eventually at home again in Annomabu.

Yet it is highly probable that down below Covent Garden, with its glittering assembly, somewhere in the darkness at that very same hour, a slave ship was clearing the port of London with a cargo of helpless victims for the Americas.

A romantic eighteenth-century fashion might now care to paint the "noble savages" of Africa as persons of primeval innocence and childish joy. But the men with the money knew better, and their notion was very different. These were the years when a systematic and instrumental racism was born in Europe and America, forging another fateful link in the chain of cause and effect. For racism was born out of the need to justify the enslavement of blacks, after the enslavement of whites had long become a crime. From the first, in other words, racism was a weapon of exploitation.

Fattening on that trade, the men with the money all agreed upon their own righteousness. They were doing no harm. On the contrary, they were doing good. Were they not removing from Africa a mob of miserable beings for whom

*Whydah or Ouidah, an important 18thC port for the sale of Africans into enslavement in the Americas. Now in the republic of Benin, Whydah was on what the Europeans called "the slave coast".*

slavery was a natural and permanent condition? Were they not transporting them to a superior civilization in the Americas? That is what the men with the money said in their clubs and drawing rooms, in parliamentary debates, in furious letters to *The Times* and every other newspaper they could reach.

And the argument took. It took widely. Men and women without the money, whether in Europe or the Americas, grew accustomed to seeing black people only as slaves delivered from the ships, wretched and exhausted, dazed by their sufferings and speechless in any European language. Or they saw them as slaves on plantations, faceless gangs with often ferocious reputations, safe only when within reach of the overseer's whip. What else but slavery could such creatures deserve?

Year after year for decades, even for as much as two centuries, matters remained thus. And this was when the older attitudes of "different but equal" were forgotten, and were replaced by other attitudes. Now the blacks were seen as "different and inferior": naturally inferior, as God was now said to have made them. Forged by the slave trade, the weapon of racism cut into the tolerance of earlier times.

### The price of slavery

Delivered aboard a slaver in 1756 when still a child, Olaudah Equiano later recorded his first impressions. He saw

> . . . a large furnace of copper boiling and a multitude of black people of every description chained together, every one of their countenances expressing dejection and sorrow, I no longer doubted of my fate.
>
> When I recovered a little I saw some black people about me, who, I believed, were among those who had brought me on board and had been receiving their pay. They talked to me in order to cheer me, but all in vain. I asked them if we were not to be eaten by those white men with horrible looks, red faces, and loose hair. . . .

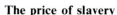

*After selection, slaves were branded with the mark of French, English or Dutch companies "so as to prevent their being exchanged by the sellers for worse . . ."*

But the real terrors were bad enough. After captives were brought from inland to the coast, a French eyewitness in the 1680s wrote:

> They are put into a kind of prison built to receive them near the beach. Thence they are taken out to a large open space where the surgeons from the slaving ships examine every part of every one of them, men and women being all stark naked.

Those "agreed to be good and sound" were then put on one side, "the rejected being above 35 years of age, or defective in their features, or grown grey, or otherwise imperfect". Next came the stamp of ownership:

> Then the good and sound are marked on the breast with a redhot iron, imprinting the mark of the French, English or Dutch companies, so that each buyer may distinguish his own, and so as to prevent their being exchanged by the sellers for worse, as the sellers are apt to try.

And "in this particular", adds our eyewitness, "care is taken that the women, as tenderest, be not burnt too hard."

No longer captives now, but branded cattle for enslavement, the victims might then wait many days for a ship. At last, however, they would be put into canoes, "stripped naked without distinction of men or women, although in orderly ships they are allowed a piece of canvas to wrap about their waists, which is very acceptable to the poor wretches."

Once aboard, fear and hatred reigned on either side. No year passed without its furious outbreaks of revolt either before or during the "Middle Passage" of the ocean. "When our slaves are aboard," recalled a Captain Thomas Phillips at the end of the seventeenth century,

> we shackle the men two and two while we lie in port and in sight of their own

*Conditions on board a slave ship bound for Brazil.*

country, for 'tis then they attempt to make their escape, and mutiny: to prevent which we always keep sentinels upon the hatchways, and have a chestful of small arms, ready loaded and primed, together with some grenade shells; and two of our quarter-deck guns, pointing on the deck, and two more out of the steerage.

Phillips fed his captives twice a day, and that "was the time they are apt to mutiny, being all upon deck." He had his crew stand to their arms, "and some with lighted matches at the great guns loaded with partridge shot, till the slaves have eaten and gone down to their kennels between the decks."

Death on shipboard – for crews as well as captives – depended largely on the length of the passage. Yet it got no smaller as the quality of ships improved, for shorter passages were accompanied by what became known as "close packing", which often resulted in high death rates. A typical "close packing" was reported as late as 1829 by a British anti-slaving patrol. This naval vessel stopped a slaver and found that it held 505 men and women captives, and had thrown 55 overboard during 17 days at sea. The captives

were all enclosed under grated hatchways between decks. The space was so low that they sat between each others' legs, and stowed so close together, that there was no possibility of lying down, or at all changing their positions, by night or by day.

Most had no more than one square foot of sitting space for weeks on end, and all suffered from an acute shortage of drinking water. Yet headroom for captives on this slaver was as much as three feet and three inches, and, because of this, veterans on the naval patrol ship judged that it was "one of the best they had seen". What could the worst have been like?

Imagination is not even necessary. There are accounts in many archives. The Cuban historian Moreno Fraginals unearthed the fearful story of the *Amistad* slaver in his researches of the 1960s. Towards 1820 this Spanish vessel had embarked 733 captives in West Africa. Of these, after a crossing of 54 days, only

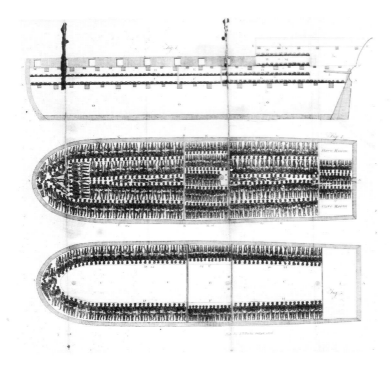

*Cutaway section of a slave ship (above) c. 1808, showing the method of "close packing" whereby the captives had "no possibility of lying down or at all changing their positions, by night or by day". A bill of sale (above, right) dated 1835, shows the sale of 9 Africans for an average price of less than $600.*

188 remained alive when the *Amistad* docked in Havana.

Once landed, captives were sold by prior agreement or auctioned in a "scramble", with each buyer jostling for the captives he fancied most. Then came plantation slavery and, for many, a mercifully rapid death.

### Consequences for Africa

Onwards from 1650 the overseas demand for captives grew by leaps and bounds. As we have seen, this caught African rulers in a double bind. To ensure their supply of European manufactures, they had to sell captives. But to guarantee the necessary supply of captives, as well as to defend the country from raiding neighbours also in search of captives, each ruler had to buy guns and gunpowder, and then more of the same. New insecurities and violence were the unavoidable result.

Some could gain from this, but even those who gained were bound to live in a new brutality. Life became cheap. The old domestic servitude of former times, an easy-going personal bondage for the most part, gave way to a far worse captivity. No few coastal communities were dragged into moral disintegration.

Within areas affected by the coastal slave trade, depopulation could be extremely severe. In the worst cases, whole polities and populations were wiped out or cruelly maimed. That was what happened, for example, to the kingdom of Ndango in west-central Angola. "This kingdom is very extensive," a Portuguese bishop reported to the Pope as early as 1640. "At one time it was rich. Now it is completely ruined." In some areas the slave trade brought about such extensive depopulation that even today it has still to be made good.

Church and State combined in these ravages. By 1700 all missionary enterprises in Angola were supported by slavery: they made money by dealing in slaves, and they used slaves for field labour as well as domestic service. The whole practice became endemic. "We claim", remarked a Portuguese governor in 1800, "to be bringing all the blacks of Angola to the lap of Holy Mother,

while, at the same time, we promote and maintain the slave trade; two aims which contradict each other."

*An early print shows a slave dealer auctioning captives from an improvised platform.*

Such rebukes fell on deaf ears. The good clergy consoled themselves: were they not baptizing their victims? The bishops of Luanda could wave a baptismal hand over the heads of captives as these were rowed below them, in boatloads, on their way to enshipment. There was even a marble chair on the wharf at Luanda for the bishops to sit in while they did so; it was still there as late as 1870.

In coastal communities such as these, the political and social consequences of the slave trade could be little else than violence and despotism. But the economic consequences for Africa as a whole were probably still worse.

Historians calculate that about 10–12,000,000 captives were landed alive in the Americas during the four centuries of the slave trade. We have estimated that another 2,000,000 or more died on the Middle Passage. As for those who died in Africa before enshipment, or as a result of slave raids and wars, the total was certainly large but is impossible to estimate.

When divided into some four centuries, this total loss of upwards of 20,000,000 people does not amount to a general depopulation of the African continent. Rather more than 20,000,000 people emigrated from Britain between 1812 and 1914, yet the British population in 1914 was considerably larger than it had been in 1812. If some communities were crippled, the fertility of others could still make good the loss in numbers. But this "average way" of calculating losses to Africa during the trade can be very misleading.

To start with, captives were taken only if they were young, healthy and of sound physique. They were those not only most able to have children, but also those most able to do productive work. Either way, productive capacity was removed from communities which needed as much of both as they could get. The ground for economic development, in other words, was continually undermined.

### An export of skills

The American historian, Professor John Hope Franklin, has pointed to another aspect of African loss and slave-owners' gain. He emphasizes that the captives who became slaves "did not come to the New World empty-handed":

> In language, music, graphic arts, sophisticated patterns of agriculture and other economic pursuits, and an understanding of the functions of government, they early became a part of an evolving New World culture in the islands and on the mainland [of the Americas].
>
> Perhaps equally important, they brought with them the energy, industry and the will to persevere that were at least as great as those qualities of human character brought by their European enslavers.
>
> Africans did not stand still in history in the Old World; and they surely did not stand still in history in the New.

The captives brought skills as well as aptitudes, the most important of which were in tropical agriculture, and it was with these that they made their largest contribution to the promotion of American wealth. In this respect it was not only their capacity to withstand tropical climates and fevers that made them invaluable. Still more, it was their Africa-acquired capacity to farm in conditions entirely strange to European experience.

Surprisingly, the same was often true of mining. In 1818 a Swedish mining engineer, returning home after long service in the great mining province of Brazil, Minas Gerais, wrote that the province of Minas Gerais "seems to have been the last in which the usability of iron ore and the extraction of iron was learned from African Negro slaves".

These captives enslaved from the ships applied their Africa-learned skills across a wide field of productive enterprise, including the search for minerals and gems. A Brazilian witness tells us:

> When a Negro is lucky enough to find a diamond of the weight of an octavo [$17\frac{1}{2}$ carats], much ceremony follows. He is crowned with a wreath of flowers and carried in procession to the administrator, who gives him his freedom by paying his owner for it.

John Hope Franklin has also emphasized that slave skills in the North American colonies were either brought from Africa, or else developed locally:

> Many plantations had their slave carpenters, masons and mechanics; but the skilled slaves were to be found mostly in the towns. There were slave tailors, shoemakers, cabinet makers, painters, plasterers, seamstresses and the like.

There were even slave inventors. In 1835 and 1836 one Henry Blair, designated in the records as a "coloured man" of Maryland, received patents for two corn harvesters which he had developed.

### Trade in economic regression

The situation in Africa was further undermined by the nature of the goods that were imported in exchange for this export of productive capacity. These were goods of a "non-developmental" kind that were more likely to promote economic regression. What came in – apart from guns, alcohol and luxury adornments for the powerful men of the trade – were cottons that supplanted local clothing industries, and metal bars and other goods that weakened the local mining and smithing industries.

In view of these facts, then, the slave trade should be seen as instrumental in promoting an early form of colonial exchange. Europe poured its manufactures into Africa. In return Africa sent out its most precious raw material – the productive capacity of young men and women. All the elements of an unequal exchange were present: a trade that was highly profitable on the European side, building capital for a multitude of entrepreneurs, but which, on the African

side, merely obtained consumer goods for a privileged minority.

An incident of 1826 well illustrates this "anti-developmental" aspect of the trade from the African side. It occurred in one of the small Niger Delta states that flourished along the mangrove-lined shores of creeks and estuaries, where Europeans lived in "trading hulks" or vessels moored within easy reach by canoe. These kingdoms had come to life in response to the opportunities of sea-going trade, and had early fallen into the meshes of the slave trade.

In 1826 the ruler of one of these kingdoms was offered a daughter in marriage by the neighbouring king of Warri, who had heard, in the words of a contemporary account, of his "amazing wealth and extensive connections with the Europeans". The king of Warri wanted to acquire his neighbour's favour through marriage, and the latter, to show his future bride's father how much he appreciated the honour thus conferred upon him,

. . . loaded canoe after canoe with rare and most valuable treasures: English, French, Spanish and Portuguese merchandise were extracted from his warehouses – gold and silver plate, costly silks and fine cloths, embroidered laces and other articles too numerous to mention.

Having sent this to his neighbour, the expectant husband then awaited the bride and her father, the king of Warri, on their nuptial visit. Meanwhile he turned his own royal residence at Bonny into a veritable festival of high living. As he told a

*African slave mineworkers. The slave trade deprived Africa of valuable skills as well as of people. It was said that in Brazil "the usability of iron ore . . . was learned from African slaves."*

visiting European in the trade language now customary along the coast:

That time I first hear, Warri's canoes come for creek, I fire one gun from my house – then all Bonny fire – plenty powder blow away you no can hear one man speak.

I stand for my house – all my house have fine cloth. Roof, walls, all round: he hung with proper fine silks. No possible look one stick, one mat: all he covered. My Queen's Father stand for beach. His foot no touch ground. He stand on cloth. All way he walk, he walk on cloth.

I give wine, brandy, plenty puncheon – pass twenty. I give for my people and Warri's. All Bonny glad too much. Every man, every woman, for my town, I give cloth – pass one thousand piece I give that day. Pass twenty barrel powder I fire that day.

It must have been a notable occasion; and the Bonny king's partners overseas, plantation owners in Jamaica or rising businessmen in England, would have thoroughly sympathized, for they, in their own way, were doing just the same.

Yet a crucial difference stood between. For while the Bonny king's gains from trade were the consumer goods in his warehouses, the businessmen in England turned their cash into productive capital, and with that capital they helped to build an economic revolution. Its early fruits were already on the scene. By 1768, in England, Hargreaves had invented the spinning jenny, which enabled one operative to use many spindles simultaneously. In 1776 Watt produced his mechanical pump, and in 1803 Trevithick made a steam locomotive that ran on iron rails. A new era had opened; but the kings of the Niger Delta had no share in its productive power. In that same period of rapid productive progress in western Europe and America, Africa fell ever more fatally behind.

Fatally, because the ending of the slave trade turned out to be linked with the onset of a new European ambition. Using African labour outside Africa had begun to seem a vastly inferior enterprise to using African labour inside the black continent. Why not go in and use it there?

There was an ironic coincidence that perfectly expressed this shift in European attitudes. The last slaving ship from Africa was creeping westward to the Americas, illegally, with smuggled cargo, at the very same time as the assembled powers of Europe, meeting in Berlin, arranged to partition the continent among each other. One chapter ended as another, leading directly out of it, began.

That was in the 1880s, but much had already occurred to prepare for the colonial era.

# Chapter 13

# Exploring inner Africa

In 1796 a young Scots surgeon named Mungo Park contrived, against every kind of obstacle, to get himself by horseback and on foot from the Gambia river, on the West African coast, to the banks of the distant but still mysterious Niger. At that time little or nothing was known in Europe about the vast interior of Africa, but leading maritime powers, with Britain at their head, were beginning to be curious. What really lay behind the skylines of the coast?

In the single matter of the Niger, geographers since ancient times had believed that it flowed from east to west, and probably into the Atlantic by way of the river known as Senegal. But was this true? Mungo Park settled the question. Travelling inland from the upper waters of the Gambia, his journey was immensely difficult, but finally proved to be thoroughly worthwhile. Arriving at last within sight of the magnificent river at Ségu, he "saw with infinite pleasure the great object of my mission – the long sought for majestic Niger, glittering to the morning sun, as broad as the Thames at Westminster, and flowing slowly *to the eastward.*"

Park met with kindness on his journey, but also with threats and perils. Moving from one community to another across the plains of the Western Sudan, he might have fared much worse. He had arrived in the period of major political reorganization that had followed the decline of the old trading empires and the development of new constellations of powers. These were still establishing themselves, and stray travellers, with motives hard to credit, often met with understandable suspicion. If they were not traders with goods to prove it, or learned men in search of wisdom with sufficient proofs of that as well, what could they be but spies?

Kings and governments might ask themselves such questions, but for ordinary people, more often than not, the rules of hospitality came first. Park was in a sorry plight by the time he reached the Niger, for he had travelled with the slenderest of means and lost most of them on the way. Resting under a tree within sight of the river, alone and hungry, he was noticed by a woman returning from work in the fields:

Perceiving that I was weary and dejected, she inquired into my situation, which I briefly explained to her; whereupon, with looks of great compassion, she took up my saddle and bridle, and told me to follow her. Having conducted me to her hut, she lighted up a lamp, spread a mat upon the floor, and told me that I might remain there for the night.

Finding that I was very hungry, she said she would procure me something to eat. She accordingly went out, and returned in a short time with a very fine fish; which having caused to be broiled upon some half-embers, she gave me for supper.

The rites of hospitality being thus performed towards a stranger in

*Hospitality for Mungo Park (below), the Scottish surgeon who in 1796 travelled from the West African coast to the upper waters of the Niger. A sketch by Park (above) of a bridge over the Bafing river.*

distress, my worthy benefactress (pointing to the mat, and telling me that I might sleep there without apprehension), called to the female part of her family, who had stood gazing at me all the while in astonishment, to resume their work of spinning cotton.

The good woman's daughters sang as they worked, and one of the songs they sang "was composed extempore, for I was myself the subject of it." As is still usual on such occasions, one singer invented the verses, and the others joined in a chorus:

> *The winds roared, and the rains fell.*
> *The poor white man, faint and weary,*
> *Came and sat under our tree.*
> *He has no mother to bring him milk;*
> *No wife to grind his corn.*
> *(Chorus)*
> > *Let us pity the white man,*
> > *No mother has he. . . .*

Park was touched, as well he might be, and "in the morning I presented my compassionate landlady with two of the four brass buttons of my waistcoat; the only recompense I could make her."

He then prepared to cross the Niger to the city of Ségou. Waiting for a ferry, he gazed at the spectacle of the city on the far bank, and was impressed.

> The view of this extensive city; the numerous canoes upon the river; the crowded population, and the cultivated state of the surrounding country, formed altogether a prospect of civilization and magnificence which I little expected to find in the bosom of Africa.

The king of Ségou, as it happened, saw no reason to receive this stranger, but contented himself with sending Park 5,000 cowrie shells for the purchase of food, and the offer of a guide to take him further down river to the city of Jenne. The sensible Park thought this generous, for why should the king believe that he had made this painful journey simply for the satisfaction of seeing a river?

> He argued probably, as my guide argued: who, when he was told that I had come from a great distance, and through many dangers, to behold the Joliba [Niger] river, naturally inquired if there were no rivers in my own country, and whether one river was not like another.

Even so, added Park, "this benevolent prince thought it sufficient that a white man was found in his dominions, in a condition of extreme wretchedness; and that no other pleas were necessary to entitle the sufferer to his bounty."

Such brief but telling insights are a corrective to a later, rather common view, that the period of the Atlantic slave trade was merely one of ruthless inhumanity in the continent.

*The township of Ségou, visited by Mungo Park long before the colonial era, "formed altogether a prospect of civilization and magnificence which I little expected to find in the bosom of Africa".*

# Exploring inner Africa

## New states and empires

Another European traveller, Heinrich Barth, who came to West Africa some 50 years after Mungo Park, found an extensive production and trade system linked to a regional network reaching far across western Africa. Of Kano he wrote:

> Commerce and manufacture go hand in hand, and almost every family has its share in them. There is something grand in this kind of industry which spreads [its products] to the north as far as Murzuk and Ghat and even Tripoli; to the west, not only to Timbuktu but in some degree even to the shores of the Atlantic; and far to the east and south.

He was describing a regional economy organized across many frontiers and within many communities. It was not exactly a West African "common market", since customs dues and state taxes were imposed by governors, but effectively it functioned as such. There were few communities, however small or remote from the trading routes, whose markets were outside the range of its supply or demand. Cowrie shells were generally used as a trading currency. This regional economy formed, to a great extent, a single monetary zone based on the cowrie – a "cowrie zone".

Covering most of western Africa south of the Sahara, this "cowrie zone" was the product as well as the vehicle of steady economic and social expansion since medieval times. The breakdown of the old empires, chiefly after the Moroccan invasion of the Songhay empire in 1591, had released new energies and created new opportunities,. On the upper and middle reaches of the Niger Park found the relatively new kingdoms of the Bambara, a people previously subject to the Mali or Songhay empires. Elsewhere he found new Muslim states, such as Bondu, formed by other eighteenth-century initiatives in reorganization.

*Heinrich Barth, 1821–65, visited West Africa over 50 years after Park and was equally impressed by the sophisticated level of commerce and industry.*

Some of these new states were doomed to failure. Their governments came unstuck from a lack of political experience, or proved unable to build on firm political ground. Others put down roots and acquired stability and wealth. They might have been well aware of the coastal slave trade, and even have been peripherally affected by its costs and gains, but their own development had little to do with either. This development reflected the needs of thriving populations and their ability to produce more goods, whether for local use or for trade with neighbours, near or far. After about 1600, here in the inland country, there was both social and economic expansion.

South from the walls of Kano, before Barth or any other European reached them, the trails led to the lower reaches of the Niger and beyond. Here, too, the onward development of production and trade among expanding populations had caused new political departures and social innovations. The old travellers went by donkey or on foot, for wheeled transport was still not used.

For some distance south of Kano the grassland plains of the Sahel continue to stretch away into the distance. But towards the great river there is steadily more vegetation of bush and trees, or, at least, it was so in the past. Towards the river, too, we leave the country of the Hausa and Fulani, and begin to meet communities closer to the cultures and languages of the forest lands. It was in these forest lands, which extend to the distant coast, that the magnificent kingdoms of Ife and Benin had developed.

Today all this is part of the splendidly varied community of Nigeria; beyond the river the lands of the Yoruba begin, a people millions strong with a known history reaching back into the time of Europe's Middle Ages. Ancestrally loyal to the Yoruba king of Ife, the Yoruba have always lived in many different states of their own. But after about 1580 there came a development that would enclose most of them, for two centuries, within a single Yoruba state or empire. This was centred on the city of Oyo, north of Ife, and ruled by the king or *alafin*.

This huge state of Oyo, reaching from the inland Niger almost to the coast at

*Barth's illustration, 1853, of the market place of Sokoto, now in Northern Nigeria.*

modern Lagos, was another aspect of internal reorganization that reflected growth and change in the seventeenth and eighteenth centuries. Partly its success derived from a large expansion of local effort in the spinning, weaving and dyeing of local cotton, as well as other crafts. But the growth of Oyo also depended on a steady increase in trade which it was well placed to promote and exploit, being in a "middleman" position between the forest lands and the cowrie zone of the grassland plains to the north. Oyo could, for instance, import horses from Hausaland in exchange for Yoruba cottons, as well as trading in a variety of foodstuffs and other commodities.

These economic strengths were combined with shrewd political skill. As in other African states, but perhaps with more consistent success, Oyo politics managed to restrict the power of authority with effective "checks and balances". The *alafin* kingship was undoubtedly strong and well able to assert itself, being armed with powerful military forces capable of harassing neighbours and preventing invasions. Yet there were constraints, sometimes narrow, on the *alafin*'s freedom of action.

The *alafin* had his own governing apparatus of "king's men", a bureaucracy of governors, sub-governors and servants of the executive. But against these was set a range of chiefs and chiefs' appointees who could if necessary counter or even cancel the authority of the "king's men". The non-royal appointees in their turn were ranged in mutually opposing ranks, which gave the royal government political space for manoeuvre. They could combine against the *alafin* and even cause him to be dethroned (by sending a ritual present of parrot's eggs). But this could only happen if royal incompetence or misrule was generally agreed to have passed beyond reasonable limits. The system proved secure and flexible.

It should perhaps be emphasized that this kind of political reorganization,

*The splendour of an Asante king recalls the powerful kingdom almost unknown to Europeans before the 19thC.*

building on the simpler structures of an earlier age, was not restricted to Nigeria. Famous kingdoms grew in strength, such as Asante in the country that is Ghana today. Others, such as Denkyira and Akwamu, became little more than a memory, although well known to visiting Europeans of the seventeenth century. Similar changes occurred in Africa's other great regions, and, generally, reorganization brought larger structures of power within more clearly marked boundaries of influence or administration. It is a complex picture that was almost completely misunderstood by Europe until fairly late in the nineteenth century, after the expeditions of Barth in West Africa, Livingstone in Central Africa, Burton in East Africa, and some very notable French explorers. Yet even they (with the exception of Barth) uncovered little sound information, and some of them, like Burton, were profoundly confused by the racist mythologies of which they had become the victims.

In the old lands of the Zimbabwe culture, on the central-southern plateau of modern Zimbabwe and western Mozambique, the strong kingdom of the Rozwi rulers, Urozwi, remained independent of outside intrusion until the 1830s, while the northerly kingdom of the Mwene Mutapha (Monomotapa) succumbed to Portuguese infiltration up the Zambezi river as early as the seventeenth century. Somewhat further north, in the wide belt of wooded grassland running east-west along the southern fringe of the Congo basin rainforest, new concentrations of political power produced a cluster of new kingdoms, the strongest of which was that of the *Mwata* Yamvo in the region of the upper Kasai river in what is now north-eastern Angola.

An offshoot of that particular kingdom took shape in the south-eastern province of modern Zaire, Shaba (formerly Katanga), where a line of kings

*The textiles of W. Africa were superior in design and quality to most contemporary Western work.*

ruled whose title was Kazembe. The power of the Kazembe derived partly from control of the east-west trading routes through the interior of this "Middle Africa", and it was considerable, as the first European to reach him (or, at least, the first to leave any extensive record of having done so) was able to note. In 1831, wearing a uniform of "blue nankeen and white breeches" (which must have been uncomfortably warm), and riding on a donkey, the gallant Portuguese explorer Antonio Gamitto was received by a parade of 5,000 warriors and the Kazembe himself:

> Many leopard skins served the king as a carpet, the tails pointing outwards to form a star; and over these was an enormous lion skin, and on this a stool covered with a big green cloth. On this throne the *Mwata* Kazembe was seated, in greater elegance and state than any other *Mambo* [central African monarch] I have seen.
>
> His head was ornamented with a kind of mitre, pyramidal in shape and two spans high, made of brilliant scarlet feathers; round his forehead was a dazzling diadem of beads of various kinds and colours. . . . *Mwata* Kazembe looks fifty years old but we were told he is much older. He has a long beard, already turning grey. He is well built and tall, and has a robustness and agility which promise a long life; his look is agreeable and majestic, and his style splendid in its fashion. We certainly never expected to find so much ceremonial, pomp and ostentation in the potentate of a region so remote from the seacoast, and in a nation which appears so barbarous and savage.

On the other side of the continent, the Sudan remained beyond European reach until the middle of the nineteenth century, and the first modern description of the kingdoms of Ethiopia (then called Abyssinia) became available only in the

157

1770s when, as we have seen, the Scots nobleman James Bruce returned from a long stay there. Bruce reported a political and military dispensation apparently so comparable to aspects of European feudal history that his tale was largely disbelieved at the English royal court, where polite society could not credit the notion that any part of inner Africa had raised itself above the level of "savage barbarism". Bruce retired to his ancestral home to write a five-volume account of his experiences – a work that is generally regarded as one of the great classics of travel literature and remains highly readable to this day.

Historians today recognize that, throughout the period preceding the European explorations of the middle and late nineteenth century, considerable reorganizations of power were in process in much of Africa. These reorganizations were, however, of a quite different kind and level from the immense and even revolutionary transformations that early capitalism and industrialism had initiated in western Europe. Many African states were becoming stronger than before, but the gap in effective military and technological power between western Europe and most of Africa, already wide, was growing still wider.

Huge invasions and interventions now lay ahead, but Africa's capacity to confront or contain them remained primitive in comparison with Western mechanical skills and organization. Nowhere was this to be clearer than in the lands soon to be enclosed within the land that became South Africa.

# Chapter 14

# The making of South Africa

Reorganization in the far south was thrust along by pressures very different from elsewhere, once the first European settlers, Dutch by nationality, had established themselves in a little community at the Cape of Good Hope. That was in 1652; and according to a white South African myth long accepted by the present rulers of that nation, the black majority – the "Bantu", so named after their language family – crossed the Limpopo from the north into what is now the Transvaal at just the same time, apparently, as those Dutchmen were stepping ashore at the Cape.

This myth is held in high affection by white South Africans, but is historically absurd. Two Khoi peoples – known to the new settlers as "Bushmen" and "Hottentots" – had lived in South Africa since Stone Age times, thousands of years earlier, while the ancestors of the Bantu-language peoples of modern South Africa – Sotho, Zulu, Xhosa, and many others – had certainly established themselves by AD400 in the territory that was to be named the Transvaal fourteen centuries later.

The two Khoi peoples had yet to enter a "metal age", and were content to live as hunters and food gatherers, or, now and then, as the masters of herds of cattle. Their way of life, organized in small family groups without any military means or potential, could present no obstacle to Dutch and then British conquest; and those living nearest to the Cape were soon reduced to slavery by the early settlers. But the Bantu-language peoples had more than a thousand years of state formation behind them by the time that the Dutch arrived on the scene, and were in any case the possessors of a competent iron-forging technology capable of making spears as well as hoes. They had formed and developed strong little states, and were able not only to resist white infiltration but also to hit back with cattle raids.

By the 1770s, early clashes had raised a frontier of hostility between intruding whites and indigenous blacks in the Great Fish River region of what is now the eastern Cape province. In 1779 there came the first large-scale fighting between them, known in white history as "the first Kaffir war", the word *Kaffir* being borrowed from the term for heathen used by Arab traders along the East African coast. This fighting was inconclusive, but served to envenom hostility between whites bent on seizing land and cattle, and blacks determined to prevent them.

Many other "kaffir wars" followed, as settlers and colonial troops – British after 1806 (and the Battle of Trafalgar which put paid to French claims of a year earlier) – pushed gradually northward and north-eastward into the lands of the Xhosa and their neighbours. Victory on balance went to the British, who had guns and good military organization, and for a while there was even a little British colony called Kaffraria in the eastern Cape. But resistance and rebellion

continued, and a century of virtual warfare fills this long chapter of the making of what was to become South Africa.

More British settlers arrived in 1820, and with the gradual establishment of a Cape Colony in which slavery was banned (following anti-slavery campaigns in Britain), the settlers of Dutch origin grew dissatisfied. Their form of Christianity taught them that enslavement of the "sons of Ham" (the black peoples) was in accordance with the unalterable will of God, a belief which proved most convenient to a farming community whose "birthright" in this new land had been taken from Africans by force. Finding the liberalism of the Cape government both inconvenient and un-Christian, groups of Dutch-speaking settlers began moving north in 1836 in a ragged migration known in their history, rather pretentiously, as the "Great Trek". By this time their original Dutch language was becoming a local variant (soon to be known as Afrikaans), and these migrant farmers or Boers, whose early ideal was to live "beyond the sight of one's neighbour's smoke", were beginning to evolve a nationality of their own.

From this time onwards, history in South Africa became a three-sided affair. There were the Boers or Afrikaners who founded the Republic of Natal in 1838, and, when that was annexed by the British five years later, continued northward and westward to found the republics of the Orange Free State and the Transvaal (the land north of the Vaal river). There were the British of the Cape Colony who, for reasons varying from a need to impose their power to a desire to enclose the diamond and gold fields discovered in the 1870s and 1880s, felt it necessary to "go after" the Afrikaners and dispossess them of their republics: out of which, eventually, there came the Anglo-Boer War of 1899–1901.

*An ox wagon (left) typical of the kind that carried migrant Afrikaner (Boer) farming families (above) northward on the so-called "Great Trek" away from the anti-slavery liberalism of Britain's Cape Colony.*

Thirdly, there were the Africans who had to resist both Afrikaners and British, although at times they tried to use the second against the first, an understandable manoeuvre which nevertheless did them no good in the end.

Such was the violent making of South Africa. Its violence is nowhere better illustrated than in the confrontation with the Zulu people.

### The Zulu drama

The fertile uplands and flowing rivers of Natal – broadly, the eastern region of South Africa bordering on the Indian Ocean – had seen the slow formation of small states of Bantu-language peoples long before the appearance of any Europeans. They were metal-age farmers whose principal wealth consisted of cattle, and whose political organization comprised numerous chiefdoms with fairly well accepted boundaries between them.

By the middle of the eighteenth century these peoples found themselves facing a number of new pressures and problems. It seems that one of these problems arose from a new shortage of, and consequently rivalry for, land, caused by the steady growth of population and of cattle herds. Hitherto the land available had appeared to be limitless, and peoples short of land could always find more. Related to this problem was a new awareness of the advancing frontier of white settlement and white land enclosure. The year 1799 saw the third "kaffir war" of whites against blacks, with a fourth in 1812 and a fifth in 1818.

These pressures argued for political reorganization, and the leading promoter of this was a chief of the Mtetwa – a group of the Nguni segment of the Bantu-language peoples of the region – whose name was Dingiswayo. He

*The powerful Zulu empire built up by Shaka (above) in the 1820s, was based on regiments of highly trained infantrymen (right).*

seems to have become an important chief in northern Natal (as the region would eventually be called) at some time after 1780. Having visited white-settled areas and observed their customs and intentions, Dingiswayo became convinced of the need to unify neighbouring chiefdoms into a single kingdom; he "rationalized" this ambition in the following way, according to an English observer who knew him:

> It was not the intention of those who first came into the world that there should be several kings equal in power, but that there should be one great king to exercise control over the little ones.

Dingiswayo set about becoming an important king, and succeeded in many small wars against his neighbours. Eventually he was slain by a neighbouring chief, but before this happened he had appointed to command his army a man who was to become far more famous in the annals of South Africa. This was Shaka of the Zulu clan, who succeeded Dingiswayo as king, and continued the work of unification with a skill and ruthlessness that far surpassed anything that had gone before. Shaka was a seasoned warrior who revolutionized warfare in terms of weaponry, discipline, and tactics.

Hitherto, warfare in those parts had been seen as a rather courtly procedure whereby two sides lined up against each other and threw spears until there were no more spears to throw, after which there was a tendency for everyone to feel that it was time to go home. Shaka put an end to this apparent lack of devotion to death and duty. He made his warriors carry a short stabbing spear and fight at close quarters, instituting a régime of arduous physical training and total submission to orders. His regiments, or *impis* in Zulu, carried all before them with a wanton slaughter of anyone who got in the way; and the many wars of

conquest that he set going became known as "the wars of crushing", in which one people after another went down in defeat, to be scattered into migration or reduced to subjection.

Shaka and his methods may have been history's answer to the equally ruthless and ever advancing frontier of white settlement and dispossession that continued to come from the south; and it may even be that Shaka and his commanders had an inkling of the same idea. However that may be, by the middle of the 1820s Shaka had built a powerful concentration of military and political power, the Zulu empire, and was unchallenged within wide dominions. North of him the Swazi people developed their kingship along the same lines, but were generally untroubled by Shaka and his regiments. South of him the Boer intruders had to toe the line or move away, and preferred on the whole to settle in lands to the west and north-west which became, in due course, the Orange Free State and the Transvaal.

But the British, in their still greater imperial power and pride, were in no mind to tolerate an independent Zulu kingdom, much less a Zulu empire. The first big clash came after Shaka's time, when Cetshwayo was the Zulu king. Finally, in 1879, a British invasion army of some 5,000 British troops and 5,000 African auxiliaries moved northward into Zulu territory. They seem to have expected a ceremonial military parade, for they marched through Zulu country without the least effort to gather intelligence about what the Zulu might be doing. Cetshwayo's regiments fell on them at Isandhlwana, routing them with fearful losses, and came near to repeating this a few days later at Rorke's Drift.

Satisfied with this effective defence, Cetshwayo now saw that discretion would be the better part of valour, and asked for peace. The British had been his

*Reinforcements search for English dead on the battlefield of Isandhlwana (above) shortly after the disastrous defeat of the invading British force by Cetshwayo's regiments in 1879. Only a few soldiers escaped, but Cetshwayo was afterwards forced to surrender (below).*

*Deep Transvaal gold mines (above) brought wealth to South African whites, but for the cheap black labour forced to work in them they were physically exhausting and socially disruptive.*

friends in earlier years, and had even approved his enthronement. The British invasion of his kingdom had now suffered defeat, but Cetshwayo had no desire to prolong hostilities. Yet those were the days of British imperial grandeur, and the worst military disaster in Britain's whole African involvement had to be avenged. New troops were brought from Britain and placed under the command of a new and, it was hoped, less incompetent general. To make sure, more artillery was added to the new invasion force, including some of the machine-guns that were now coming into European use.

While Cetshwayo held back his regiments and talked peace, this second army of invasion advanced on his capital at Ulundi; and this time the machine-guns carried the day, as they were soon to do on many other colonial battlefields. Fruitless charges by Cetshwayo's regiments, trying vainly to get to close quarters against Britain's redcoats, left 1,500 dead and many more wounded. It was the end of an independent Zulu nation, and Britain's way was now clear for its next great target: the Boers. That was achieved after provoking war with the Transvaal Republic in 1899, and in 1902, in the wake of a costly British victory in this Anglo-Boer War, modern South Africa was born.

### Towards South Africa today
Modern South Africa was born from a compromise; but it was not whites and blacks who compromised, but British and Afrikaners, for the central issue of white supremacy over the black population was never in question. What imperial Britain wanted was the political power that could guarantee safety of investment and export of profits, above all in the Transvaal where capital-intensive mining of deep-seamed gold had more than proved its value in the

1890s. Britain was accordingly determined to dispossess the Afrikaners of any political or administrative power to thwart these operations and ambitions; once that was assured, peace and reconciliation with the Afrikaners were high on the British agenda.

The Afrikaner republics made peace in 1902, and acquiesced in their own disappearance, because they could do no other, while the British, for their part, welcomed into cooperation such Afrikaner leaders as were ready to offer it, notable among whom was a future prime minister of South Africa, Jan Smuts. The next few years were spent, politically, in shaping a South African state – a union of the four constituent countries: Cape Colony, Natal, Transvaal and Orange Free State – in which the British would achieve their economic aims and the Afrikaners would be assured of continued white supremacy. The two white communities – Afrikaans-speaking and English-speaking – would remain at arm's length, nursing old bruises and suspicions, but they would combine in a shared exploitation of African land and labour. They would quarrel, and often hate or despise each other, but their greatest interest would always remain common to both.

The new South African state came formally to birth with an Act of Union in 1910, and its white minorities were given a sovereign power to do whatever their parliament might decide. What that was going to be became clear almost immediately in laws that systematized anti-black discrimination in every field of life, though nowhere more clearly than in distribution of land-ownership rights. Acts to "regulate labour" – in plain language, to secure a ready supply of defenceless black labour – followed at once upon the Act of Union, and in 1913 came the Land Act which was to form the structural basis of the new system.

*A South African propaganda photograph (c.1920) of a "native open-air school" in one of the so-called "Native Reserves" – the tiny fraction of South African territory allocated to the black majority.*

165

# The making of South Africa

*Jan Smuts, c. 1910, one of the Afrikaner leaders prepared to cooperate with the British after the Anglo-Boer War, later became prime minister of South Africa.*

This awarded some 90 percent of the whole land surface of South Africa to white ownership, leaving less than 10 percent (since enlarged to 12 or 13 percent) for African ownership. Outside that fraction, Africans were to have no civic freedoms, but be subject to an increasingly dense network of pass laws and comparable regulations.

This 10 percent of the land surface "reserved" for African ownership was divided into many geographical particles known as "Native Reserves" or, with the evolution of full-blown apartheid (Separateness), as "Bantu Homelands". In the 90 percent of South Africa outside the "Reserves", Africans could "minister to" the white minorities, as the official language put it, but, as servants, were strictly on sufferance there. The complete doctrine of apartheid, with all its inevitable repressiveness and intolerance, was introduced by law only after 1948, when the Afrikaner minority acquired full parliamentary power for the first time; yet in all issues and questions bearing on the daily life of Africans it had taken shape long before, and very obviously by 1920.

Three peoples were to escape direct application of racist doctrine, at least so long as they stayed at home, and, for various reasons of imperial politics and convenience, would remain in as many British "protectorates": Bechuanaland (independent as Botswana in 1966), Basutoland (independent as Lesotho in 1966), and the kingdom of Swaziland (independent under that name in 1968).

Westward, the peoples of Namibia had no such luck. Enclosed within the German colony of "South West Africa" after ferocious wars of conquest early in the twentieth century, this region ( Namibia by its African name) came under South African rule after German defeat in World War I. At first it was a mandated territory of the League of Nations, and later a trusteeship territory of the United Nations; but in spite of these high-sounding labels the country continued to be ruled directly by South Africa as a colony in all but name.

# Chapter 15

# From the Bible to the gun

The transition from the slave trade to the colonial invasions was a complex one. But an African trade unionist, J.H. Mphemba, looking back in 1929, believed that the essentials of the story, from an African standpoint, could be comparatively simply stated:

First, the white man brought the Bible. Then he brought guns, then chains, then he built a jail, then he made the native pay tax.

The saying passed into African folklore. When the whites first came, it was said, "They had the Bible and we had the land. After a while, we found that things changed round. Now they have the land and we have the Bible." The Ethiopian emperor Theodore made much the same point when, facing British invasion, he said: "I know their game. First, it's traders and missionaries. Then it's ambassadors. After that, they bring the guns. We shall do better to go straight to the guns."

The missionaries may have begun the process, but scientific inquiry came first. One June evening of 1788, at a meeting of the Saturday's Club – a scientific society that was also interested in geographical questions – the members decided to form an Association for Promoting the Discovery of the Interior Parts of Africa. The task proved long, but by the 1870s the Association's successor, the Royal Geographical Society, knew a great deal about the principal topography of Africa, even if much detail had still to be explained.

The explorers followed African trails, and the missionaries came after them or, like Livingstone, took part in the work of geographical research. Great numbers of missionary societies were founded in France between 1816 and 1870, while Portugal and Spain, as well as Italy, Germany and the Scandinavian countries, launched many others. Saving the Africans from themselves became something of a popular craze in those high evangelical times.

The driving inspiration, as we can now see, came from a perverse interpretation of the history of the slave trade. Europeans had initiated and promoted the Atlantic slave trade, but this was forgotten. Following the line of pro-slaving apologists of earlier times, it was held that the trade was only an extension of what was mistakenly believed to be the ever-present practice of slavery inside Africa itself. Europeans must therefore help Africans to liberate themselves. And by now, of course, the argument had some colour of truth, for the slave trade had indeed extended the condition of slavery inside Africa.

Geographical exploration and missionary zeal combined in the work of "liberation". Financing an expedition up the Niger from the sea in 1832, the British government ordered it "to make treaties with the native chiefs for the suppression of this horrible traffic; and to point out to them the advantages they will derive, if, instead of the wars and aggressions to which it gives rise, they will substitute an innocent and legitimate commerce."

# From the Bible to the gun

*The Royal Geographical Society (right) employed missionaries in geographical exploration, and the Bible played its part in the 19thC colonial invasion of Africa, as well as the gun. To Africans on the receiving end of the invasion, such as the Ethiopian ruler Theodore (below), it seemed "better to go straight to the gun", and cut out the "traders and missionaries".*

But soon it appeared that exploration and missionary zeal were not the only forces at work, for now the European coastal traders came in with loud demands. They were particularly active along the coastland of the Niger Delta, where an "innocent and legitimate commerce" in palm oil – much needed in nineteenth-century Europe for soap and lubricants – had taken the place of slaving. The Europeans had obtained a monopoly on the sea, and were now determined to achieve a monopoly on land as well, which meant that firm action would have to be taken against African producers and traders. In 1861 the British seized Lagos Island and proclaimed it a colony. Step-by-step invasion of the mainland duly followed.

There were missionaries who welcomed the colonial invasions as a blessing to the peoples thus invaded, and there were others who did not. There were those who were perfectly convinced, like Wardlaw Thomas of the London Missionary Society, that Africans were so deeply sunk in primeval barbarism as to be perfectly incapable of any progress until they had accepted the message of the Gospel. "Ignorant, degraded, corrupt", declared Thomas, "their life darkened by their belief in evil spirits and witchcraft, cursed by the slave trade, the inhabitants of Central Africa make their mute but powerful appeal to the Church of Christ to come over and help them."

There were other missionaries, among them Bishop William Tozer of the Universities Mission to Central Africa, who took a milder view, or had perhaps acquired a different experience. Writing home from Central Africa, Bishop Tozer asked awkward questions:

What do we mean when we say that England or France are civilized countries and that the greater part of Africa is uncivilized? Surely the mere enjoyment of such things as railways and telegraphs and the like do not necessarily prove their possessors to be in the first rank of civilized nations. . . . Nothing can be so false as to suppose that the outward circumstances of a people is the measure either of its barbarism or its civilization.

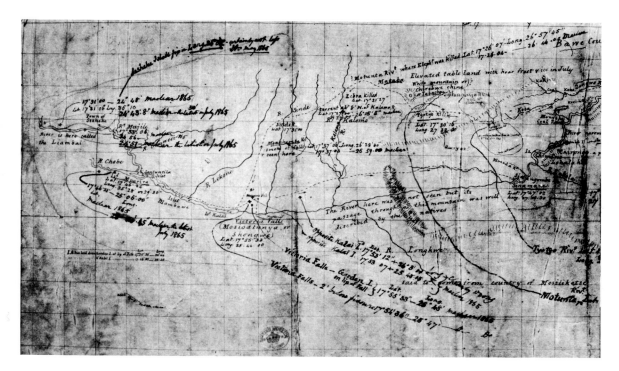

But those who thought like Wardlaw Thomas were more numerous than those who agreed with Bishop Tozer; the missionaries who entered Central Africa from the east coast had, as it happened, some powerful reasons for disagreeing with the bishop.

## A scene at Bagamoyo

Descending gently, a narrow road goes from the little East African town of Bagamoyo to the edge of the Indian Ocean. Old houses of timber, some of them with finely carved front doors, stand on either side of the road. They seem to be relics of an old history, although in fact Bagamoyo is a product of the early and middle nineteenth century.

A new slave trade began in East Africa late in the eighteenth century and grew massive in the nineteenth. Bagamoyo became one of the terminals of this slave trade from the interior to the Swahili shore of the ocean. Today, the heat of the midday sun, here on the last stretch of the sorrowful trail to the sea, seems to clog one's thoughts, as though memory were better not recalled. Yet Bagamoyo, for all its evil history, is also a shrine to the cause of human solidarity.

In 1872, in Central Africa many hundreds of miles away to the west, the great Scots missionary David Livingstone breathed his last, and was found by his African companions beside his cot. Sickness and exhaustion had overtaken him at last. His companions, led by Chumah and Susi, now took an extraordinary decision. It was their duty, they decided, to carry their revered master's body to the coast, so that it could find a last resting place in Livingstone's own country. Having eviscerated the body and buried the heart, they exposed the corpse to the sun for two weeks, then wrapped it in bark and cloth, and set out to walk to the coast.

It was a long, arduous journey, and many months passed before they safely delivered the body to the British consul in Bagamoyo, who sent it by British

*David Livingstone (below), the great 19thC Scottish missionary and explorer, was also an accomplished map maker. His map of the Zambezi river (above) shows the Victoria Falls.*

*A new slave trade (above), initially launched by Arabs settled along the east coast, ravaged Africa in the mid 19thC. Chuma, a liberated slave, and Susi (below), Livingstone's faithful servants in his last years, carried the explorer's body to the coast, but were not permitted to accompany it to Zanzibar.*

warship to Zanzibar for onward despatch. Chumah and Susi and the others were curtly dismissed, and the manner of their dismissal is revealing: "No sooner did they arrive at their journey's end," wrote Horace Waller, the editor of Livingstone's journals, "than they were so far frowned out of notice that not so much as a passage to the Island [of Zanzibar] was offered when their burden was borne away."

Even Livingstone had shared a certain racist attitude. He wrote:

We come among them as members of a superior race, and servants of a Government that desires to elevate the more degraded portions of the human family. We are adherents of a benign holy religion, and may, by consistent conduct and wise patient efforts, become the harbingers of peace to a hitherto distracted and downtrodden race.

Livingstone was no crude racist, yet such were his convictions. Partly they came from the European spirit of those times, and partly from mere misinformation. Partly they agreed with the convictions of Livingstone's contemporary explorers, particularly Burton. But above all they came from another consequence of the curse of Columbus.

In 1806 Britain had begun the abolition of the overseas slave trade with a ban on its practice in British ships. Other slaving nations slowly followed suit, encouraged by the presence of British naval patrols that tried to prevent competitors from indulging in a profitable vice which the British had now denied themselves. Landing freed captives year by year in Sierre Leone, these patrols rescued tens of thousands of men and women. But just as the West Coast slave trade began to dwindle and die, a new slave trade, operating along the East Coast, spread far into central Africa.

This new plague was partly the work of Egyptian raids southward through the eastern Sudan. At about the same time, in the 1830s, Arabs from Oman established themselves on Zanzibar and gradually brought the Swahili coast under their domination. Whether for clove plantations on Zanzibar or for

## A scene at Bagamoyo

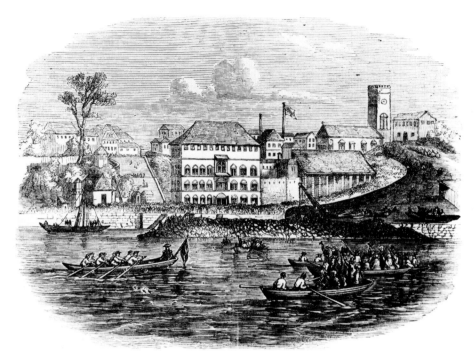

*Freed slaves made up much of the population of mid-19thC Freetown in West African Sierra Leone.*

export overseas, huge numbers of captives were seized by an Arab-Swahili partnership and delivered to the coast.

A new and pitiless violence now pushed into the quiet lands of the interior. Arabs were largely responsible, but Europeans came in to complete the damage. A deal in the 1750s between the king of Kilwa and French planters on Mauritius saw the beginning of European slaving in the area, and this was greatly expanded after 1806 by the Portuguese in Mozambique. For some 40 years, up to 1850, the Portuguese are thought to have exported to Brazil, every year, a total of some 25,000 captives from these eastern lands.

The trails followed by Livingstone, and by explorers such as Burton and Stanley, were the same trails that were opened or enlarged by the slave traders and raiders. Misery and death stalked along them; fear and hatred went beside. Wide regions were indeed "distracted" by the 1850s when Livingstone first got there, and many of their peoples sorely "downtrodden". It was mistakenly thought that matters had always been like that.

There had been a small export of slaves from East Africa since the earliest recorded times, but convincing evidence from various sources suggests that it remained small and sporadic until the last decades of the eighteenth century. Early Chinese records refer to black slaves who were "doorkeepers", and always "sad"; and there are early Indian references to black slaves who made themselves into kings. With a solitary exception, all the eastern records indicate that the requirement was for domestic or military slaves, and that these were never in large numbers. The exception was ninth-century Iraq where, for a time, numerous black workers were imported as slaves for plantations. Otherwise there were no plantations in the east which could use slave labour on anything like the scale approaching that of the New World. Before the late eighteenth century, in short, the East Coast slave trade was a small affair.

But although of far briefer duration than the western slave trade, this new eastern hunt for captives probably became more destructive. It laid waste whole

# From the Bible to the gun

*In East Africa, Portuguese slavers of the 19thC were exporting some 25,000 captives a year to Brazil. Henry Morton Stanley (below), the famous explorer, pressed for the ruthless commercial exploitation of Africa.*

zones of peaceful trade and cultivation. It dismantled the frail defences of peoples who had known nothing like it in the past. It fed every European prejudice of a racist kind. Seeing the wretched survivors, Livingstone could easily become convinced that he belonged to "a superior race".

The early missionaries were appalled by the devastation that they found, and considered it their obvious duty to succour these ravaged peoples and, through the blessings of the Christian message and trade without slavery, to raise them to levels of civilization they could not, as it was believed, ever hope to reach by their own unaided efforts. Yet the missionaries were themselves to be the victims of another kind of mission, a new and very different one that Livingstone could never have foretold.

We move now into modern times. These were going to be times of warfare and upheaval on a previously unimaginable scale.

### "A gigantic steeplechase"

In 1878, six years after Livingstone's death, the assembled businessmen of Birmingham in their chamber of commerce were treated to an address by the famed explorer, Henry Morton Stanley, who boasted of the gateway to Africa that he had thrown open to their enterprise, if only they would go through it. Were they frightened for their money? Did they think he was exaggerating? Had they any reason to disbelieve him? Their doubts were absurd. Raising his voice, and in characteristically abrasive tones, he told them:

> There are forty million naked people beyond that gateway, and the cotton spinners of Manchester are waiting to clothe them. Birmingham's foundries are glowing with the red metal that shall presently be made into ironwork in every fashion and shape for them, and the trinkets that shall adorn those dusky bosoms: and the ministers of Christ are zealous to bring them, the poor benighted heathen, into the Christian fold.

But the businessmen of Birmingham were not convinced, not yet; and they

# "A gigantic steeplechase"

turned him down. Whereupon Stanley went off to work for King Leopold of the Belgians, whose attitude to seizing bits of Africa was well defined in a letter he had written to Baron Solvyns a year before. "I mean to miss no chance", wrote the king, his eyes already on the limitless forests of the Congo, "to get my share of this magnificent African cake."

Leopold did not miss his chance, and others were inspired by his example. Then began what the prime minister of France, Jules Ferry, was to call a "gigantic steeplechase into the unknown". Commenting on the African share-out that took place at the Conference of Berlin in 1884–85, *The Times* coined a memorable term: "the scramble for Africa".

This new imperialism seemed a glorious enterprise to its participants. Others had a different view. "The plundering goes merrily on," wrote Belfort Bax in William Morris's socialist *Commonweal* of 1885: "The explorer reconnoitres the ground, and the missionary prepares the soil, the 'trader' works it. The time is then ripe for protectorates and annexations."

Soldiers were now needed, and further wars. Invasions had already penetrated the extremities of the continent, with the settler wars of seizure in the south, and, in the north, a comparable French invasion of Algeria in the 1830s. Elsewhere there were British raids and incursions, such as the march into the Asante kingdom in 1874, and many similar marches into the Western Sudan by French forces. In addition there were Portuguese and Italian operations of the same kind, and many others too numerous to be listed here.

The invaders met resistance in all regions, and often bloody warfare. In the worst cases, such as the expedition of Captains Voulet and Chanoine through Upper Volta into Niger (as it is today) there were wild scenes of murder. But everywhere, even when the invading forces practised restraint, a new and insidious weapon was brought to bear by the Europeans. In the words of General Henri Meynier, writing in 1911 of a military advance through lands that would soon become French West Africa:

*The French conquest of Dahomey (above), 1892, marked a stage in the colonial invasion of Africa. King Leopold of the Belgians (below) employed Stanley to help him get his "share of this magnificent African cake".*

# From the Bible to the gun

*Racial superiority pervaded the attitudes of the 19thC European colonialists. King Prempeh and the Queen Mother in Kumasi are forced to submit ritually (above) to the invading British in 1896.*
*French soldiers (below) proudly display the severed head of an Ivory Coast freedom fighter, c. 1905, "as an example to the others".*

From the very first encounter, the Europeans established as a principle their superiority over the black race. They affirmed it by a profound contempt for the inferior race. And soon enough, using their force, they reduced the Africans to slavery, justifying this by the right of the strong, asserting their moral supremacy.

The missionary cause had become a racist cause. The Bible had given way not only to the gun, but also to the all-excusing weapon of racial superiority. Priests and poets hastened to embellish it:

*Take up the White Man's burden*
*Send forth the best ye breed*
*Go, bind your sons in exile*
*To serve your captives' need;*
*To wait in heavy harness*
*On fluttered folk and wild,*
*Your new-caught, sullen peoples,*
*Half-devil and half-child.*

Nevertheless, the colonial conquest was not completed easily or quickly. Many years were needed, and without the new machine-guns, first the hand-cranked Gatling and then the fully automatic Maxim, it might scarcely have been achieved at all. This factor was something that would later be forgotten, but it was critical at the time. The English poet Hilaire Belloc offered a satirical comment that made the point:

*Whatever happens we have got*
*The Maxim gun and they have not . . .*

Such guns were widely needed, for refusal was generally the reply of African

## "A gigantic steeplechase"

rulers when called on to submit. Typical is the response of a Yao chief, Mazemba, in the country that is Tanzania today, when faced with a German demand for submission:

> I look for some reason why I should obey you, and find not the smallest. If you want friendship, then I am ready for it, today and always. But to be your subject – that I cannot be. If it is war you want, then I am ready for that, but never to be your subject.

> I am Sultan here in my land. You are Sultan there in yours. But listen: I do not say to you that you must obey me, for I know that you are a free man. As for me, I will not go to you, and if you are strong enough, then come and fetch me.

Masemba was neither "wild" nor "fluttered", not devil, nor child, but he had to be dealt with – hammered, as the British called it. Yet military operations proved costly; and they posed a moral problem for Europeans who preferred to see the colonial experience as a work of mercy: a work, in any case, for which the recipients should be thankful. Could there not, perhaps, be ways of taking up the White Man's burden other than by using the gun?

An Englishman called Cecil Rhodes believed that he might have the answer. He was not in the least averse to using the gun, as events would soon prove, but thought that money and deception might achieve still more. The son of an Anglican clergyman of Bishop's Stortford, Rhodes had come to South Africa at the age of 17, attracted by glowing prospects of easily won wealth.

He began by growing cotton, but soon moved to the newly opened diamond fields of Kimberley, already the scene of an extraordinary "diamond rush" by adventurers from Europe and America. There he began to conceive his two ambitions: to make an enormous amount of money, and then to use it in order to spread the blessings of British rule from Cape Town to Cairo. A few years later he wrote a "confession of faith" which shows what he had in mind:

> I contend that we are the finest race in the world and that the more of the

*The superior fire power of automatic weapons such as the Gatling and the Maxim gun (above) was a chief reason for the success of the colonial conquest, which nevertheless took many years to achieve.*

*Lobengula (right), king of the Matabele (Ndebele) people, was an obstacle to Rhodes's expansionist ambitions. His adviser, the Rev. Charles Helm (far right) of the London Missionary Society, suffered from divided loyalties. The LMS desired the overthrow of Lobengula.*

world we inhabit the better it is for the human race. Just fancy those parts that are at present inhabited by the most despicable specimens of human beings: what an alteration there would be if they were brought under Anglo-Saxon influence . . .

He rapidly fulfilled his first ambition, and made a fortune by gaining control of the Kimberley diamond concessions to such effect that he was ready, by the end of the 1870s, to embark upon his second, more grandiose, project. His next move was to attempt to secure mineral concessions north of the Limpopo river, then as now the northern border of the South African countries. Prospectors had brought back reports of important gold finds there, and the possible value of these was blown up by tales of "King Solomon's Mines" that were beginning to return with the few Europeans who had seen the great ruins of the Zimbabwe Culture north of the river.

But there was one great obstacle. Some 60 years earlier a branch of the Zulu nation called the Ndebele, or Matabele, had broken away from Shaka's rule and crossed the Limpopo in search of a new homeland. Settling in the south-westerly part of the country, they founded their capital at a place named Bulawayo, the headquarters of their warrior king Mozelikatse. A second Matabele king, Lobengula, had come to the throne by the time that Rhodes's active interest was aroused. Rhodes sent emissaries to Lobengula, asking for permission to dig for gold. The king at first agreed, subject to conditions that he believed were binding. But it was not long before it became clear to him that the white concession hunters had plans that went beyond the words they used.

### The fly and the chameleon
King Lobengula had a Christian adviser at his court in Bulawayo, the Reverend Charles Helm of the London Missionary Society. Trusting Helm, Lobengula discussed with the missionary this apparently major conflict of interests: on the one hand there were Rhodes's emissaries with their demand for mineral

The fly and the chameleon

concessions (while rivals of Rhodes opposed and intrigued for concessions of their own); on the other was the growing probability that the concession hunters would use his consent further to undermine his authority and open his kingdom to European infiltration. At the same time his own people were divided, but a clear majority of his fighting men were against making any concessions. Lobengula wavered in his policy towards the whites: not because he was weak, but because he was puzzled.

Lobengula was a strong ruler. Raised to be king of the Matabele (as the English called the Ndebele), he possessed every quality of kingship. Visiting Europeans were not misled by the fact that he was often naked save for a skin about his loins: "He walks quite erect," wrote Sir Sydney Shippard, "with his head thrown back and his broad chest expanded, and as he marches along at a slow pace with his long staff in his right hand while all the men around him shout his praises, he looks his part to perfection." Another visitor, who had seen "many European and native potentates", affirmed that "with the exception of the Tsar Alexander, never have I seen a ruler of men of more imposing appearance."

He needed to be a strong king, for he had to rule a warrior offshoot of the Nguni people, trained in the tradition of Shaka Zulu. Although they had been pushed northward over the Limpopo by Zulu quarrels and the advancing front of white settler penetration, the Ndebele had taken their warlike habits with them. In the 1830s they overthrew the last kings of the western Shona – those who had ruled from Khami and other *zimbabwes* built long before – and settled around Bulawayo.

But by the 1870s the Ndebele had lost much of their aggressiveness. They continued to extract tribute in cattle from their Shona neighbours to the east but, like the Danes in Anglo-Saxon England, were usually content to clash their spears and make off home again, if suitably mollified with payment.

Now the settler penetration seemed poised to cross northward over the Limpopo, sending mining agents in advance of it. Well knowing what disasters had befallen Africans in South Africa, including the Zulu, Lobengula had every reason to be anxious. His warriors believed they could beat the whites in war if it should come to that, but Lobengula thought otherwise. Could he still beat them by diplomacy? He doubted that too.

"Did you ever see a chameleon catch a fly?" he asked Helm. "The chameleon gets behind the fly and remains motionless for some time, then he advances very slowly and gently, first putting forward one leg and then another. At last, when well within reach, he darts his tongue and the fly disappears. England is the chameleon and I am that fly." Lobengula weighed most of twenty stone but the comparison was still a good one.

The details of the English chameleon's strategy were hidden by distance and discretion, but Lobengula knew that the British government, considering all these lands north of the Limpopo within its "sphere of influence", was determined to "protect" Lobengula's sovereignty. In this way Britain would stop all rivals, particularly the Portuguese in Mozambique, from playing the chameleon. But how was Rhodes to persuade Lobengula to extend his consent for mining concessions into a treaty which would allow a step-by-step colonial enclosure, while, of course, concealing this purpose from Lobengula and Lobengula's emissaries? Rhodes multiplied his inducements, but Lobengula, increasingly uneasy about what was really intended, still held back. All through 1889 he baulked. Meanwhile Rhodes's rivals at Lobengula's court suggested that the king might write to his fellow ruler in Britain, Queen Victoria. Let him complain to her, and see what she would do for him. Lobengula thought this sound advice, and sent two of his chiefs to England with a letter and a verbal message to the Queen. Rhodes's agents tried to stop these messengers in Cape Town, but they got to London and explained to Queen Victoria that their king was much troubled by her people, who were asking permission to dig for gold in his country. What should he do?

### A correspondence with Queen Victoria

It was, by all accounts, a touching scene. There, in the midst of England's imperial majesty, the legendary monarch received two of her "fluttered folk and wild", and everything was done to make them happy. Regimental cannon were fired for them, the doors of the Bank of England were opened to their curiosity, and titled ladies bade them welcome. A reply to their king's letter was required, so a reply was written for the Queen to send. Its text has survived.

Written in March 1889, Queen Victoria's letter to Lobengula was a relief to him. Opinions about the wisdom of giving Rhodes a free hand were still much divided, largely due to pressure from Rhodes's competitors, and the Queen's reply was unfavourable to Rhodes's scheme. She wrote that "she had heard the words of Lobengula", and understood his worries. He should be careful:

Lobengula is the ruler of his country and the Queen does not interfere with the government of that country, but as Lobengula desires her advice, she wishes him to understand that Englishmen who have gone out to Matabeleland to ask leave to dig for stones have not gone with the Queen's authority.

That, at least, was plain and clear. And there was more:

The Queen advises Lobengula not to grant hasty concessions of land or leave to dig. A king gives a stranger an ox, not his whole herd of cattle.

*A prospector's licence issued by Rhodes's company empowers the holder to search for metals in Lobengula's territory.*

Convinced that the great white ruler was on his side, Lobengula hastened to write back. He again complained that "the white people are troubling me much about gold", but he wanted her to know, in case he might be misrepresented, that "if the Queen hears that I have given away the whole country" – the "whole herd of cattle", in the Queen's terminology – "then it is not so". And he concluded by thanking her for advising him "that I am not to let anyone dig for gold in my country except to dig for me as my servants".

But the chameleon now advanced another foot, again most discreetly. Rhodes bought out his competitors, who forthwith joined him in the realization of his master plan. This was to secure a royal charter for the formation of a company, to be called the British South Africa Company, that would have powers to rule whatever territory, north of the Limpopo, it could eventually enclose. Opposition to it in London was now at an end, and the charter was granted and formally confirmed at Westminster on 29 October 1889. Like nearly everything else about this company, its name was misleading. It was not to operate in South Africa at all, but north of the Limpopo; and although it was called a company, it possessed powers which also made it, potentially at least, a fully-fledged instrument of government.

These powers authorized the company to make "treaties" with African kings or governments north of the Limpopo, but these "treaties" were interpreted, not only by Rhodes but also by the British imperial government, as being tantamount to a surrender to British rule. Quite without consulting Lobengula or any other African authority, the Company was likewise authorized by Queen Victoria's charter to make and enforce laws, raise and maintain a police force, and undertake "public works" as well as opening mines. If African kings or governments should then object to any of this, that would be called rebellion.

Missionaries like Helm were well aware of all this, at least in outline and intention, but they were in a dilemma. Some might wish to be, and act like, Lobengula's friends, but all were now convinced that there could be no substantial conversion of the Matabele to Christianity unless the power of

Lobengula was undermined, and the coherence of Matabele traditional society brought to an end. In this they were very probably right, and indeed represented the universal missionary policy throughout the continent. So long as the traditional authorities of the African peoples held firm, their cultures would tend to resist any large-scale conversion to Christianity. The Bible, in short, could not succeed without the gun, however much individual missionaries might deplore the fact.

*Missionary societies bent on bringing Christianity to the Africans (above) actively approved Rhodes's policy of undermining traditional African authority.*

While missionaries at Lobengula's court tried to confuse or deceive him, Lobengula himself at last saw clearly. The royal charter had just been granted, though nobody had informed Lobengula of the fact, when he received a second letter from Queen Victoria containing very different advice. The Queen now recommended, in so many words, that he should concede whatever Rhodes's men might demand, because:

> Wherever gold is, or wherever it is reported to be, it is impossible for [Lobengula] to exclude white men and therefore the wisest and safest course for him is to agree, not with one or two white men separately but with one approved body.

Just what the "one approved body" would consist of became rapidly clear. Even before receiving this second letter, Lobengula had made up his mind, powerfully helped in that direction by his own army commanders. He repudiated the mining concession he had given earlier to Rhodes's men. He would give them nothing. He closed the frontier.

### Invasion

Rhodes now faced his own dilemma. He had the charter, but not the land in which to exploit it. Should he still try to outwit Lobengula, or should he challenge him? He chose the second way, acting through his henchman Dr Starr Jameson. A "pioneer column", raised in South Africa, was to cross the Limpopo under arms and advance, not into Lobengula's country in western

Zimbabwe, but into Shona country in the centre. The invaders were to occupy the country of the Shona, who were not thought capable of stopping them, and establish Company rule there.

Two hundred "pioneers" were raised from a mob of eager applicants, mostly English. Each was promised 15 gold-prospecting claims and a 3,000-acre farm, never mind from whom they took it. To ensure their success, 500 armed British police were sent with them.

As empire-builders of the period, the pioneers were typical enough. In the words of a British eyewitness:

Such a mixed lot I never saw in my life, all sorts and conditions, from the aristocratic down to the street arab, peers and waifs of humanity mingling together like the ingredients of a hotchpotch.

Yet they and their police escort proved sufficient for the purpose. The Shona, not in the least knowing what was afoot, let them pass without resistance, while Lobengula's *impis* remained to the west of their chosen route. On 12 September 1890 they reached a place they named Fort Salisbury. Here they raised the British flag and formally "took possession" of Mashonaland, the country of the Shona, with all that it contained.

The rest followed as foreseen. On behalf of Rhodes and the Company, Jameson claimed a boundary line between Mashonaland and Lobengula's kingdom. Lobengula angrily protested:

Who gave him the boundary lines? Let him come forward and show me the man that pointed out to him these boundaries.

This was impossible, of course; no boundaries had ever been fixed. Soon there were clashes, recriminations, and the onset of the war that Rhodes and Jameson had thus provoked.

Eleven years earlier, the Zulu *impis* of Cetshwayo, Shaka's successor, had shattered an invading British force at Isandhlwana. But it turned out otherwise for Lobengula's *impis*. Jameson's invading columns, moving west into

Lobengula's kingdom, were armed with field artillery as well as machine-guns. Lobengula's best regiments were wiped out. "I must record", commented a British eyewitness, "the pluck of these two regiments which was simply splendid, and I doubt if any European troops could have withstood for such a long time as they did the terrific and well-directed fire brought to bear on them."

So Matabeleland was added to Mashonaland: not of course through conquest, as it was duly explained to the few English critics of the policy, but by a reasonable and indeed necessary act of British self-defence. As for the king, he withdrew from the scene and died. "It was said to be smallpox of which he died", the British historian Philip Mason has recalled, "but perhaps it would be true to say with the fairytales that he died of a broken heart." His surviving chiefs made peace with Rhodes; there was nothing else for them to do.

The peace was harsh. Within a few years, "virtually the whole of Ndebele land and by far the greater part of Ndebele cattle", in the words of another British historian, Professor Terence Ranger, "passed into white hands." Such lands as were left to the Ndebele in "native reserves", after the South African pattern, was described by an official commission at the time as "badly watered, sandy and unfit for settlement". In the rest of the country, now to be called Rhodesia, the Shona fared little better.

Before the invasions these two peoples had possessed 300,000 head of cattle. By 1897, after a brave but vain war of resistance – labelled a "rebellion" by the British – and an epidemic of cattle disease, they were thought to possess fewer than 14,000. Having taken land and cattle, the settlers then went for their next target, African labour. This they took either directly by force, or, thinly camouflaging the force, by imposing taxes in cash on people who could find this cash only by working for wages: that is, working for the whites.

This last was another of Rhodes's inventions, and it was widely imitated. It rested on a further doctrine of the new racism, namely, that the "natives" were idle both by habit and nature. These "natives" had toiled and laboured on their

*Lobengula's envoys sue for peace at Fort Tuli after British "self-defence" had broken the power of the Ndebele king.*

*Ndebele (Matabele) prisoners held in Bulawayo (right) after the failure of the Matabele "rebellion" of 1896. A* Punch *cartoon (below) celebrates Rhodes's dream of expanding British power in every country "from the Cape to Cairo".*

own account for generations, but now it was said that they only worked if they worked for the whites. They did not want to work for the whites, but "the gentle stimulant of the labour tax", as Rhodes put it, would change their minds. As prime minister of Cape Colony, where a labour-tax law was passed in 1894, Rhodes had addressed his parliament thus:

> You will remove them from that life of sloth and laziness, you will teach them the dignity of labour and make them contribute to the prosperity of the State, and make them give some return for our wise and good government.

As for that, the Ndebele and the Shona had now lost everything that could have given them wise and good government of their own: their land and their cattle, their right to exploit their own labour, and their independence.

Rhodes was triumphant, bestriding the map of southern Africa as the hero of settler and missionary alike. So it was that Rhodesia was born in duplicity and violence. And thus would Rhodesia come to an end 90 years later.

### The share-out

Rhodes died in 1902, and was buried in the Matopo Hills where he had made peace with the Ndebele, whose lands he had seized after their "rebellion" of 1896. His dream had been to raise the British flag in every country "from the Cape to Cairo". The dream was to be realized in 1918, when Britain took over Germany's East African colony of Tanganyika, and thereby joined South Africa and the two Rhodesias – Southern and Northern, (now Zimbabwe and Zambia) – to British East Africa. From there, by way of Britain's control over the Sudan and Egypt, the chain extended to the gates of Cairo itself.

The whole African shareout was more or less complete by 1901, when most frontiers were settled by agreements between the new colonial powers. Only two countries remained under governments of their own, Ethiopia and Liberia, and the latter was little more than a dependency of the USA.

The British, on the whole, got the best and biggest bits to the south of the

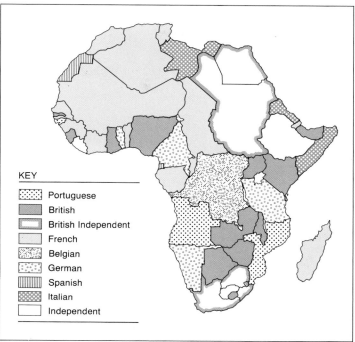

KEY

- ▨ Portuguese
- ▨ British
- ▢ British Independent
- ▨ French
- ▨ Belgian
- ⣿ German
- ▥ Spanish
- ▨ Italian
- ▢ Independent

*Map of the colonial partition of Africa (above). The Belgian king Leopold's brutal mismanagement of the Congo (left) became apparent even to the other colonialist powers.*

Sahara. The French took all of North Africa west of Libya, while Italy seized Libya in military campaigns that had to be carried on for some 20 years. South of the great desert, the French laid claim to territories that were huge on the map, if sparsely populated. Coming late into the game, the Germans invaded Namibia, or South West Africa as it was then called, and completed their occupation after a truly murderous campaign. The conflict left two peoples, the Nama and the Herero, sorely depleted; over 70 per cent of the Herero died in a war of resistance, most brutally repressed, in 1904. The Germans also took Kamerun (Cameroun), Togo and Tanganyika.

As in earlier times, the Portuguese put in claims which were as large as their own country was small. In the end they managed to get Angola, Mozambique, Guinea-Bissau and two groups of Atlantic islands. Italy was able to instal its colonial rule not only in Libya but also in Eritrea, along the Red Sea, and in much of the country of the Somalis. An attempt to swallow Ethiopia as well led to much pain, and more Italian soldiers are said to have died in the Ethiopian victory at Adowa, in 1896, than in all the battles for the unification of Italy 40 years earlier. King Leopold of the Belgians had meanwhile got possession of enormous tracts of the Congo Basin, known as the "Congo Free State", from the free-trade stipulations made by rival powers. After that he proceeded to misgovern the Congo to such a point that he had to hand it over to the Belgian state in 1908. Spain, the only other contender in the share-out, was satisfied with small territories in northern and western Africa.

Looking back on it all, one has the impression of a veritable fever of aggression, and indeed to some elder statesmen it seemed so at the time. But although they disliked it, they were dragged along by an inflamed public opinion. Addressing the City of London a few years after the 1885 share-out conference of Berlin, the veteran Lord Salisbury allowed himself to be sardonic:

We have been engaged in drawing lines upon maps where no white man's foot has ever trod; we have been giving away mountains and rivers and lakes

*European greed and the African share-out: a cartoon view from America (*right*) and Germany (*far right*).*

to each other, only hindered by the small impediment that we never knew exactly where they were.

These lines on the map of Africa had been made good by force, and now they would have to be maintained by force. And yet there were few people in Europe for whom the colonial share-out seemed anything but a good and great adventure, God's work and civilization's duty. By this time, moreover, there were plenty of miseries in Africa to convince them they were right. A confident euphoria was the hallmark of the share-out years, reaching its climax in the grand year of Queen Victoria's Jubilee, 1897. One of countless tributes written then may stand for all the rest, and the more convincingly because it was not a British tribute. A Frenchman enthused:

*In sixty years, O Fairy Queen!*
*Under your spell, what have we seen?*
*Wondrous changes of vast import,*
*Rich in blessings of every sort. . .*

Not many Africans shared this view. "The old slavery", wrote a Gold Coast African newspaper in 1900, "is dead, but a more subtle slavery may take its place. The demand of the capitalist everywhere is for cheap and docile labour." A little further north, in the lands behind the Gold Coast (the old lands of the caravans of gold) an African poet put the matter more directly:

*A sun of disaster has risen in the West*
*Glaring down on people and populated places.*
*Poetically speaking, I mean the catastrophe of the Christians.*
*The Christian calamity has come upon us*
*Like a dust cloud . . .*

There followed the full colonial period. It would give rise to huge internal contradictions and furiously opposed opinions. Only now, long afterward, are we beginning to see our way through that dust cloud.

# Chapter 16

# "This magnificent African cake"

Opinions about the colonial partition of Africa were various at the time, and have remained so ever since. It is scarcely surprising. Around 1885, and quite suddenly, as it seemed, seven European powers decided to invade a continent of which they knew little, and often nothing. A review of the contemporary records can even give the impression of a kind of collective hysteria, a wild rush for other people's property.

So what was it all about? The answer depends to some extent on who one is. Pondering the question in 1978, one of Britain's most influential former colonial officials, Sir William Poynton, gave his explanation: "The objectives of our colonial policy have been summed up in a number of different formulae, but the shortest and simplest is 'nation-building'." Britain's aim, in brief, was to take the poor Africans in hand, and show them how to live in prosperity and peace, for this was no less than Britain's moral duty. Other empire builders have affirmed the same conviction on their own account. Explorers and missionaries of the nineteenth century had found an Africa ravaged by the consequences of the European and the Arab demand for slaves, and wide regions were lost in pain and conflict. What could still those tumults but an outside hand?

As a diagnosis of "colonial fever", this sort of explanation may have seemed plausible, but with hindsight it now looks unsatisfactory, or at least incomplete. Moral duty, after all, was scarcely what impelled King Leopold of Belgium to reach for his "share in this magnificent African cake".

Another British colonial official, Mr D.A. Sutherland, a senior member of the Gold Coast administration who was well placed to know the inside story, pointed to rather more tangible motives in a confidential report of 1951. He calculated the profitability of British and other foreign-owned mining industries, and found it high. In the case of gold, diamond and manganese mining, about half of the total export values every year went into "remittances abroad": that is, profits to investors, none of whom was African. From that standpoint the truth behind the colonial mission looked a good deal more like Cecil Rhodes's definition – "philanthropy plus 5 per cent" – except that the real percentage, as records in many colonies prove, was often closer to 50 per cent.

## King Ja Ja's problem

Even in the early years of the colonial partition, there were Africans who accepted the case for "nation-building", and welcomed it. Africa needed to be modernized and launched upon new paths of progress. Europeans had progressed by becoming nations, and Africans must do the same.

A distinguished West African, the Reverend Attoh Ahuma, argued for this in a memorable book of 1911. He appealed to his readers "to emerge from the savage backwoods and come into the open where nations are made". It was an

# "This magnificent African cake"

*A* Punch *cartoon (*above*) shows how imperialism came to be seen as a moral duty in late 19thC Britain. A Ugandan missionary school (*right*) illustrates the godfearing claims of the new colonialism.*

appeal that found a vivid response among Western-educated Africans in those days, or at least those in British colonies. Here were some of the origins of the nationalism that would later sweep the continent. Remodelled on the pattern of nationalist Europe, Africa should be able to face the twentieth century and all that might come after. Loss of independence might be painful, but for a while it could be desirable.

After absorbing the shock of defeat, the kings or emirs of northern Nigeria discovered that British rule could also be far from comfortless. Confirmed in their control of local government, they were able to add to their powers and privileges. The *alafin* or king of the old Yoruba empire of Oyo, much reduced after years of internal warfare, made the same encouraging discovery. Almost from the first he reached a pleasant understanding with "his" British authority, a certain Captain Ross, who saw his own prestige as being closely dependent on the king's. They walked together in early colonial Nigeria, and enjoyed the mutual benefits.

But one central point was firm and clear from the first. Whatever the colonial enterprise might be thought to mean, there was to be no rivalry for the profits. Any well-placed person who tried that game soon found himself in trouble. King Lobengula of the Ndebele lost his kingdom through trying to maintain his control of mining concessions. Even more instructive was the case of King Ja Ja of Opobo in the Niger Delta of southern Nigeria.

Like other leading men of that region, King Ja Ja had managed to exploit the ending of the slave trade by the construction of an entirely new economy based on palm oil production for export to Britain and other industrialized countries. Palm oil had grown into big business, so big indeed that the Delta estuaries along which it was produced were known as "the oil rivers" – almost a hundred years before the oil in question became petrol.

Europe's market for palm oil, which was then essential for soap and lubricants, had become seemingly limitless. European sea-traders competed

186

*A new economy based on palm oil for export to the European industrialized countries flowed down the "oil rivers" of West Africa in the late 19thC, filling the vacuum left by the abolition of the slave trade.*

furiously for its purchase in the Delta estuaries. But although in competition, they also did their best to combine together so as to keep the buying price as low as possible. They aimed, in short, at a monopoly of purchase. King Ja Ja, a leading palm-oil producer, took the point. Against the European sea monopoly of purchase, he set up his own land monopoly of sale and, being an efficient operator, had much success.

Ja Ja's response was an updated version of the trading "contract" of earlier times. It assumed African control of the land with its wealth, and European control of the overseas market, allowing a reasonable bargain on the prices of goods exchanged. Yet times had changed by the 1880s. In the case of the Delta, Britain's interest no longer lay in buying captives for sale in the West Indies, but in buying palm oil for sale in Europe; and a British desire to gain direct control of the areas of production had become correspondingly strong. Conveniently for this aim, something else had changed. Britain now considered the Niger Delta as her own "sphere of interest", seeing it in practice, if not yet in theory, as a British possession. No African control of production was going to be accepted there for any longer than was necessary.

King Ja Ja went ahead regardless, apparently taking the colonial objective of modernization at face value. He modernized in every way he could. Having built his land monopoly on the pattern of the European sea monopoly, he went further. He persuaded one of the European trading companies to break ranks and deal with him separately. He next attempted to arrange his own European shipping, so as to get round the shipping "ring" of the European merchants.

His drive and skill were found intolerable. Outraged British traders took their woes to the British consul in nearby Lagos, an offshore Nigerian island annexed by Britain in 1861. The consul decided that Ja Ja's enterprise was an affront to British imperial prestige, and, of course, to British merchants with access to the newspapers and parliament in Britain.

An extraordinary scene now unfolded on the Opobo river. On one bank, at a

British trader's "factory", was the consul, Harry Johnston, who had travelled from Lagos. On the other stood King Ja Ja's capital town of Opobo. In between, anchored where the river estuary broadens, was HMS *Goshawk* and a crew of 77 bluejackets with loaded cannon trained on Ja Ja's town. Johnston invited the king to a parley, promising no British use of force. Ja Ja accepted the consul's invitation, evidently thinking himself safe to go and to return. Nevertheless, he crossed the river with an escort of 27 war canoes manned by 700 men, being a king who liked to do things with a flourish.

Johnston received the king in an improvised court room, rather as though Ja Ja were already on trial, and instead of opening negotiations for a mutually acceptable agreement about peaceful trade immediately produced an ultimatum. While the *Goshawk* stood by to fire on Opobo town, the consul gave the king two choices: he could either make himself Johnston's prisoner, or he could

*The West African king Ja Ja of Opobo became a leading palm-oil exporter in the 1880s (*top and opposite*), but the success of his enterprise led to his deposition by the British. British-controlled palm-oil trading-posts (*right*) took over the exiled king's business.*

return to Opobo town. In the latter case, Britain would declare him her enemy, bombard the town, confiscate his goods and pursue him as an outlaw.

Perhaps Ja Ja might have resisted and got away with it, but the price could only have been heavy for his people. He thought it better to surrender, whereupon the consul sent him to Accra in the Gold Coast and had him put before a British colonial court. This court found the king guilty of grave offences to peace and good conduct, and deported him forthwith to the West Indies. The British road to occupation of the mainland was open, and was duly followed.

Ja Ja's fate illustrates the central contradiction in the whole imperial design. Wherever something more than simple plunder was involved, the colonial mission was said to be justified by the claim that it was modernizing Africa, throwing wide the gates of progress after the miseries of the slave trade. Yet here were the British dispossessing and deporting one of the most advanced of all the African modernizers of that time. According to the logic of the colonial mission, they should have cherished Ja Ja: instead, they removed him from the scene and installed their own monopoly in place of his.

Consul Johnston's high-handedness was not to everyone's taste in London. There were some who thought it little more than brigandry, and among these was the Foreign Secretary, Lord Salisbury – a man who belonged to a time when brigandry had been less appreciated. But Salisbury was carried along on the imperial tide, regardless of his own opinions.

"Simply approve his conduct," he minuted on the consul's despatch reporting Ja Ja's removal. "We need not discuss the principles involved in this despatch. They amount to this, that when a merchant differs from a native chief as to their respective rights, the native chief is to be deported."

## Occupation and resistance

The colonial frontiers might be settled on the map, as they mostly were by 1901, but the colonial powers had still to occupy and take possession of the countries enclosed by those frontiers. More violence followed, and new wars. Africans had resisted colonial invasion; now they resisted colonial occupation. To men like Consul Johnston this resistance seemed often perverse and always deplorable; they assigned it, generally, to a natural African wickedness or a tendency to what they called "tribal warfare". Their own wars of colonial occupation were labelled "campaigns of pacification".

In all this there was little difference in policy or practice among the various colonial invaders. Each liked to claim that its doctrine of government was more admirable than its neighbours', but each in fact had the same problems. These

# "This magnificent African cake"

*Colonial occupation of East Africa. Frederick Jackson, James Martin and Archibald Mackinnon persuade the Kikuyu chief Kamiri to sign a treaty establishing a British administration in Kenya, 1889. In general the occupation proved far from peaceful.*

were to establish a military control that none of its rivals could contest, and to silence all internal protest. Each solved these problems in much the same way.

Like the others, the British "hammered" any people who resisted. Many peoples suffered this fate, but Kenya's experience may stand for most of the rest. Here the aims of the British were to establish full control to tax Africans in order to meet the costs of exercising such control, and to extract cheap African labour for settler and administrative use. To achieve this there had indeed to be a great deal of shooting.

The Nandi people were among those who caught the brunt of it. They were ready to resist all three British aims, and they had to be "hammered" relentlessly. A British officer called Sir James Sadler took the matter in hand. Rather oddly, in view of what Sadler did to the Nandi, the settlers called this man "Flannelfoot". But by the end of "Flannelfoot's" campaigns against the Nandi, in 1906, this farming people had lost 1,117 killed as well as 16,000 cattle, 36,000 sheep and goats, and 4,956 homes and grain stores.

Then it was the turn of the Embu, another of the settlers' targets for land and labour. They lost 407 killed, while the colonial forces, thanks to their Maxim machine-guns, lost only two. Another Kenya people, the Kisii, lost about 100 killed during a further campaign of "pacification"; and the bloodshed seemed set to continue. But there were those in London who thought it was going too far. A junior colonial minister in 1908, the youthful Winston Churchill, responded to news of the "hammering" of the Kisii with a telegram to the Kenya government: "Surely, it cannot be necessary to go on killing these defenceless people on such an enormous scale?" he wrote. It seemed, however, that it was necessary.

"Pacification" had to continue in many colonies until the late 1920s. Peace was made after countless small wars and several major ones. Resistance in Libya and Somalia continued for 20 years. As late as 1926, French and Spanish armies totalling some 800,000 men were finally required to overcome the resistance of Abd al-Krim and his "Republic of the Rif" in northern Morocco. If Africa had known much warfare before the colonial invasions began, it had to suffer far more after them.

### The way things were

Eventually, however, silence fell. After about 1920, all the colonial powers found it possible gradually to replace military control with civilian colonial government. This, of course, could not be any kind of democratic government, for that would necessarily have undermined colonial control. Two of the colonial powers, Italy and Portugal, were in any case fascist regimes, entirely hostile to democracy. Here was another of the contradictions of the colonial mission, above all within the British and French empires. In theory, the mission was supposed to prepare African peoples for European forms of democracy; in practice, it could operate only by dictatorship.

All the resultant systems of colonial rule, at least when seen from an African standpoint, came to be essentially the same, even if there were many differences of circumstance and, on the European side, of "doctrine". This was because all the systems had basically similar aims, and these aims were naturally reflected in similar behaviour.

One aim was to expropriate African farming land wherever large-scale white settlement was found possible and desirable. Another was to force out African labour from the countryside wherever railways or roads had to be built, mines exploited or plantations manned. A third was to develop export crops, such as cocoa or cotton, wherever these could be grown by African farmers who would otherwise have grown food for themselves and their neighbours. A fourth aim was to tax Africans so as to meet the costs of achieving all this and, at the same time, pay for police and troops to put resistance down. And a fifth aim, remembering at last the colonial mission, was to provide some primary education (with a little, here and there, at higher levels), some health services, and some other aspects of what Cecil Rhodes had called "our wise and good government".

Before summarizing the results of these policies (briefly, since whole libraries would be needed to explain them in detail) we should consider some of the human factors involved in this contact between colonizer and colonized. Among the many novels and memoirs about these issues, Joyce Cary's *Mister Johnson*, Castro Soromenho's *Camaxilo*, and Muga Gicaru's *Land of Sunshine* are particularly interesting. Better than most writings of the same kind, they illustrate a central drama: in effect, a drama of interpretation. The executives of colonial rule, always European and therefore few in number because expensive to maintain and pay, had invariably to rely on local African clerks, interpreters, police constables, and other servants. There grew up in all colonies a group of African intermediaries between government and population; and these men, as happens in such cases, acquired powers and privileges which, generally, they abused. Dictatorships have never been able to work in any other way.

There was a wide sense in which these intermediaries became the true agents of colonial rule. If you were a villager desirous of some favour from your white

# "This magnificent African cake"

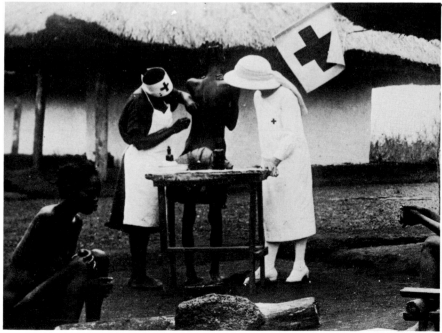

*Two views of colonial Africa: massive mining operations (*above*) combined with the expropriation of African farming land and with cash-taxation which forced Africans to provide cheap labour; "bush surgeries" (*right*) provided a vestigial health service in return for taxes which also paid for police, troops and colonial officials.*

*British justice comes to Africa: trial of a West African "native" at a British consular court in the 1890s.*

District Officer or *Commandant de Cercle*, a dignitary whom you would never normally talk to or even see, you would carry a suitable present to his clerk or messenger. Or if you were the dignitary in question, relying on that clerk or messenger for information and a quiet life, you would be careful not to enquire too closely into the man's credentials or behaviour. Either way, the petty decisions of colonial rule were decided less and less by white officials, and more and more by black employees.

That was how things were, and we should not be too quick to censure, for that is the way such systems have to function. The black employees naturally looked first to personal and family interests, and made the most of their power to bully and take bribes. The white officials, often overworked and poorly paid, were additionally harassed by a host of problems, personal or public – tropical fevers, recalcitrant populations, unreliable local chiefs, and an often painful longing for the comforts of home in Europe.

Many white officials worked devotedly and faithfully for the ideals which they believed they served, and were admirable men. Yet all depended on a constant push-and-pull between colonial policies designed to achieve higher rates of profitability, and other policies, far weaker yet still present, which called for schools and clinics, orderly government, and whatever might be understood by welfare.

In the last resort, moreover, all depended on events and processes beyond anyone's power of control or foresight, such as great wars begun in Europe and extending to Africa, or the fate of the world's banking system. World War I hit Africa hard; so did the great economic slump of the 1930s, and then World War II, not to speak of lesser troubles. Who can wonder, really, that colonial rule had to march along trails of confusion and disaster?

White officials and black clerks constituted the human factors shaping the everyday dramas of life; but beyond this was an irreversible trend that was well

# "This magnificent African cake"

*Local Gold Coast Africans employed in colonial administration (*above*). Black clerks and interpreters, rather than white officials, made many of the day to day decisions of colonial rule both in British and in French West Africa.*

advanced in Africa by the end of the 1920s, and was going to be strengthened by all the years that came after. This trend was towards an increasingly profound dependence on the outside world. We need to keep this well in mind, for it was the primary cause of some of the toughest problems facing Africa today.

The American historian Immanuel Wallerstein has argued, in my opinion rightly, that this African dependence on the outside world – specifically on the "developed world", as we rather strangely call it – began as long ago as the rise of capitalism in the seventeenth century. For the rise of capitalism meant the rise of the slave trade, and the slave trade undoubtedly brought wide bands of coastal Africa into an ever-deepening dependence on the markets of Europe and the Americas. That opened the way for the colonial invasions; and then the colonial systems engulfed the continent. Dependence became complete.

# Chapter 17

# The black man's burden

Little of this was understood at the time. Europeans and Americans, other than those with money to invest, regarded Africa as a curious zoo of no importance, and in any case they had plenty of troubles of their own. Moreover, Africa was difficult to visit; none of the colonial powers encouraged unofficial visitors from home, and tourism was virtually unthinkable.

There was practically no reliable public information about the continent, other than about its animals, and attempts to gather such information were disliked and discouraged. When I was preparing, as late as 1951, for an initial visit to Northern Rhodesia (Zambia today) I could find only one serious book on the subject of its government. There were no few occasions, in those years, when colonial officials of this or that territory were far more eager to show the door to a traveller from Europe or America than to welcome him through it. They were only doing their job, but they made understanding hard to win.

Colonized Africans found understanding of their true position harder still: partly because they were debarred from all useful sources of factual information, but also because they were generally prevented from travelling outside their own territories, and sometimes even outside their own areas of residence. In this respect World War I proved something of a help, even if the price in human life was high, for large numbers of Africans were conscripted into European armies, whether in Europe or Africa, and those who survived the experience had much to think about.

Yet the lessons these Africans learned were of limited value because all the colonial powers – except for Germany, whose colonies were taken from her – came out of the war with renewed imperial ambitions. Each closed more firmly on itself, and stiffly barricaded the gates of its empire. Even the traditionally free-trade British were driven into what was called "imperial protection". Competitive tariffs became the order of the day.

That was only logical, for the colonies were regarded as so many "estates of the Mother Country", and Mother's duty was naturally to keep out all poachers, rivals, and critical observers. Only thus, it was agreed, could the "estates" be made to yield the maximum advantage to their owners. Many forms of "protection" were devised, as for example in the case of cotton grown in the Portuguese colonies. Wishing to develop their own textile industry in Portugal, the Portuguese turned to their colonies for the raw material. Cotton had been grown there since long before colonial times, but in small quantities. The Portuguese colonial system now enforced the large-scale production of cotton by compelling African farmers in Mozambique and Angola to grow cotton at the expense of food and other crops they needed for themselves. Any refusal was met by the customary methods of "pacification".

The large quantities of cotton thus produced were paid for at prices fixed

*African involvement in European wars: Germans recruit East Africans (*above*) in 1916 with solemn oaths sworn on the Koran; mutilated and decorated veterans of the Allied side (*opposite*) remember the dead of Flanders Field.*

artificially low by the colonial administration, and were then shipped to Portugal to be manufactured into clothing. Some of this was then sent out to the colonies and sold at prices fixed artificially high through the exclusion of all non-Portuguese competition. So the cotton was bought cheap in the first place; all the value added to it by manufacture was retained in Portugal; and this value was enhanced by "protecting" the Portuguese overseas market.

That example could be generalized. It applied in greater or lesser degree to all the colonies and to all that they produced. Every significant system of African production became a system for transferring wealth from Africa to Europe, and this indeed was what colonial dependence really meant, no matter what high ideals and good intentions may have gone along with it. A "poor" continent became truly poor. Not for nothing did African farmers in Mozambique, forced to grow cotton at give-away prices, call that cotton "the mother of poverty".

Much later, after World War II, the cotton-growing areas of Mozambique became areas of famine. Even a most prudent and pro-colonial clergy grew disturbed. Writing about conditions in his diocese late in the 1940s, the very orthodox bishop of Beira told his readers:

I know a region which used to be a granary for lands afflicted with hunger. After the cotton-growing campaign was begun there, the fertile fields ceased to supply food for the neighbouring populations, and the people of the region itself also began to feel hunger. There belongs to my diocese a region in which for six months the black spectre of hunger reaped the lives of the population.

196

The black man's burden

# The black man's burden

*Cotton grown for export (*right*) transferred wealth from Africa to Europe according to a system known by the locals as "the mother of poverty". Mines extracting precious metals and minerals (*below*) benefited British, American and French companies, but not the local peoples.*

## Two zones

Gradually, as the mechanisms of colonial wealth-transfer took shape, a general pattern evolved. In most, if not all colonies, two different zones developed. One of these consisted of the areas where export-based profits could be made: zones where minerals could be extracted, phosphates mined, or agricultural products grown for export to the "Motherland" and its commercial partners. Such export zones were the jewels in the imperial crown; they were vividly cherished, being linked to the sea by railways or roads, and planted with little towns for Europeans to live in. These, in short, were the zones of colonial development.

Sometimes they were little more than tiny patches on the map, as with the Italian banana plantations in coastal Somalia, a territory otherwise thought incapable of yielding any gain. Sometimes they were distant from the sea, as with the diamond deposits of Angola in the remote inland province of Lunda. Or else they were solid pockets of territory such as the plantations developed by Lever Brothers in the Belgian Congo, or by African cocoa-farmers in the central areas of the Gold Coast. Others were strong mining enclaves opened by British, American and French companies exploiting gold, copper, manganese and various other minerals.

But the profitable zones were generally small in size when compared with the second kind, the so-called "underdeveloped zones". These were often vast in area and known for the most part only to the rural peoples who lived in them. Such zones were governed as cheaply as possible, and here the blessings of colonial rule were few indeed. An occasional missionary station might attract a convert now and then, or build a little school room or install a nurse or doctor. Otherwise, the direct colonial impact was barely felt at all.

Yet the indirect impact was felt increasingly. These unprofitable zones were indeed found to have a value, for the profitable zones began to need far more labour than they could recruit locally, and the unprofitable zones, by taxes or other means, could be made to yield their men. Better still, these men could be extracted as single men, on their own, by the simple device of forbidding them to

*Migrant workers (above) at a Johannesburg mine perform a traditional dance of the lands they have been forced to leave. The migratory system provided cheap labour for the colonial mining enclaves and export zones, but according to a contemporary colonial report "undermined the fabric of the old order of society".*

take their families along. They could be paid bachelor's wages in the profitable zones, even though, back at home in the bush, they had a wife or several wives and quantities of children.

The "undeveloped" zones, in other words, could be made to enlarge the export profits of the "development" zones, and at bargain-basement wage costs. So the two zones in each colony were in no way independent of each other: on the contrary, they were like two sides of the same coin. It was simply that they furnished different products: one supplied exports, while the other supplied labour.

### The labour network

A map of the population movements that ensued would show a complex network of "labour migration" back and forth across the continent. Wide rural areas regularly fed their menfolk into mining and plantation zones. These were the reservoirs of cheap labour that worked the mines of Rhodesia and South Africa. Other areas of recruitment serviced the mines and plantations of the Congo Basin and East Africa. Others again provided labour for cash-crop zones in West Africa or North Africa, or wherever else men were needed. In all this, as the patterns of migration scored their track more deeply on the map, the colonial frontiers counted for little or even for nothing.

The consequences of this consuming drive for labour were not to be fully seen until the 1950s. But they were clear in outline as early as the 1930s. Many protests were launched against the migratory system. Those initiated by African action were entered in the records of "pacification", and may be read about in police archives (or in the few such archives which survived the end of colonial rule). The protests of worried colonial officials were simply ignored. But they tell the same story.

In 1935, for example, the members of an official committee concerned with Nyasaland (Malawi today) were moved to remark that the migrant-labour pattern was ruining the stability and self-sufficiency of local populations. They affirmed from inside evidence that

. . . the whole fabric of the old order of society is undermined when 30 to 60 per cent of the able-bodied men are absent [on labour service] at one time.

. . . [This migration], which destroys the old society, offers nothing to take its place, and the family-community is threatened with complete dissolution.

The report enlarged on the wastefulness which thus allowed employers to produce their exports by cheap labour rather than make any effort to "utilize the potential income-creating powers of all sections of the community", and discussed the resultant evils. But the report might as well never have been made.

Tides of men began to be sucked across the continent, back and forth, in a pattern that would continue for decades. Many left their villages to be swallowed by tumultuous new towns, and a vivid folklore has remembered their sorrows. In the words of a popular Zulu song recorded by Hugh Tracey half a century ago:

*Ulele emangewabeni . . .*

(*Lying in the graves*
*Lying in the mine dumps*
*The lover of my child . . .*)

Women were also sucked into the tides of migration, and other songs told of daughters lost to decency and self-respect in some distant city. A Zulu song about "Goli" (as Africans have called Johannesburg, the city of gold) says:

*Kwathi phesheya kwendonga ze Tigwa . . .*

(*Beyond the banks of the Vaal*
*We came to the great city of Goli*
*As the sun was setting*
*I saw my child Mary*
*And thought of her childhood days . . .*)

*Main street of a village in one of the so-called "unprofitable zones" of colonial Africa. As many as 60 per cent of the men in these areas could be absent on labour service at any one time.*

There is really no way of measuring the pains of the migratory system. It thrust its tentacles into the most remote regions. I have even come across its influence among peoples living as far away as the plains of eastern Angola, "the lands at the end of the Earth", as the colonial Portuguese used to call them.

Yet no matter how sad its consequences, the migratory system proved indispensable to the profitable zones and acquired in time a dynamic of its own. Men and women began to follow its trail of their own free will, curious about this "new world" beyond the bush, ready to accept its miseries in exchange for the cash that could buy clothing, pots and pans, even a bicycle. For male migrants its very perils became a test of manhood, and even grew to be seen as "initiation rites" whereby a woman could try her man's ability and courage, or a man could prove them to his woman.

The colonial systems had always advanced by force of police and troops;

# The black man's burden

*A European couple in Kenya survey the locals near Nairobi, Kenya. "It must be remembered," wrote a senior official, "that Europeans will not do manual labour in a country inhabited by black races".*

after the 1920s, they increasingly advanced by force of circumstance. Their impact drew an indelible line between past and future.

## Two types of colony

Internally, there were many differences between the various European colonies: differences caused by climate, terrain, human culture and custom, or various aspects of colonial rule. But none of these differences had as profound an influence as that which was caused by white settlement. In point of fact, there were really two types of colony: those with European settlers, chiefly farming settlers, and those without.

The essential doctrine of white settlement in Africa was laid down by the French conqueror of Algeria, Marshal Bugeaud, as early as 1840. That robust man of war had no hypocrisies or hesitations. "Wherever good water and fertile land are found," he lectured the French parliament about Algeria, "settlers must be installed without questioning whose land it may be."

And that is what happened. By 1890 about 20 per cent of all Algerian land reckoned as profitably cultivable had passed into settler ownership; by 1940, with the process of expropriation still continuing, the proportion would be about 33 per cent. In South Africa – from a colonial standpoint the Algeria of the southern part of the continent – the process went far beyond that. Its Land Act of 1913 secured for white farmers or businessmen an exclusive ownership of 90 per cent of the country. South Africa's blacks, four times as numerous as the whites, could now own land only in the remaining 10 per cent.

Elsewhere the proportions varied, largely because white settlers were often hard to find and harder still to finance. But wherever settlers came, even in clusters of a few hundred or a few thousand, their interests were invariably placed first by colonial government. They might be placed first in theory as well as practice, as with the Portuguese and the French colonies. Or they might be put first only in practice, as with the British in East Africa where, in theory, settler interests were supposed to defer to African interests. The theory made little difference.

In 1903 a senior official in the then very new colony of Kenya complained to his governor, Commissioner Sir Charles Eliot, that incoming settlers from Britain were taking African land and usurping African rights "to such an extent that at the present time incoming settlers are threatening to disturb the peace of the country". They should be restrained, he continued, since "we are here to safeguard the native interests".

Commissioner Eliot replied warningly to this: "You quite forget that what we have to do is to *attract* people [from Britain]. Your regime would stop people from coming." So settlers continued to arrive then and later, and the peace of Kenya was mightily disturbed. This was not only because they needed land; they also needed labour. The settlers were ready to manage and steer and drive, and rough it when they had to, but work in the fields was not for them. So labour was extracted from otherwise self-sufficient African farmers by force or by taxation, and those who did not like it were duly "hammered" into a proper frame of mind.

Yet what other way was open to colonial government, once settler interests were established as coming first? In reply to London protests against "hammering", the same liberal-minded senior official who had himself protested about the settlers in 1903, had to explain: "It must be remembered that Europeans will not do manual labour in a country inhabited by black races." Manual labour went against everything that the settlers thought about themselves. Most were very middle-class people; they had certainly not left Britain to join the labouring poor.

In other colonies this general pattern was repeated with minor variations. Southern Rhodesia (Zimbabwe today) had won full local powers as a settlers' colony in 1923. Africans there, notwithstanding some paper "safeguards", ceased to have any legal means of self-defence against whatever the ruling white minority might take or do. Northern Rhodesia, in apparent contrast, stayed under the direct rule of the British Colonial Office and its governor. Yet a leading Northern Rhodesian settler, Sir Leopold Moore, was stating an obvious truth when he addressed the all-white legislative council in 1927:

> The natives do not come into contact with this House. They are governed by the people of this country: not governed in the sense that they are legislated for by the people [this was done, constitutionally, by the British colonial administration], but they are governed by the people who employ them.

It may read strangely, since nine-tenths or more of the people of Northern Rhodesia were "natives". Yet the good Sir Leopold was not thinking of them: for him, "the people of this country" were himself and his fellow settlers. The blacks might be useful as cheap labour; they were otherwise entirely absent from the white man's scene.

The large settler minorities took it for granted that any advance towards self-government or eventual independence must necessarily confirm them in power. That was what had already happened in South Africa and to a large extent in Southern Rhodesia. Three years after Sir Leopold Moore had explained who really governed Northern Rhodesia, another member of that same legislative council, Captain T.H. Murray, spoke for all his kind:

> I cannot conceive the remotest possibility of Africans being able to sit in the Legislature in twenty, or even fifty years' time.

All this was to lay up trouble for the future.

# The black man's burden

*European merchandise for West African consumption journeys up river to be sold at prices fixed by the colonial government.*

### West African exceptions

Matters in the other, non-settler, type of colony went rather differently. The most important of these colonies were in West Africa, where there were no settlers from Europe save in small pockets of the French Ivory Coast, Guinea, and Cameroun. This was partly because of the climate with its well-earned reputation as "the white man's grave", remembered in the traditional English sailors' shanty:

*Beware and take care*
*Of the Bight of Benin*
*For one that comes out*
*There are forty go in.*

Another reason for the absence of white settlement in West Africa, and one that proved more important, was the strong resistance offered by well-organized African peoples.

Colonial government in West Africa was just as dictatorial as elsewhere, but was generally content with a supervisory role. Having seized control of all these African economies, above all in the large-scale marketing of produce, British and French interests could concentrate on the profits. Large trading companies were formed and became increasingly monopolistic in their mode of operation as the years went by. Their aims were to promote African production of crops for export, and to buy this produce at prices fixed by themselves for sale abroad. In return they imported manufactures from Europe and sold these to Africans, once again at prices fixed by themselves.

Though excluded from any share in export-import profits, there were Africans who could still make some solid gains. All these economies suffered from the export of their wealth to Europe (and, in the case of mining, also to the USA), but not all sectors felt the same degree of loss. Gold Coast cocoa-farmers, Africans to the last man, were repeatedly successful in bringing new

land under cultivation after the introduction of cocoa in the 1890s, raising their levels of productivity until the Gold Coast became the world's greatest cocoa producer of that crop. Nigerian farmers went into groundnut production with a comparable vigour, and so did other farmers in Senegal and elsewhere. There was increasing production of crops for export, and consequently diminishing production of food for local use; and in this, too, lay trouble for the future.

*West Africans became efficient producers of export crops according to 19thC concepts of free enterprise; but their efforts were not always approved by their colonial masters.*

Some limited political rights were possible in the British West African colonies: Nigeria, Gold Coast (Ghana), Sierre Leone, The Gambia. As a matter of principle, Britain had always accepted that these colonies would eventually become independent, even if their day of freedom might be indefinitely delayed. So long as the overall system held firm against "agitators" – by whom was meant any effective local critic – British governors were ready to grant a few concessions. They allowed "suitable" Africans to sit in advisory legislative councils, or to launch and edit newspapers, or to form cultural and even political organizations of their own.

These were small concessions, made to handfuls of Western-educated men (and occasionally women) in these colonies. But they were useful and, in determined African hands, they were going to be important in shaping the future. They explain why the major tides of African nationalism after World War II, demanding independence and eventually getting it, first began to flow in the British West African colonies.

### Dr Mottoulle's doctrine
Meanwhile, inside the colonial systems, the biggest problem for Africans was to gain a clear understanding of how the systems worked. A simple understanding was easy enough, for day-to-day events provided it. But a sure and sophisticated grasp depended on education, and education above the elementary level was very hard to get. As late as the 1940s there were only two or three secondary schools in all of West Africa, and fewer still (except for the children of whites) in East and Central Africa. This was not necessarily for lack of money: copper-

*General Probyn and his staff at Freetown, Sierra Leone, c. 1910. "Suitable" Africans were permitted a lowly part in the colonial administration of British West African colonies.*

rich Northern Rhodesia (Zambia), for example, was exporting huge mining profits all through the 1930s and 1940s, yet this territory could still enter the 1960s without a single secondary school capable of preparing African students for higher education.

The real obstacle had nothing to do with money, nor was there any lack of understanding by colonial governments of the value of education. On the contrary: it was precisely because colonial governments understood the value of education that they were reluctant to provide any, at least above the elementary level. Allowing Africans a little knowledge would always be dangerous; allowing them a lot might well be fatal.

I doubt if many colonial officials, devoted to their mission, saw anything wrong in such an attitude. Most, in my experience, genuinely thought that "their" Africans were far better kept in the safety of innocence; and this is where we reach another of the human factors in the colonial story. The raw contempt and indeed the overt racism of the nineteenth century had become an ingenious, though stiff, paternalism. This was paternalism in its most literal sense, for it was generally held by the masters of colonial rule that blacks were incapable of growing up. The British, for their part, seldom liked to say this, but others were more forthright. "The raw native," affirmed a Portuguese colonial authority as late as 1950, "has to be regarded as an adult with a child's mentality." Such was God's dispensation, and there was nothing, sensibly, that could or should be done about it: consequently, for their own good, blacks must not be given the tools of understanding, since they would certainly misuse them.

All the spokesmen of colonial authority put forward this view in one form or other, but perhaps the doctrine was best set forth by Dr Léopold Mottoulle, who was for many years in charge of social and medical services for the great Belgian Congo mining corporation, Union Minière. Dr Mottoulle, as I remember him from the 1950s, was a kindly man of warm attachment to the "mining natives" under his care. He had long denounced the evils of the migrant labour system, and had induced the Union Minière to abandon it in

favour of long-service mining villages where men could live with their families. He spent his days in devising charters of social care and public health, and his proposals, set forth with tremendous energy and a truly Belgian shrewdness of expression, were not always ignored.

Mottoulle loathed violence and thought its use a plain proof of administrative failure. The colonizer, he held, "must never lose sight of the fact that the Negroes have the minds of children", and nothing could be got from children by violence. The blacks, he preached, "are big children from whom one will get more by a kindly word addressed to their good sense and still more their self-respect than by insults, anger or brutality: each of which, in any case, reveals a weakness in the man in charge."

The man in charge, the European, "must always show himself calm and thoughtful, good without frailty, benevolent without familiarity, combining action with method, and be above all just in repressing faults as in rewarding good service." Mottoulle would then complete his lecture with a shake of his little pointed beard and an admonitory wave of a pencil-wielding hand: he knew what was best, and liked to let you know that he knew it. Being children, the natives must above all be saved from the infection of politics. Any kind of politics (for one thing always leads to another) could only be subversive. And a truly immense effort was expended, whether in the Belgian Congo or anywhere else, in preventing any political movement from starting up, or if it had somehow done so, in watching and supervising, note-taking, police-tailing, reprimanding, incarcerating, and generally acting to dissuade.

A British historian of the colonial service, A.M.H. Kirk-Greene, has inspected the record. "Politics, for the average British colonial administrator," he writes, "was something of a dirty word, with 'politician' not far removed from 'trouble-maker'." Mr Kirk-Greene was being generous, for this was really the least that could be said, and in any case refers only to the British West African colonies. Elsewhere, politics was quite simply a matter for the police.

Even mild critics were met with suspicion. Stray researchers from home were

*Master and servant in colonial Africa: an early 20thC Luba carving (below) recalls the familiar sight of the colonial official and his driver (above).*

# The black man's burden

guarded wherever possible from contact with the "natives"; or, if they managed to evade their shadows, they were called to account and threatened with deportation, or, of course, deported.

Racism had always been a weapon of domination. Now with colonial rule in full swing it also became a systematic method of oppression. It was this method that maintained colonial rule in the troublesome run of daily life.

# Chapter 18

# Deepening crisis

And what were "the big children" really thinking? They were thinking quite a bit, as may be seen in what has been said and written since. Yet the realities beneath the surface of events were hard to analyse, and there was much confusion at the time.

This is what may best explain the apparent perversity of some of the anti-colonial protest of high colonial times. People, especially rural people, could see that something had gone badly wrong with their world. An evil had been loosed upon them that was obvious in its effects – labour service, land loss, taxation and the rest – but by no means so obvious in its origins. What were the hidden causes of this evil? Where had people sinned in bringing it on themselves? Whose baleful sorcery had willed it?

In line with their beliefs they applied to the shrines of oracles and ancestors, and ascribed to witchcraft whatever was painful or destructive. The hunt for witches became ever more widespread as the adverse consequences of colonialism multiplied, and physical or political insecurity merged with an agonizing spiritual insecurity. Much the same mood had troubled Western Europe during the great social and cultural upheavals of an earlier period. With their world turned upside down, people became gripped by fear and despair, oracles multiplied and anxieties spread.

Christian influences had already taken a new turn. Having found that European missionaries were part and parcel of the colonial systems, African Christians rejected their European mentors and formed Christian churches and communities of their own. This movement for separatist churches had begun long before in South Africa – now it evolved in many colonies. An African pastor of Nyasaland (Malawi today), whose baptismal name was Charles Domingo, explained its motives as early as 1911. Speaking of the senior colonial official in his province, Domingo said:

> Poor Resident, he thinks too much of his skin and not of his heart. What is the difference between a white man and a black man. Are we not all of the same blood and all from Adam? . . . There is too much failure among all Europeans in Nyasaland. The three combined bodies, Missionaries, Government, and Companies or gainers of money, do form the same rule to look upon the native with mockery eyes. If we had power to communicate ourselves to Europe we would advise them not to call themselves "Christendom" but "Europeandom".

Domingo, as it happened, escaped official wrath. Others who thought and said the same were less fortunate.

If there was much anxiety and fear, there were also sharp contrasts in the individual experience of Africans. Such contrasts covered a wide range of good and bad fortune, and two examples from the opposite ends of the range may

*Separatist African Christian churches (*right*) began to form once the missionaries had been identified by Africans as part of the colonial system. A Luba carving (*below*) shows a missionary with brandy bottle and glass attracting his flock with alcohol, or possibly taking it away from them – in either case an unflattering view of the "official" Christian church.*

serve to illustrate the great complexity of those years.

**Dr Busia and Mr Sandele**

Dr Kofi Busia, M.A., D.Phil (Oxon) was an acquaintance of mine in the Gold Coast of the early 1950s. He belonged to West Africa's outstanding group of Western-educated persons, and was a man of genuine erudition. Admiringly or enviously, such persons were known among their fellow countrymen as "been to's" because, having been to England and acquired a higher education, they had won unusual privilege, or the chance of it.

"Been to's" were no more than a trickle before World War II, and even fewer managed to get an education in the USA. Bold characters among them went into nationalist politics as early as the 1930s, and challenged colonial rule in a period when it still seemed beyond challenge. Others accepted the kindly lessons of Oxford and walked in the paths of righteousness. High among the latter was Kofi Busia.

He deserved great success, and achieved it. In 1942 the Gold Coast Governor, Sir Alan Burns, appointed him, together with another notable Gold Coaster, Yaw Adu, to be Assistant District Officer. These two were the first Africans to achieve senior rank in the British colonial service. Shortly

# Dr Busia and Mr Sandele

afterwards Busia extended his field of action, carrying out a sociological survey of the port of Sekondi that remains a model of its kind. Busia later went into the politics of independent Ghana and in 1969 became its prime minister. In this, for once, he revealed no talent, and was removed for incompetence in 1971. Thereupon he recognized his error and returned to Oxford where, as he rightly said, he had found his spiritual home. And in Oxford he happily remained until his death.

Busia's career represents one extreme of the colonial experience; at the other, more thickly inhabited, end of the spectrum is the case of Mr Sandele.

Sandele, a skilled carpenter of central Angola (then a Portuguese colony), set down his story in a written memoir. He was the parishioner of a remarkable American medical missionary, Dr Merlin Ennis, who had lived in central Angola for many years. In 1942 Sandele brought a long text to Dr Ennis, who translated it from Umbundu into English and later entrusted it to me.

*Dr Kofi Busia, an Oxford-educated African who in 1942 became one of the first Africans to reach high rank in the British colonial service.*

Sandele's account began in 1940, when he was about 30. A diligent man, prized for his skill in carpentry, he found work at a district administrative centre not far from his home village. There he learned that the District Officer or *chefe*, a Portuguese named Lelinho, expected him to work without pay. Sandele thought this wrong and went away, whereupon Lelinho sent police after him and locked him up for 45 days.

He was then taken by the police to Cuma, a little town on the fringes of the Angolan upland, where he was put in the lock-up for a few more days, and then set to work again, once more without pay.

The Ovimbundu are a stubborn lot, and Sandele held to his refusal to work for nothing. With considerable daring, he went to the provincial capital of Nova Lisboa (Huambo today) and laid his complaint before higher authority. Higher authority found Sandele's case a good one, and ordered District Officer Lelinho to send him back to his village without more ado. But Senhor Lelinho, feeling himself badly put down, took Sandele and another carpenter to his own headquarters, where he began a process of instruction. Sandele wrote:

> We were taken into the lock-up, and there we passed the night. When it was morning we awoke. At about nine thirty we went to the office with the wire about our loins. There we found the administrator [Lelinho]. We stood. He said: "What did you go to Huambo to do?" I said: "We went to ask about our pay." He reviled us and said: "I do not want speeches in here."

After further dialogue along these lines, Lelinho called for an African policeman to "bring the *palmatória*". That was a familiar administrative weapon in those parts, consisting of a piece of flat wood with a handle. The flat disc was pierced with tapering holes in the pattern of a five of dice; when struck against bare flesh, the holes applied an effect of suction, producing much pain. Sandele continued:

> The *cipaio* [policeman] came with the *palmatoria*. When he was tired with beating my comrade, I came in for it. Seventy blows with the *palmatória* were given to me. Then he said: "Take off your trousers," and when we were naked he said, "Lie on your faces". Then the *palmatória* was applied to our backsides, blow upon blow, thirty apiece. He said, "Take off your shoes."
> We took them off and he filled them with filth.

After that the two carpenters were sent to forced labour in the far south of the country, and only in 1943 did they manage to return home.

Those who seek to discover the details of what most Africans experienced in the colonial era will have to follow an uncertain course, for very few were able to record their own story as Mr Sandele did. But the outer margins of that wide and diverse ground will be found to lie, I think, with the examples of Dr Busia on the one hand, and of Mr Sandele on the other.

# Deepening crisis

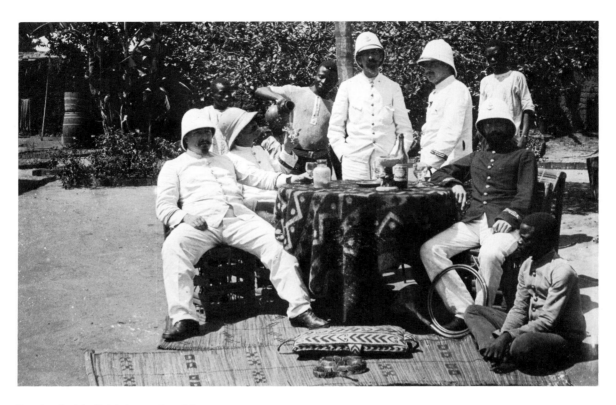

French colonial officials in Dahomey (modern republic of Benin) during the high days of European colonialism.

## A crisis opens

Gradually, as the colonial years rolled by, Africa's deepening dependence on the outside world was accompanied by other developments. Old confusions expanded into new confusions. Labour migration, land expropriation, and all the dislocations that went with them, gradually wrecked the earlier stabilities of African community life and reproduced, although of course in new and different forms, the ancient miseries of the slave trade.

By the 1950s, in many colonies, all this gathered into a profound crisis affecting every part of African society. Over wide areas villages grew forlorn and hungry. Filling with migrants from those rural areas, colonial towns swelled into monstrous slums and shanty suburbs where people clawed for a living, and tried to make sense of what was happening to them. The tumult brought much dismay.

Nobody had intended any of this, least of all the colonial officials, who were increasingly distressed by what was happening. They set themselves to halt and hold back these furious tides of change, but the tides proved too strong for them. Great economic disasters, originating outside Africa, had marked the 1930s. The world depression, which began in 1929, had a profound impact on the dependent African economy. Between 1929 and 1931 the export trade of Britain's four West African colonies slumped from a value of £56,000,000 to one of £29,000,000. In the same two fearful years the export trade of six British East African colonies also fell by half. Fourteen French colonies had their exports cut from the equivalent of £30,000,000 in 1929 to less than £18,000,000 in 1931. Other colonies suffered in much the same degree.

All social services, insofar as they had evolved by 1931, had to be severely cut, and poverty spread widely as prices fell. The slump continued and it seemed that nothing could alleviate its pains. And then, as slow recovery at last

appeared towards the end of the 1930s, a new disaster struck.

World War II had many consequences for Africa, but in terms of this deepening crisis of African society its principal consequence lay in the intensive "war effort" that was demanded of African rural producers. The colonial aim now was to increase still further the production of cash crops for export or, as in the case of the French West African colonies, to achieve substitution for imports not now obtainable. It is hard to exaggerate the impact of this "war effort". It was felt in most colonies, but a single case may stand for the rest. In 1945 the Jesuit Father J. van Wing, speaking to the Belgian Royal Colonial Institute in Brussels, summarized what had happened in the Belgian Congo. He was addressing a select Belgian audience who had been deprived of contacts with the Belgian Congo for more than four years, and who now hoped for good news from there. But Father van Wing had no good news:

> For five years, our populations were subjected to an extremely intense and varied war effort. The whole black population was mobilized to produce as much as possible as fast as possible, in order to send the Allies what they needed and make good the loss of imports.

He went on to explain that internal wages, and prices paid to peasant producers, had been kept so low that "only coercion enabled us to reach the end of the war without great damage". Colonial rule had survived, at the cost of the deepening crisis of the 1930s. That crisis now became irreversible, not just in the Belgian Congo but everywhere else as well.

*A shanty town outside Accra, Ghana, in the 1950s. The colonial systems led to rural poverty which increasingly swelled the populations of the cities, many of which trebled in size during the decade after 1945.*

### Flight to the towns

From about 1940 onwards, and ever more rapidly after 1945, the cities grew enormously, doubling and trebling their populations in a decade or less. Yet they were cities only in name. Their cores might consist of business and residential quarters for Europeans, often comfortable and well equipped with clubs and restaurants – in some of the French and Belgian colonies you could even enjoy oysters flown from Europe. But the vast peripheries of these towns were a different world. Sprawling across squalid acres of trampled mud, numberless shacks and hovels offered primitive shelter to the multitudes who had fled from village hunger, and who now had to try to survive, though officially unemployed, by means of menial services, charity, petty crime, or whatever family solidarity might remain.

Some of these new towns were huge conglomerations such as Léopoldville (Kinshasa), Lagos, Nairobi, Dakar, and Abidjan. Others were smaller, but all were bad to live in. Outside the European centres there were no public services: no transport, no electric light, no sanitation, not even any street names. In 1954 I found that the Portuguese colonial port of Lobito, where the trans-Angolan railroad reaches the Atlantic, had some 20,000 Africans packed into its steaming *senzala* or black township. I walked around and counted the water taps in the streets (there were no taps, of course, in the huts), and checked my estimate with a local missionary: the taps totalled 16, or about one for every 1,250 inhabitants. Yet I doubt if Lobito was exceptional.

People continued to arrive in these towns, no matter what the discomforts, and nothing seemed able to stop them. Shattered officials began to talk about an "urban revolution". Colonial pressures might have set the flood moving, but all too clearly it had acquired its own momentum. A Belgian anthropologist, Professor Louis Marquet, found that "the young people go off to the towns because

> life dies out in villages which are sad and comfortless, without enough food, where forced-labour services pile up without any hope of a man's seeing an end to them, where sickness is widespread without the Europeans fighting it, and where the old people, the sorcerers, and the beneficiaries of Native Custom combine to prolong their tyranny.

Far from being an exaggeration, this seems to me a true description of very extensive rural areas by the 1950s. These conditions represented Africa's real situation, at the bottom of the heap, when the colonial systems began to near the end of their time.

### "The white man's God"
Despite this deepening crisis, pessimism was not necessarily the order of the day. Quite the reverse: the towns could often seem exciting and colourful to their newly arrived inhabitants. Riotous they might be, and upsetting to the right and proper, but seldom dull. One found a vivid resilience there, a very African resilience. Africa was in furious transition, but somewhere along the line, amazingly enough, people were enjoying it. Once again, the Belgian Congo of the 1950s provides an example.

When visiting their village homes, "these people of the towns make a good impression", wrote a thoughtful African in *La Voix du Congolais* of 1956:

> They are well dressed. They jabber in French, the language of the Europeans. They reveal the secret of their condition: money, the white man's God. In the towns, they say, you can get anything for money.

So this "urban revolution" also seemed to have its liberating side, and this, I think, was especially true for women, even in ways that may appear perverse.

Rural women were Africa's truly oppressed classes. Generally, they were far more exploited than anyone else; and the colonial systems made life worse still for them, since the migrant-labour pattern often obliged them to do the field-work that absent menfolk would otherwise have done. Women were at the very bottom of the colonial heap, and yet the new towns apparently had something

*A* Swahili *fille de joie at* Zanzibar. *The dislocation of traditional African society led to unexpected freedom for some African women drawn to the expanding cities.*

to offer them too.

Large numbers of "newly urbanized" women took to independent lives of their own, by whatever means they could find; and often, in the circumstances, prostitution was the only way open to them. These prostitutes were known as *femmes libres* (free women), and not for nothing. I observed at the time:

Audacious, fickle, frivolous, seizing life with both hands, these *femmes libres* dominate the city life of Congo Africans. They flock to the bars, laugh the innocents out of their fears, initiate the village boys new to the city, organize in their own defence, fleece the lascivious European, and generally carry on in gross defiance of Morality and Family Order.

According to official estimates, as many as one-quarter of all the women in the great conurbations of Elisabethville (Lubumbashi) and Léopoldville (Kinshasa) were *femmes libres*, and Professor Georges Balandier reported much the same situation from the neighbouring French Congo capital of Brazzaville.

All this was deplorable, but it was something more as well. I found another distressed male observer, M. Bonaventure Makongo, descanting on the case of a certain Catherine who, he feared, might be typical of her kind:

Another thing about Catherine is that she has been to school. Of course she has misunderstood and misinterpreted those destructive words, "equality and emancipation". Now she believes she is the equal of a man, and as free to do what she likes as he is.

Money, M. Makongo considered, was at the root of the evil. Others agreed with him. "Everything", remarked another commentator, M. Henry Bongolo, "is dominated by money." The price of brides had soared, and the lifestyle of the *femme libre* had become "an ideal", so that "in these conditions, to ask the hand of such girls in marriage is like asking for the daughter of a Maharajah".

The crisis of African society had all these sides to it, and many more. Much ill was spoken of the vivid ladies of famous bars such as La Délicatesse and La Joie Kinoise in Léopoldville, and of the mutual-aid associations of *femmes libres* in Brazzaville, such as the "Lolita" and the "Violette". The resentment was understandable, since the condition of most men in these towns was probably, for once, far worse.

For a last insight into the African situation on the threshold of independence we may turn with good reason to the 1955 report of a British Royal Commission on East Africa. The commissioners found much to bother them. They found, for instance, that cash earnings in British East Africa per head of the African population, "amounted to only £3 3s as compared with £8 8s in the Belgian Congo". They found worse. Employed workers in Nairobi were sleeping "under the verandahs in River Road, in noisome and dangerous shacks in the swamp, in buses parked by the roadside, and fourteen to a room in Pumwani, two to a bed and the rest on the floor."

Such conditions "have been deteriorating over a considerable period," they observed. But there was worse again; and the royal commissioners concluded with an implicit judgement on 60 years of colonial rule:

> The wages of the majority of African workers are too low to enable them to obtain accommodation which is adequate to any standard. The high cost of accommodation relative to wages is, in itself, a cause of overcrowding, because accommodation is shared to lighten the cost. This, together with the high cost of food in towns, makes family life impossible for the majority.

And then, in the midst of this crisis, the colonial governments began to make ready to pack their bags.

# Chapter 19

# The rise of nationalism

The scenes of colonial departure were set in many different dramas over many furious years. Not much was simple in the process, nor straightforward, nor even done without violence. Few expected that departure, and only later on, often much later on, did all the reasons for it become clear.

Each of the colonial powers at the end of World War II seemed fully capable of holding on to its possessions. The only exception was Italy whose Fascist regime, crushed by the Allies, had also suffered total defeat in Somalia and Ethiopia during 1941: Italy lost its colonies, just as Germany had done in the wake of World War I. But the major colonial powers appeared no weaker than they had been before.

That was soon to be revealed as an illusion. Beneath the colonial calm when the battles ended, and the soldiers returned home, great changes of opinion and of interest were at work. One of the first clear signs of this was small in size but large in influence. The event occurred in 1948 at a sleepy crossroads in Accra, capital of Britain's "model colony" of the Gold Coast, where indeed any sign of change was least expected. The symbol of the crossroads was to acquire a continental meaning.

### Incident at the crossroads

The date was 28 February 1948, and the prospect nothing in the least dramatic. From the walls of the great castle of Christiansborg, where the British governor had his residence, a little road called Castle Drive led to the intersection for Accra. And Castle Drive was as peaceful and empty as usual.

Or almost so. Down at the crossroads, quite unusually, there stood a posse of armed African police under the command of a British inspector. They were waiting for trouble, although still hoping to avoid it. At about three o'clock on what had turned into an irritatingly clammy afternoon the trouble began to arrive. The head of a column of some 2,000 marchers from the town appeared, walking here on a route forbidden to them by the police.

The men were unarmed, but were marching well, for they were veteran ex-servicemen of Gold Coast brigades that had fought hard battles against Italian Fascist armies in East Africa, and afterwards against the Japanese in Burma. Led by former sergeants, and wearing their campaign medals, they were carrying a petition concerned with grievances over jobs and war pensions, and they intended to present this to the governor.

Their mood was resolute and became angry when the police stopped them at the crossroads. When they pushed against the handful of police, the British inspector, beginning to lose his head, ordered the use of tear gas. But the wind was wrong and the crowd answered with a hail of stones. At this the inspector entirely lost his head and opened fire with a rifle snatched from one of his men,

*President Roosevelt and Prime Minister Churchill on board the USS Augusta in 1941 (above). The result of their meeting was the Atlantic Charter, promising "the right of all peoples to choose the form of government under which they will live." Roosevelt insisted that this should apply to people under colonial as well as under Fascist or Nazi rule.*

*Christiansborg Castle. (right) in Accra, residence of the British governor of the Gold Coast, and scene of an incident in 1948 that, though small, indicated a fundamental change in the African acceptance of colonialism.*

killing a former sergeant and a youth who happened to be in the crowd, and wounding several others. The marchers, who had come with no violent intentions, turned back.

In itself this was a very small colonial killing, a mere spatter of blood compared with much that was to follow elsewhere; yet it was to have a tremendous significance. For it proved to be the prelude, and in part the provocation, for huge upheavals in Accra and other Gold Coast towns, and rioting went on for days. And these riots led, if indirectly, to a strong political demand for independence. The confrontation at the crossroads, however unexpectedly, heralded the first stage in the subsequent decolonization of the Gold Coast, and, with that, the eventual end of direct European rule everywhere else.

But what were the wider causes?

## A war for freedom

Probably few people today remember the Atlantic Charter, but it was considered important enough at the time. In August 1941 President Franklin D. Roosevelt received Prime Minister Winston Churchill aboard an American warship off the coast of Newfoundland. It was a desperate time for Britain, who had no ally against the Germans and Italians save, very recently and as yet doubtfully, the Soviet Union, invaded two months earlier by the armies of Hitler, and sorely defeated in battles east of Poland. Would the United States make at least a gesture of support?

Roosevelt made that gesture, and the Atlantic Charter emerged from their meeting on the warship. That was a solid gain for Britain, but Churchill had to pay a price for it that he afterwards regretted. For the Charter contained a clause whereby the two great signatories undertook that, when the war was won, they would

respect the right of all peoples to choose the form of government under which they will live.

Churchill later sought to apply this only to European peoples overrun by the Nazi and Fascist armies, but Roosevelt saw no reason to exclude the peoples under colonial rule. And the latter, or at least those of them who could make their voices heard, claimed at once that this clause amounted to a clear promise of freedom after the war was over.

British wartime propaganda confirmed this belief that the winning of the war would mean anti-colonial change. Appealing for African troops, the British seemed to make large promises. Thousands of African volunteers – together with far more conscripts – joined in a war which the British now called, as in their Swahili propaganda message, *vita vya uhuru*, "a war for freedom".

Nine brigades were raised in the British West African colonies, and still more from those of East and Central Africa. These were the troops who stormed the Italian divisions on the Juba river, and drove the Fascists to complete defeat in Somalia and Ethiopia, later going on to face the Japanese in Burma. And in all this they learned new lessons about human equality and the prospects of a different future.

Not a few of them wrote home to say so. "We all overseas soldiers," wrote a Nigerian private in India to Herbert Macaulay, the pioneer of Nigerian nationalism, "are coming back home with new ideas. We have been told what we fought for. That is 'freedom'. We want nothing but freedom."

India became independent, Ceylon (Sri Lanka) and Burma as well. Why not the African colonies? No one had asked for it. But winning the war had greatly weakened Britain, and France still more, while across the Atlantic the new superpower of the USA was seen to have little interest in sustaining other

*Dr Kwame Nkrumah, just after his election as prime minister of modern Ghana (formerly the Gold Coast) in 1957.*

peoples' empires. Inside the African colonies, too, much had changed, not least in the soaring growth of towns and cities as hungry peasants flocked in from villages impoverished by the war, and where forced-labour service often remained heavy and repellent.

The nationalists of the 1930s were now joined by younger men with stronger demands, and these found for the first time a mass audience whose numbers were further swelled by ex-servicemen returning from distant battlefields. The politics of nationalism moved, at this point, firmly into the streets.

### The importance of Kwame Nkrumah

Historians are understandably shy of personalizing history, but great events nonetheless tend to crystallize around persons. Through the vast and varied process of decolonization there was a number of such persons, but none of them in those years proved more influential than Francis Kwame Nkrumah.

Much loved in his time as well as much hated, Nkrumah came to epitomize the cause of African nationalism and its campaigns promised by the Atlantic Charter. I knew him well over many years and found him, behind the barriers of official rhetoric and propaganda, a tolerant and gentle person in whom a real devotion to learning was inspired by a grand vision of the possibilities of African development. He had the faith that could move mountains but, like all good prophets, he also had his feet on the ground. More than anyone else, he became "the man of Africa" when the black continent broke through its colonial silence after World War II, and the wide world sat up and for the first time took notice of what was going on there.

At the time of the "flurry at the crossroads" in February 1948, Nkrumah had lately returned to the Gold Coast after eight years in the USA, chiefly in universities, and two years in Britain. He was 38 when he returned, and mature

# The importance of Kwame Nkrumah

in his opinions and beliefs, which, broadly, were that the time had come for black peoples to win the independence without which they would never be able to realize their potentials. The Gold Coast must become independent, but Gold Coast independence must lead to an all-African independence, and this all-African independence must find its guarantee and future in an all-African unity. While still in Britain, he had helped to organize a new Pan-African Congress, held in the city of Manchester.

*Election fever on the eve of Ghanaian independence. Ballot boxes are transported across a river by canoe.*

In Britain he won a reputation for efficiency and drive. Hearing of this, the leading nationalists in the Gold Coast asked him to come home to be secretary of a newly formed party called the United Gold Coast Convention (UGCC). These were prudent persons, lawyers or suchlike, who had perceived that Britain's post-war government was ready to concede a certain amount of constitutional advance in the four West African colonies of Nigeria, Gold Coast, Sierre Leone, and The Gambia. They saw that Britain's plan was to move by small and slow steps towards an eventual concession of self-government. Their own plan in the Gold Coast was to hasten these steps by a suitably cautious pressure until power should eventually accrue to a nationalism embodied in themselves.

Arriving in 1947 with a vision conceived during his years in the New World, Nkrumah took the job that the Old Guard of Gold Coast nationalists had offered him, but he had a plan different from theirs. He wanted rapid progress, an urgent drive for independence whose power would come from mass influence and pressure. He set about organizing the UGCC away from its somewhat nominal existence into a dynamic political movement with many local branches, lists of rank-and-file members, designs for demonstrations, strikes, or anything else that could be useful, short of violence. His very respectable employers soon began to regret their new secretary, and before long a rift

*Participants at the celebrations marking Ghana's independence,1957.*

opened between them.

The violence of 1948, in which Nkrumah and the UGCC had no part at all, broke upon the scene while this rift was emerging. It was at once widened still further by the governor of the Gold Coast, who ordered the arrest of six prominent leaders of the UGCC, including Nkrumah, on the grounds that they were promoting a "communist plot". Given the opinions and the record of the six imprisoned leaders, this charge was patently absurd, and a commission of inquiry quickly had them released.

The Old Guard, coming out of prison after this brief though unpleasant experience, decided that they had better get rid of Nkrumah, but with the wind of mass support behind him, Nkrumah outdistanced them. In 1949 he formed his own nationalist party, the Convention People's Party (CPP), and went from strength to strength. With the rise of this new and popular nationalism, demanding independence, Nkrumah and his CPP won an overwhelming electoral success in 1951, and soon afterwards became the party of government.

This was not yet independence for the Gold Coast, but a compromise in which both sides, the British and the CPP, saw crucial gains. The nationalists had secured internal self-government with the promise of full independence to follow. The British, for their part, had bought a respite in which they could measure this new situation produced by the unfamiliar pressures of a popular nationalism, and could consider how best to deal with it.

There followed six years of difficult, exciting but often productive experience for the new African government until Britain was at last ready to concede full independence. Much was achieved, and the Gold Coast became a place of hope and encouragement throughout the colonized continent and, outside Africa, wherever black communities suffered from discrimination and abuse. Independence duly came in 1957, when the Gold Coast became a Dominion of the

# The importance of Kwame Nkrumah

*A traditional Ghanaian king celebrates Independence in full regalia (above) The newly-independent colony was re-named Ghana in honour of the ancient West African empire of that name. African history had begun again. Nigerian independence (left) followed three years later in 1960.*

British Commonwealth, and, in 1960, a sovereign republic. Its name was changed to Ghana in historical honour of the ancient West African empire of the same name; and this change of name seemed very right and natural, for Africa's history, on that memorable day of Ghana's independence, could indeed claim to have begun again.

That is how it seemed in those euphoric days when Nkrumah, speaking on the day of independence, had told his people, "Your beloved country is free for ever." And perhaps that is how it really was. True enough, five countries in northern Africa had already taken the same road: Libya, Egypt, Sudan, Tunisia and Morocco, but Ghana was the first colony in "black Africa" to break free. Nkrumah held to his vision. The independence of Ghana, he declared, would be "meaningless" without the full independence of the continent.

Ghana became a magnet for nationalists in other colonies. A young man called Robert Mugabe was one of many who came to this new home of independence. A native of Southern Rhodesia, he had been teaching in an African school in Northern Rhodesia where another seven years would pass before it became Zambia. In 1982, when I asked Robert Mugabe, by that time the prime minister of a newly independent Zimbabwe, why he had come to teach in Ghana, he replied:

> I went to Ghana to see the experiment which Ghana was proving to the rest of Africa: that a former British colony could sustain itself on the basis of African rule without any political help from anybody.
>
> And so it was really very enchanting! Against the background of the [white-settler ruled Central African] Federation imposed here [Southern Rhodesia] against the will of the majority of people, what Nkrumah was trying to do in Ghana became our desirable goal. . . .

Mugabe went on to speak of the value for nationalists at that time of the Pan-African ideas and aims which Nkrumah had set up as targets. And I think that Mugabe was reflecting the thoughts of anti-colonial Africans in all the empires, even within the shuttered colonies of Portugal, for many told me so.

With the Ghana breakthrough, nothing in political Africa could be the same again. The proofs came rapidly.

### Progress in Nigeria
Nationalists in the giant colony of Nigeria – in fact an assembly of several large territories under a single British umbrella – were already on the move. But here the situation was more complex by reason of the sheer size of Nigeria and its great diversity of cultures. Early on in the colonial period the country had taken shape as two large entities, the largely Muslim north and the geographically smaller but still very considerable south where few peoples, at that time, were either Muslim or Christian. This division was further sharpened by rivalries and hostilities between the British colonial officials in north and south. Those in the north held fast to the aristocratic attitudes of what was called indirect rule – government through local chiefs and kings who were ready to take orders from the British – while those in the south were obliged to have a far more direct and even democratic contact with the peoples over whom they were set to rule.

Nationalists in the south, notably Nnamdi Azikiwe, had begun calling for Nigerian self-government even before the war was over, and they increased their pressures as soon as peace came. Their problem was a double one: they had to win independence but, at the same time, they also had to forge a unity of action and of loyalty between the chief constituent parts of Nigeria. They found the first part of the problem very much easier to solve than the second. Nigeria was a geographical giant which, in other circumstances, might well have been carved into several different colonies at the time of partition; beyond that, the

division between the south and north was by this time deep and even bitter.

As it turned out, progress in the south went a lot faster than in the north, where powerful kings and chiefs tended, not unreasonably, to see in the drive for independence – with all the democratizing influences that must follow – a lively threat to their traditional powers and privileges. In a succession of constitutional concessions, the two southern regions (the largely Yoruba west and the Igbo-led east) advanced to internal self-government, with British approval, in 1957. Two years later, if with many doubts, the aristocratic leaders of the wide northern region felt obliged to follow suit. Independence for a Nigerian federation of all its regions was agreed by Britain in 1960, although none of the problems of inter-regional unity were anywhere near solution. This legacy of suspicion and rivalry between the political pacemakers of the big ethnic units such as Yoruba, Igbo, Hausa and others, together with lesser but equally explosive rivalries among the smaller ethnic units, was to weigh heavily on the future. In the circumstances a confrontation was probably inevitable; and at least the problem of decolonization was solved.

Little time was then required for the other two West African colonies of the British empire to acquire their own sovereignty: Sierra Leone in 1961 and The Gambia in 1965.

### The French empire south of the Sahara

Pressures against continued French rule after 1945 had to follow a different course. Even though the French and British colonial systems were closely alike in their essential aims, much divided them in practice. South of the Sahara the French had conquered two vast regions, the first covering a large part of western Africa, and the second enclosing much of central-west or "equatorial" Africa. "French West Africa" consisted of eight territories under the supreme

*Independence in the Gold Coast, Nkrumah believed, should be the first step not only towards all-African independence but also towards all-African unity.*

*Arriving in London for the Commonwealth Prime Ministers' Conference in 1957, Kwame Nkrumah was warmly greeted by the English people.*

control of a governor-general in Dakar, the capital of Senegal, together with the small UN "trusteeship territory" of Togo, while "French Equatorial Africa" had four territories under governors ruled by a governor-general in Brazzaville, capital of Middle Congo (now Congo Republic), together with the large UN "trusteeship territory" of Cameroun. There were thus two colonial federations consisting of 12 units, or 14 with the UN trusteeship territories.

African political involvement became possible in 1946 thanks to the centre-left coalition government of France that emerged from the anti-Nazi resistance in occupied France. It expressed itself most effectively through a new multi-territorial party called the *Rassemblement Démocratique Africain* (RDA) with *sections* (or local parties) in most of the constituent colonies of the two federations. When forced labour ended in 1946 and the electorate widened, dynamic political leaders could take their seats in the French National Assembly or its lesser Chamber, known as the French Union Assembly.

But these men – Gabriel d'Arboussier, Félix Houphouet-Boigny, Mamadou Konaté, Léopold Sédar Senghor and others – still had to operate within another context of the French colonial system. This presupposed that the destiny of progressive change in French Africa must carry its inhabitants to the status of citizens of France – of *la plus grande France* as it was sometimes called – and not to any national independence of their own. History decided otherwise.

Three phases may be distinguished in the advance of these colonies to political independence. In the first phase, from 1947 (when the wartime Resistance Coalition collapsed in France with the onset of the Cold War) until about 1954, successive governments in Paris and their governors in Africa tried hard to reverse the democratizing currents of 1945–56. Strong measures were taken to suppress the more demanding of the new African territorial parties, such as the *Partie Démocratique de la Côte d'Ivoire* led by Houphouet-Boigny

and the *Union des Populations du Cameroun* led by Reuben Umnyobé, while a nationalist insurrection in the great island of Madagascar was put down by military force with the loss of many thousand lives.

Yet by 1954 it was clear that this policy of the mailed fist could have no future. French defeats in distant Vietnam were accompanied by armed uprisings in North Africa, leading to the concession of national independence to Tunisia and Morocco in 1956. Partly under the influence of what was happening in British West Africa, notably in Gold Coast and Nigeria, African political leaders south of the Sahara turned from demands for French citizenship and autonomy within a French Union to demands for much more.

A second phase opened in 1956 when Paris decided to grant far-reaching powers of local and internal self-government to each of its 14 sub-Saharan territories (or 15 with Madagascar). This duly took place in 1957 against the efforts of those African leaders, such as Sékou Touré of Guinée and Djibo Bakary of Niger, who wanted to convert the two colonial federations into two autonomous groupings which, in due course, should become (rather like multi-regional Nigeria), independent federations. But Paris, for obvious reasons of national interest, preferred 14 weak territories to two strong ones.

Events then accelerated with the collapse of the Fourth French Republic in 1958 under the hammer blows of its colonial war in Algeria, and the return to power of France's wartime hero, General Charles de Gaulle. In this third phase, De Gaulle moved quickly towards conceding independence to Algeria at a time when France herself was being torn apart by the consequences of that war; at the same time, he hastened to over-reach the new nationalists south of the Sahara. He promised each of the territories a greater degree of local autonomy within a "French Community"; and this offer, under the threat of a withdrawal of all French aid and support from any who rejected it, was duly accepted.

*General Charles de Gaulle (above), architect of the so-called French Community of former French colonies, receives Abbé Fulbert Youlou, president of French-speaking Congo (Brazzaville). Sekou Touré (below), the leader of formerly French African Guinée, chose full independence in 1958 rather than membership of de Gaulle's French Community.*

*A statue of Nkrumah, pulled down but later re-erected, reflects the changing reputation of Ghana's famous first prime minister.*

One territory – Guinée, led by Sékou Touré – preferred outright independence even at the cost of French economic reprisals, and Guinée thus became a sovereign republic at the end of 1958. This set an example that the other territories felt bound to follow, but the sovereignty they achieved in 1960 was rendered nominal by their dependence on France within the "French Community". As "associated states" of France, they remained subject to French controls. These were exercised first through a joint currency known as the "colonial franc" that was tied to the French franc; then through French military controls organized by "defence agreements" and the continued presence of French troops; and finally through political controls operated less obviously but nonetheless commandingly by individual and party influences.

So the termination of the French tropical empire in Africa was far less clear and complete than in the British case. Most of these mini-republics, some of which were very small in population (if often large in geographical size) and practically without any visible means of economic support (save for French subventions), assumed a form of independence which Africans were soon regretting, vainly for the most part, as a new if less direct form of colonial rule. They called this "neo-colonialism", a term of abuse which was afterwards, and with good reason, far more widely applied.

It could scarcely have been otherwise. Once the African plan of 1956 for two large federations had failed to win French assent, a continued if indirect supervision by Paris was in practice unavoidable. Many of the new African leaders welcomed this supervision as their only effective means of staying in power, or even of facing the problems of government; and the result was a half-way independence that was bound to endure for many years.

Only a major restructuring of post-colonial Africa along broad federal lines, blurring or re-drawing most of the inherited frontiers, could have provided the basis for an advanced independence; but no such reorganization was possible then, or appeared even thinkable for a long time into the future. Not a few of the former colonies of the British African empire found themselves caught in the same situation. The nationalism borrowed from Europe had proved a doughty weapon in helping these peoples to escape from direct colonial rule. But the same nationalism was now to prove a major factor in obstructing their development into viable communities. Yet at least the problem of political decolonization had been solved, as in British West Africa, with little violence. Elsewhere the road ahead proved far less peaceful.

# Chapter 20

# Challenge of the settler minorities

While West Africans were winning one constitutional concession after another with little or no loss of life, huge conflicts lay ahead in all the territories of large European settlement. African pressures for independence in Algeria provided one of the earliest of these conflicts, and by far the worst in bloodshed and destruction.

Fearful clashes in 1945, beginning on the very day of the war's official ending in Europe, had confirmed a total French control. Neither Arabic nor Berber, the languages of the great majority, was allowed any official existence, even in primary schools. Most of the nationalist leaders of the 1930s were silenced or demoralized; and the large settler minority was stridently supreme in every field of public life. Far-seeing men and women in France might regret all this, and see in it a portent of renewed disaster; but governments in Paris, one after the other, let things slide. Algeria's future must be French; more exactly, white-settler French. But once again history took another view.

## Insurrection

In 1944, while war still raged in Europe, General de Gaulle met an African who would be remembered. The future president of France was presenting medals for valour to Free French troops who had fought the armies of Hitler in costly battles across Italy. These had been well deserved against an equally courageous enemy, and casualties had been high. Among survivors in the French regiments, a handful of men were personally decorated by de Gaulle.

One of these was an Algerian, Warrant-Officer Ahmed Ben Bella, especially commended for bravery and devotion to duty by his commanding officer, Captain (afterwards General) de Villaucourt, one of those French soldiers who had rescued the fair name of France from the humiliations of Nazi defeat and occupation. Yet this Algerian, as he afterwards explained, was fighting for more than France. "I was fighting," he recalled, "for democracy and national freedom." The enemy, he added, was "Nazism and whatever stood in the way of progress". To Ben Bella this meant progress for the Algerians of Algeria.

No national freedom came: on the contrary, Algeria was to remain a possession of the French, seemingly for evermore. Early in the 1950s, despairing of any advance by peaceful means, some Algerians turned to war. Ben Bella was among them.

In July 1954, 10 years after his encounter with de Gaulle, Ben Bella was one of a half a dozen men gathered most discreetly in a run-down hostelry in the Swiss capital of Berne. So secretive were they, in fact, that the rascally hotelier guessed them to be Algerians up to no good, and pressured them into paying double the normal price. They vanished a day or so later, but they had taken some momentous decisions. They had agreed to form a Front and an Army of

*Ahmed Ben Bella (right), a Free French Army veteran personally decorated by de Gaulle, was a key figure in the struggle to overthrow French dominion in Algeria. Freedom fighters in the Aurès Mountains (below) were often half-starved and under-equipped.*

National Liberation. Ben Bella would go to Cairo to raise funds and arms from his friend Gamal Abdel Nasser, who has just become president of a strongly nationalist Egypt, and the others would slip back into Algeria to complete their preparations. The insurrection they had planned broke out four months later.

Filtering from the rock-bound Aurès mountains of eastern Algeria, guerrillas of this Army of National Liberation (ALN) attacked police posts, ambushed military vehicles, felled telegraph poles, and spread the news of their revolt. Weak at first, they found a people ready to follow them. By 1956 a tremendous struggle had developed which was eventually to involve some 700,000 French troops against 10,000 to 15,000 Algerian fighters. And as bitter fighting continued, the degradations of colonial war dragged both sides into ever more ruthless violence.

Against an overwhelming repression, the Algerians managed somehow to hold out, although by 1960 many of their fighting units were surviving only by a miracle of courage and determination. One of their field commanders, Captain Abdelkader Laribi, afterwards recalled:

> Towards the end we had nothing left to eat, and so we followed French columns and gathered the food they threw away. Then they realized this, and buried their waste food. Then we ate grass, and then they drove us into places where there was no grass. Then they began to burn down those forests, leaving us only scattered hilltops. And finally they burned those too, surrounding them and shooting to kill everything that tried to save itself, whether animal or human.

The land became a smoking ruin. Tens of thousands of Algerians died, even hundreds of thousands. Yet the Liberation Front (FLN) and its army were not destroyed. Meanwhile, with pressures for peace beginning to be felt in France, the French settlers in Algeria took to a violence of their own. They began to intrigue with certain French generals, and carried their violence across the Mediterranean into France itself. Soon they were bombing or shooting their

*A so-called 'Mau Mau' fighter cornered by British forces in Kenya, 1956.*

civilian opponents, whether in Algeria or in France. As treason spread de Gaulle was confronted by another insurrection, this time by Frenchmen and French commanders. There was now no real choice but to end the fighting in Algeria or face the threat of civil war at home.

De Gaulle had hoped for a "neo-colonial" solution such as he had just achieved south of the Sahara, but the plots and insurrections forced his hand. He had to overtake them, and in 1961 he and his government in Paris conceded a ceasefire in Algeria with independence to follow. That came in 1962 after confirmation by a referendum. An almost total majority of Algerians voted for their national freedom, and achieved it. While Ben Bella took office as the new republic's first president, France quietly removed her armies. Their commanding general was an officer whom Ben Bella remembered from 18 years earlier: his name was de Villaucourt. The promise implicit in the victories of World War II was fulfilled at last.

### Rebellion in the White Highlands
At a time when Africans in the Gold Coast and Nigeria were preparing for a peaceful transition to independence, those in Kenya on the other side of the continent were in the midst of an emergency: more exactly, of a rebellion. It was not expected by the colonial authorities but should have been, for it broke out in the so-called White Highlands, an area of dense British farming settlement in lands where the Kikuyu, Kenya's largest people, had lived for many centuries.

As much as 50 years earlier a British officer engaged in central Kenya on military "pacification", Captain (afterwards Colonel) R. Meinertzhagen, had noted in his diary:

> [The Kikuyu] will be one of the first tribes to demand freedom from European influence and in the end cause a lot of trouble. And if white settlement really takes hold in this country, it is bound to do so at the expense of the Kikuyu, who own the best land.

*The Aberdare Highlands of Kenya, farmed by white settlers on land that had formerly belonged to the Kikuyu, was the scene of a rebellion that finally led to independence.*

He was right: white settlement had taken hold and the trouble duly came, even if it erupted half a century after he wrote his prophecy.

The detailed story of this rebellion is one of enormous drama, the tale of a peasant people seeking stubbornly and often confusedly an effective means of self-defence against settler expropriation. Using old vows of solidarity and new ones of warfare, they swore to fight for the return of the land that Europeans had taken. Officially persecuted as "Mau Mau", a name of unknown origin never accepted by the rebels, they were mostly simple people. Very few of them were literate, but the records show that they were never in doubt about what they were fighting for. They called themselves the Land and Freedom Armies.

Nearly all of Kenya's qualified political spokesmen were arrested by the colonial government before the fighting actually began, and few of them, if any, had in fact supported the idea of rebellion. Concealed in the forests of the Aberdare Mountains, and along the flanks of Mount Kenya, the rebels were left to find their own leaders and to work out their tactics of resistance. In the Aberdares their leaders also formed a political committee called the "Kenya parliament", and strove to evolve a political strategy as well.

The British, on their side, saw only violence and destruction. There was much of both, increasing on either side as the Land and Freedom Armies were hemmed in by powerful British forces. No other large Kenya people came to their support, and the Kikuyu themselves were sharply divided between rebels and "loyalists". The conflict soon became a civil war as well as a struggle for land. By the middle of 1956 the rebels were all but eliminated, or had joined the 80,000 suspects held in detention camps or "protected villages".

Yet this great rebellion, although militarily defeated, proved the key to a wider political success. British business interests decided that it would be preferable to seek political compromise rather than continue to support the last-ditch intransigence of the farming settlers, while opinion in Britain, shocked by the ravages of the rebellion and repression, was in no mood to

*Jomo Kenyatta (above), first president of the Kenya republic in 1963. "Mau Mau" rebels (left) await interrogation in a detention camp. Without them, a veteran of the conflict said afterwards, "there was no way we could have got back our land".*

prolong British support for the farming interest. African political activity was legalized again, and a constitutional conference paved the route for British colonial withdrawal. Kenya's most prominent African leader, Jomo Kenyatta, whom a British governor had recklessly called "a leader to darkness and death", was released from detention to become the honoured president, of a Kenya republic in 1963.

Up in the Aberdares, on a characteristically cold and wet day of 1982, I asked one of the former rebels what he thought about it all, now that a quarter of a century had passed since the "Mau Mau" was defeated. This veteran of the

*Patrice Lumumba (above), first president of Congo/Zaire, sought military aid from the United Nations in 1960 (right). The UN force included contingents from both Western and African member states.*

rebellion was now a peasant farmer in the maturity of middle age; he took his time in reply but then spoke without hesitation. "When I look back," he said, "I see that there was no way we could have regained our land, no way for our children to have got an education, if there hadn't been a 'Mau Mau'." It is the kind of truth, perhaps, that survives when lesser truths are long forgotten.

### The tragedy of Patrice Lumumba

Among a score of colonies that became formally independent in or around 1960, the largest geographically was the Belgian Congo, wider even than Nigeria and almost 90 times bigger than Belgium itself. From the beginning, things had not gone well for this huge conglomerate of ethnic groupings around which the Belgians had been able to draw colonial frontiers. They had begun badly, and they continued worse.

Up to 1959, no matter what might be happening in the rest of the continent, the Belgians held firmly to the view that "their Congo" – a Belgian colony since 1908, and the Belgian king's more or less private estate for 20 years before – could be allowed to emerge from their control only in a distant future. They continued to rule on rigidly paternalist lines, allowing no say in politics to Belgian settlers or to the vast black majority.

Yet Africa was changing fast, and the ideas of nationalism began to penetrate even the silent provinces of the Congo basin. Quite suddenly, in 1959, the Belgians gave way to a variety of pressures and shifted their ground. Dramatically, they offered independence within a year or even less.

Was it their concealed intention to produce an independence so confused and weak as to invite collapse and a return to Belgian control? Opinions about that have varied. Yet whatever they intended, a fatal confusion ensued, and with hindsight nobody can be surprised. At that time there was not a single Congolese in the senior grade of the civil service, not a single African officer in the colonial army, no more than a handful of fully literate Africans in the whole country, and worst of all, no African with any experience of modern political practice and its problems.

Permitted suddenly to form parties and bid for the inheritance of power, mushrooming "movements" competed for influence and position. Unavoidably in a country where any concept of national unity was entirely new and unfamiliar, and where there was now no time to forge such an ideal, competition rapidly became chaos. Only one man among the leading contenders appeared to possess the vision and purpose required to achieve the beginnings of political unity; and even he had next to no political experience. He was Patrice Lumumba, chairman of a newly founded political group called the *Mouvement National Congolais* (MNC).

At independence the MNC managed to become the centrepiece of a coalition, and Lumumba was elected as the country's first prime minister. He had plenty of courage, but faced an impossible task. A "national army" that was little more than a mercenary mob renamed from the Belgian-officered colonial army, went on the rampage. A civil service bereft of nearly all its senior administrators, most of whom had decamped for Belgium, dissolved into impotence. The great mining province of Katanga (Shaba today) broke away into separatist dissidence under local politicians backed by settler interests. A second province, Kasai, followed suit.

Battling against all these confusions, Lumumba looked around for help and called for military aid from the United Nations. This arrived in the form of military contingents from African member-states, including Nigeria, Ghana, Ethiopia and others. But these found themselves at once entangled in plots and intrigues that were now dangerously compounded by international pressures. The record shows that Lumumba wished only to reach a political ground where he need altogether rely neither on West nor East. But the financial stakes were high in this mineral-rich country covering the geographical heart of Africa; and the USA, determined to exert control, reached the convenient but mistaken view that Lumumba signalled "the thin edge of Communism".

Thrust rapidly aside by a gang of rivals, Lumumba was obliged to ask for UN military protection against his one-time army commander, General Mobutu, groomed now as "the West's man" against "the threat of Lumumba". At the end of 1960 the prime minister left UN protection in a strangely careless attempt to reach the main body of his own supporters in the distant town of Stanleyville (Kisangani). Mobutu's troops seized him, and in scenes of disgraceful humiliation and brutality sent him by plane to the secessionists in Katanga, where he was summarily murdered. Mobutu took over the central government. Violent uprisings by the murdered Lumumba's followers broke out in 1964, eventually put down with the help of Belgian and American paratroops; and in 1965 Mobutu became the country's military ruler. But dissidence continued, and even in the 1980s there was still no real peace in sight.

Independent Africa mourned Lumumba as a martyr, for in all the turmoil of Belgium's formal withdrawal he was seen as having stood for a genuine sovereignty and as the victim of enemies and traitors for whom sovereignty appeared only a means of personal enrichment. The setback to African hopes was bitter, but it led on to a demand for all-African measures that could help to meet the external threats and interventions which had accompanied Lumumba to his death. If most of the new states of Africa were far too small or weak to stand on their own, could they not mend their plight by standing together? An answer came in 1963.

## A bid for unity
It was not to prove a satisfactory answer, but was still far better than it might

*Kwame Nkrumah with the Ethiopian leader Hailé Selassie. The Organization of African Unity was formed in Ethiopia's capital of Addis Ababa in 1963, and incorporated Nkrumah's pan-Africanist ideas.*

have been. There were 32 independent states by 1963, with others about to join them. Already it was clear that some agreed means of resolving disputes between them, as well as of offering a common front against the pressures of the outside world, had become more than desirable. In this situation the old ideas of Pan-Africanism came to the fore, and were vigorously promoted by Nkrumah and some others.

All the leaders of the newly independent states except one, the king of Morocco, met in Addis Ababa, the capital of Africa's oldest and most venerable independent state, and formed the Organization of African Unity (OAU). Some clauses of its founding charter, such as the provision for an all-African executive and administration, were utopian and naturally led to nothing. Essentially, however, the OAU was modelled on the United Nations Organization, and, within those limits, soon showed that it could function usefully and with some success.

Acting as a forum of compromise between Africa's governments, the OAU notched up many credits in its early years. It resolved frontier disputes; it promoted common policies on a number of issues of common interest; it gave African diplomacy the kind of political ground of its own that Patrice Lumumba had tragically failed to secure for the Congo (Zaire). Its basic policy was one of non-alignment, expressing an intention to keep Africa outside the conflicting world blocks of West and East, and thereby reduce the dangers of external intervention.

Yet the OAU, like the UNO, remained an organization of governments and presidents, and could act only within the limits set by these and by the tensions between them. As the years passed, and disagreements deepened between those governments with much independence of mind and those with little (and many of the second kind appeared), meetings of the OAU increasingly became a stage for rhetoric and propaganda. Frontier conflicts proved harder to settle as the momentum of independence faltered.

Like the UNO, its model, the OAU might now appear to have become little more than a convenient camouflage for the reality of growing disunion. All the same, as even its critics were ready to admit when pressed (and again as with the UNO), the OAU remained indispensable as an aspiration, a statement of intent, and a place of meeting. It would not be dissolved, and it could yet nourish the seeds of a more positive unity in the future.

*Freedom fighters of* FRELIMO *in the Portuguese colony of Mozambique move into position against colonial forces.*

### The wars continue

Absent from the founding of the OAU were all the countries of central and southern Africa, where one or other form of colonial dictatorship still ruled. For these, the future was to be more war and many years of it.

Among the absent ones were the two great Portuguese mainland colonies of Angola and Mozambique, the smaller colony of West African Guiné, the mid-Atlantic archipelago of Cape Verde, and the two south Atlantic islands of São Tomé and Principe. The first three of these were the scenes of the longest wars of independence, and, apart from Algeria, the most costly in the loss of life.

These were not "settlers' wars" in any primary sense, although settlers in Angola and Mozambique played their destructive part. The conflict here was different from others in several important ways, and produced a different outcome. This was chiefly because the Portuguese state and its weak economy lacked the power to make concessions to African nationalism: not being able to "neo-colonize", in other words, Portugal's rulers would not or could not decolonize. They believed that others would step into their place if they withdrew, and in this respect they especially feared the USA. They were further conditioned in this belief by an acutely provincial intransigence deriving partly from a not-so-distant Portuguese feudalism, and partly from the nature of the dictatorship that ran the country. This has been installed early in the 1930s under Oliveira Salazar on the abrasively racist model of Mussolini's Fascist state in Italy.

Little groups of clandestine nationalists appeared in all these colonies during the 1950s. Sorely harassed by the police, they seemed to have no legal way ahead. In 1959–60 a number of police massacres in each of the mainland colonies convinced nationalists that their only effective response to colonial violence must be an anti-colonial counter-violence. They accepted this conclusion with an understandable reluctance, and began to formulate a strategy of armed resistance. They found this extremely difficult, and they met at first with some fearful setbacks and disasters.

Fighting began in Angola in 1961 and continued through a period of great complexity until 1975, when the country's movement of national liberation, the MPLA, was able to declare an independent republic. Its companion movement in Guiné, the PAIGC, launched insurrectionary warfare against Portugal in 1963, and was able to fight its way to a complete and unqualified victory in 1974. A third movement, built on the same lines in Mozambique, FRELIMO, initiated warfare in 1964 that led to a comparable Portuguese defeat in 1975. The two island groups likewise became independent republics in 1975. These successes rang a death knell for the Portuguese dictatorship itself, and a democratic regime was installed in Portugal as well as in the former colonies.

All this greatly changed the balance of effective power and influence throughout the southern half of the continent, for South Africa at once lost its two great "flank guards", Angola and Mozambique, on the north-west and north-east, while the Rhodesian settlers found themselves wedged between states of a militant African nationalism. But the victories of the movements of liberation in the Portuguese colonies did more: they introduced a trend of radical thought and action that had not been seen before. Indigenous forms of social revolution had taken shape here.

The reasons for this were many and various, but one above all was decisive. In order to survive and win, the little groups of early nationalists had had to grow into wide popular movements capable of securing the active participation of many rural peoples. It had therefore been necessary to build these movements "upwards from the base" by policies and attitudes that were clearly democratic. Having achieved this with at least adequate success, the un-avoidable task then was to begin building a new form of state structure and organization to replace a colonial dictatorship that had shown itself incapable of significant reform. This task was tackled, during the wars, in large zones that were freed from colonial control and, to some extent, immune to enemy reprisals. The revolutionary states of the former Portuguese colonies emerged from revolutionary experience within these liberated zones.

Only men and women of an outstanding steadfastness and intelligence could lead to that achievement, or could pass the tests and trials that it posed. Notable among these were Amilcar Cabral of Guiné and Cape Verde, Agostinho Neto of Angola, and Eduardo Mondlane and Samora Machel of Mozambique, although the list of others who stood beside them, including a number of remarkable women, is in fact a long one. They are names that Africa's history seems likely to remember with an especial respect.

### Central African struggles

Settler minorities in British Central Africa were meanwhile facing problems of their own. They had succeeded in 1953 in winning British imperial support for the formation of a Central African Federation consisting of Southern and Northern Rhodesia and Nyasaland. This proved vastly to the advantage of the settler minority in Southern Rhodesia, able now to draw on the benefits of Northern Rhodesia's copper revenues and of the markets of the two northern components in this Federation. But the other two minorities hoped that they

*The author with the Angolan leader, Aghostino Neto, in eastern Angola in 1970, during the struggle for independence from Portugal.*

would benefit in the long run by holding African aspirations in check and eventually forming, with the minority in Southern Rhodesia, an independent dominion of the British Commonwealth.

They reckoned without the growing strength of African nationalism. By late 1963 the independence party of Nyasaland under Dr Hastings Kamuzu Banda, and that of Northern Rhodesia under Dr Kenneth Kaunda, were able to win their respective battles for African majority rule, and the settlers' Federation had to be dissolved. Nyasaland became independent as Malawi in 1964, and Northern Rhodesia as Zambia in the same year.

Dismayed at these developments, the relatively large settler minority in Southern Rhodesia had pressed the British imperial government for their own independence, but had been told that this would be granted only if the settlers committed themselves to an eventual African majority rule. In 1961, accordingly, they reluctantly accepted a constitution which gave votes to a number of Africans, and which promised a democratic outcome at some unspecified time in the future. Even this cautious concession proved too much for the acutely racist settler electorate, and in 1965, reacting against continued British refusal to grant them independence, their all-white government rebelled against Britain and declared itself "unilaterally independent".

The British reply proved weak and hesitant. Economic sanctions against this rebellious settlers' Rhodesia, duly extended by the United Nations, were at once and widely breached by South Africa and Portugal, as well as by assorted business interests up and down the world. The settlers lost no time in fashioning a racist regime on South African lines, and the Africans, or those who meant to be effective, replied with guerrilla war. Begun in 1966, this warfare had little effect until 1972, when the practical example and aid of FRELIMO in Mozambique changed the situation.

Further fortified by Mozambique's independence in 1975, the nationalist fighting movement was clearly on the way to victory by 1978. Under American

*African leaders who forced independence for their countries in British East and Central Africa; from left to right: Hastings Kamuzu Banda of Malawi (formerly Nyasaland), Kenneth Kaunda of Zambia (formerly N. Rhodesia), and Robert Mugabe of Zimbabwe (formerly S. Rhodesia).*

and South African pressure, the settlers' leader Ian Smith then attempted a last-moment compromise with Bishop Abel Muzorewa, but the manoeuvre came too late. Fighting ended in 1980; and a general election gave overwhelming success to the principal nationalist party, ZANU, and its partner (or rival) ZAPU. Rhodesia became the independent republic of Zimbabwe with Robert Mugabe, the ZANU leader, as its first prime minister. Peace came at last, even though it brought with it a legacy of acute and violent problems.

Only the Africans of Namibia, ruled virtually as the colonial subjects of South Africa, had now to free themselves from white minority racism. And, of course, the black peoples of South Africa itself.

# Chapter 21

# South African tragedy

Admitting defeat in 1974, the Portuguese chief of staff, General Costa Gomes, informed the world that his country's armed forces had "reached the limits of neuro-psychological exhaustion". They would fight no more in Africa; and the new politicians in Lisbon, where the dictatorship of half a century had been overthrown a few weeks earlier, had to accept the fact. They had to make peace; at last, they had to decolonize.

The ragged little armies of African resurgence, ill-fed, often poorly armed, outnumbered ten to one by their powerful but eventually desperate colonial enemy, had carried the day beyond any possible question of denial. They had done this, moreover, without resort to the weapon of terrorism, and, as they showed then and have repeatedly shown since, without indulging in hatred of the Portuguese as a people. This rare superiority of mind and policy had proved to be a major factor in their victory. Having risen above the confusions of racism, the leaders of the liberation movements were able to measure their colonial enemy with clear minds.

The leaders and generals on the Portuguese side, by contrast, possessed no such clarity. To the last, they were blinded by their racist contempt for the blacks. A prominent Portuguese commander, General Kaúlza de Arriaga, was characteristic. Addressing senior officers on a staff-training course in 1967, he assured them:

> Subversion is above all a war of intelligence. One must be highly intelligent to carry on subversion; not everyone can do it. Now the black peoples are not highly intelligent; on the contrary, they are the least intelligent of all the peoples in the world.

A year or so later this same General de Arriaga was sent to command the Portuguese armed forces fighting FRELIMO in Mozambique. He at once initiated a major military offensive which, he declared, was obviously going to end the war within a few months. But the offensive hit the air – or, more often, civilian villages and peasants – and FRELIMO's commander, Samora Machel, was able to win new positions. Exploiting these a little later, Samora entirely bypassed the bulk of de Arriaga's troops and cut into his communications from their rear. By 1973 de Arriaga was plainly out-thought and out-fought; within the year his troops had "reached the limits of neuro-psychological exhaustion".

As a result, by the 1980s a number of illusions about the power and real potential of white minority dictatorship in Africa had been exposed. For instance, there was the illusion, widely held outside Africa and written into official United States policy as late as 1970, that all the white regimes were "here to stay", and that African protest, however determined, would not be able to oust them. Samora Machel and others like him had made their convincing comment on that.

*Triumph in Mozambique as* FRELIMO *soldiers celebrate independence in 1975.*

There was also the illusion that the racist system inside South Africa, the bastion of white-minority dictatorship, contained within itself a self-correcting mechanism which must lead, in the end, to a dissolution of that system. With time, it was believed, the sheer expansion of the South African economy must produce an ever greater demand for skilled and professional black labour; and this would steadily destroy the colour bars and the racist mentality that maintained them. South Africa would advance to a democracy of equal citizens' rights because white prosperity would require as much.

Yet the facts, by the 1980s, clearly proved otherwise. Each major expansion of the South African economy, notably through the long and extraordinary boom of the 1950s and 1960s, had always been accompanied by new laws to repress and persecute any black people who might ask or press for equal citizens' rights. These laws were invariably harsh, and they were ruthlessly applied. The system evidently possessed no self-correcting mechanism. On the contrary, more expansion went hand-in-hand with more repression.

### The meaning of apartheid
The full meaning of that repression has been difficult to grasp or understand outside South Africa.

Full-blooded apartheid – an Afrikaner word meaning "separateness" – was introduced into South Africa only after 1948, but it was really a new term for an old tyranny. Even in 1945, in what could now well seem a time of tolerant liberalism, no fewer than 986,593 black persons were arrested, and 861,209 convicted, under one or other section of the manifold laws on anti-black discrimination, chiefly by means of one or other form of the obligatory "pass system" imposed on blacks. A few years later, in 1950 (and still before the onset of fully institutionalized apartheid), a distinguished and by no means re-volutionary specialist in the subject of Native Law at the University of the Witwatersrand in the Transvaal province of South Africa, Mr Julius Lewin, could comment without exaggeration:

The legal position today of the Africans is such that the police can arrest any of them walking down the main street of Johannesburg at any time of the day or night, and any competent prosecutor will have no difficulty whatever in finding some offence with which he could be charged.

*Oppression in South Africa under the institutionalized discrimination of* apartheid.

Within a few years, savage new laws of repression were on the statute book, and the black situation had become far worse.

Why was this? After all, no black rising had broken out; on the contrary, black protest remained strictly within the easily contained boundaries of passive and pacific objection. Quite different considerations were at work here, for the new repression mirrored large changes little noticed by the outside world.

The South African economy had grown into a power in its own right. Its old colonial-type status as an exporter of raw materials in exchange for manufactured imports had more or less entirely vanished. The middle years of the 1930s, in marked contrast to what was happening elsewhere, had initiated a tremendous upsurge in the white economy of South Africa. World War II had sustained that upsurge, while the plight of Western Europe encouraged a continued expansion of South African manufacturing capacity, which increased between 1939 and 1945 by as much as 116 per cent.

These changes brought an increasing flow of black labour into white-owned and managed enterprises in the "white areas", so called because these areas, in accordance with the infamous Land Act of 1913, consisted of 88 per cent of the whole country in which black people were debarred from land ownership, and were subject to all the laws and customs of anti-black discrimination. By 1951 about 56 per cent of the four-to-one black majority were residents of the "white areas", and their labour had become completely indispensable to the whole system. Nothing could be done without these black worker-residents: from the nursing of white children to the manning of white-owned factories.

Surely, then, the time had come for "levelling up" in order to ease social strains and guarantee continued expansion? In fact, precisely the reverse took

THE BANTU HOMELANDS OF SOUTH AFRICA

THE STEPS TO PROSPERITY

INDUSTRIAL DEVELOPMENT

HEALTH SERVICES

AGRICULTURE IMPROVED METHODS

EDUCATION ACADEMIC AGRICULTURAL TECHNICAL

**Happy homelands . . . from a geography primer.**

*A South African geography primer extols the virtues of the "Bantu Homelands" (above); a settlement in Kwazulu "Homeland" (right) shows the reality.*

place. Partly from white determination to continue profiting from very cheap black labour, and partly from the pathology of racism, anti-black discrimination continued to grow. As early as 1950 a "Group Areas Act" began to make all previous efforts at the segregation of blacks from whites – as well as of blacks from blacks according to their "tribes" – appear liberal and easy-going. By the late 1970s no fewer than 3,000,000 and probably as many as 4,000,000 black men, women and children – countless families and even whole communities – had been uprooted from their ancestral homes in the "white areas" and transferred out of sight into the 12 per cent of the country designated as Native Reserves, or "black areas" or, more recently, "Bantu Homelands". Within the "white areas", meanwhile, another 7,000,000 to 8,000,000 black people were deprived even of their rights of residence and treated, now officially, as persons without any South African citizenship. And this was done, and continued to be done, with ruthless disregard for the elementary humanities of what might pass as civilized government.

How, then, did the members of this white minority perceive the future? Were they altogether blind to the all too probably violent consequences of their laws and customs? It seems that they still thought themselves powerful enough to withstand any conceivable pressure for change. The successful advances of black nationalism in the rest of Africa had worried their rulers for a while, but the worry was brief. Soon enough they came to believe that shrewd manoeuvres and tough policies would be sufficient to contain, corrupt or intimidate any contrary currents of opinion. They also had their own plan for the future.

This plan began to take shape in the early 1960s. It was publicly outlined in 1964 by the then prime minister, Hendrik Verwoerd, and was to remain the system's long-term aim. He called for the gradual building of a "Southern African Common Market" under the economic, and therefore indirectly political, control of South Africa. There was to be a constellation of states in widening orbits around the sun of Pretoria.

Nearest to the sun, obediently in orbit, would be a huddle of helpless little

*Police break up an anti-*Apartheid *demonstration at Durban, 1949.*

fragments built out of the former Native Reserves: the "Bantu Homelands" or, in common parlance, the "Bantustans". A little further out, but almost as helpless, were to be the three former British High Commission Territories of Basutoland (Lesotho), Swaziland and Bechuanaland (Botswana), each of them a labour reservoir like the Bantustans in all but name. Further out again would be another orbit of large states consisting of the convenient Portuguese colonies of Angola and Mozambique, as well as recently independent ex-colonies such as Zambia and Malawi; and beyond these again, more or less taken for granted, there would be the enormous economic wealth and potentials of a subservient Zaire (ex-Belgian Congo). South Africa's industries would be guaranteed captive markets for its manufactures, as well as endless supplies of crucial raw materials for its industries; and Pretoria would dominate half the continent.

The plan seemed promising until it went badly awry with the success of liberation movements in Angola, Mozambique and Zimbabwe. Yet it was not abandoned. The early 1980s witnessed a consistent effort by Pretoria to redress the balance in its favour and restore the basis of its old bid for hegemony over an enormous region. Backed by powerful foreign interests, the 1980s saw South Africa effectively at war with the new republic of Angola, stonewalling on pressures for progress in Namibia, promoting mercenary sabotage and subversion in Mozambique, and, as many believed, engaged in comparable measures of destabilization in the new republic of Zimbabwe. There was now a real prospect that the violence of the South African system would engulf the whole southern-central continent; and no official pressures from the outside world appeared willing or able to counter that prospect.

In this grim situation, attention turned once again to the black majority inside South Africa.

### From passive protest to counter-violence

The earliest spokesmen of black protest in South Africa had watched the advance of the racist system with dismay, but few of them had thought of acting

*Police attack a* SWAPO *rally in Windhoek, Namibia.*

*Nelson Mandela, leader of the African National Congress of South Africa, sentended to life imprisonment in 1963.*

strongly against it. Most had believed that any "trouble-making agitation" would only frighten the whites into attitudes even more violent than those they had adopted hitherto. Characteristic of the early spokesmen was Professor D.D.T. Jabavu, whose main idea was that black collaboration with white supremacy would in the course of time bring about a white acceptance of equality with blacks.

Such attitudes persisted. Right down to the 1950s, the organizations of the non-whites – whether African, Indian or Coloured (that is, of mixed parentage) – held firmly to policies of non-violent and pacific protest, very much in the Gandhian tradition, even though not the smallest progress came of them. On the contrary, every passive protest produced its new law of repression. A widely supported and entirely peaceful campaign against the pass laws, in 1952, was met by new measures providing imprisonment, or flogging, or both. And the whole apparatus of apartheid segregation was now in powerful motion.

Patience began running out towards the end of the 1950s. Counter-violence was planned for the first time, notably by a new armed wing of the African National Congress, *Umkonto wa Sizwe.* Even before this went into action – ultimately unsuccessful, as it proved – peaceful demonstrations against the pass laws had been promoted by a new black organization, the Pan-African Congress (PAC), only to be met by police massacres on an unprecedented scale. At Sharpeville and Langa a total of 83 blacks were killed and 365 injured, many by wounds in the back when unarmed demonstrators were running from the police. In 1962 the leader of the African National Congress, Nelson Mandela, was arrested, and police informers led to the arrest of the whole "high command" of *Umkonto wa Sizwe* who were then inside South Africa. Long prison sentences were meted out in 1963, including life imprisonment for Mandela and six others.

After that it seemed that all effective black protest had been silenced, cowed by fear or demoralized by failure. Yet the early 1970s brought a resurgence of militancy among black workers in several of South Africa's relatively new

*The body of Steve Biko, Black Consciousness leader, who died in o South African prison of brain damage in 1977.*

manufacturing industries. Many such workers had been admitted to semi-skilled and even skilled jobs by the device of raising the ceiling level of the colour bars, so that skilled work would still earn low (often extremely low) wages well below the publicly admitted "poverty datum line". Meanwhile all well-paid work continued, as before, to be reserved for white workers. Now there came a black workers' drive against the wretchedness of their wage levels, and for the first time since the foundation of modern South Africa this movement was quite widely successful.

This still left political protest entirely muted; but the victories of the highly-politicized liberation movements in Mozambique and Angola, signalled in 1974 and consummated in 1975, once more brought politics back into the middle of the stage. A new militancy began to emerge in some of the vast all-black townships clustered as labour dormitories round the principal cities. Partly this was the work of black students in a number of segregated black colleges, where each college was designed by the government for a single ethnic group among the blacks – Zulu, Sotho or other – on the old principle of "divide and rule". The students worked for unity of purpose across these often artificial divisions, and had some success, notably in creating the Black Consciousness movement. Taking its inspiration from various traditions, and not least from the tradition of the African National Congress and the teachings of its exiled or imprisoned leaders, Black Consciousness sought for semi-legal or even legal ways of raising black morale after the disasters of the 1960s, and of pressing demands for change in the laws of apartheid.

To this the system replied with its usual ferocity, and soon afterwards the Black Consciousness leader, Steve Biko, died from brain damage in prison while being held naked and manacled in his cell. Yet a far wider resistance had already erupted elsewhere, beginning in the million-strong black conurbation of South West Township, or Soweto, outside Johannesburg.

Ordered to learn more of their lessons in the hated language of their oppressors, Afrikaans, secondary-school students went on strike early in 1976 and filled the streets with anti-apartheid demonstrations. Police opened fire into these marching crowds of schoolchildren, and killed several hundred of them. Yet the strikes continued and spread to Cape Town and other "locations", as black townships were called. Here again there was indiscriminate shooting by the police. But the old intimidations were now seen to have lost their power. The protests turned into counter-violence, and the counter-violence rapidly soared into the dimensions of a mass uprising.

Many more lives were lost before "law and order" were restored. Yet it was now clear that South Africa was not only at undeclared war with its northern neighbours, but also with wide sections of its own population. At the same time, emphasizing this new and potent fact, the counter-violence of *Umkonto wa Sizwe*, the ANC's "Spear of the Nation", began to operate again; and this time it began to operate with success. Its ranks had been reinforced by many hundreds of young men and women from Soweto and other townships who had escaped abroad and now returned with guns in their hands and the skills and disciplines required to use them.

Operating in small units, guerrillas of *Umkonto* began to attack selected targets, such as oil refineries, with an increasing effectiveness; more and more often they found safe cover in an evidently sympathetic black population. Some were caught by police or army, and jailed or hanged; many more, as evidence proves, got safely away. The violence of the system had produced its own response; the snake of repression had begun to eat its own tail. And there seemed to be nothing within the system that could halt the process.

**A militarized system**

True enough, a new government under Prime Minister Botha had begun, early in the 1980s, to talk a slightly different language. To the fury of many of its Afrikaner voters, this government promised some concessions to reason and good sense. Black trade unions were not exactly legalized, but at least they were allowed to exist. A plan to provide some kind of second-class parliamentary representation for Indians and Coloureds – but not for Africans – was produced and proceeded with. Minor forms of racist insult were removed, or, it was promised, were going to be removed.

Yet the basic evolution of apartheid as a system continued apace. More and more "unwanted residents" of the "white areas" were summarily bulldozed from their homes and removed to "black areas" which, often enough, were nothing more than open bush without any facilities or any hope of employment. There they were left to rot or, if they attempted to regain their homes, were driven back again by force.

Efforts were made to promote the "independence" of the various geographical fragments known as the Bantu "Homelands", even though these efforts were hopelessly eroded by the crowding in of people and cattle, the absence of industries, and the failure to provide any investment whereby such industries could be built. None of the "Homelands" had the slightest prospect of becoming independent, not even the Transkei, which was the only relatively large one; and no foreign government (except Dr Hastings Banda's government in Malawi) could bring itself to recognize any of them. The fact that they were now endowed with organs of local self-government could in no way lessen the truth that each of them continued to be subservient reservoirs of black labour for the dominant white areas.

The system, meanwhile, militarized itself still further. Under the energetic leadership of its defence chief, General Magnus Malan, new armouries of sophisticated weapons were assembled by purchase from abroad or by local manufacture on licence from foreign patent-holders. All-white professional

*Soweto, 1976: The reality of apartheid. Soldiers fire on demonstrating schoolchildren, killing several hundred of them.*

armed forces were strengthened and enlarged, and were reinforced by new measures of conscription of the white population. Little of this could have any reference to the internal situation, no matter how much counter-violence might now develop. Most of it, all too clearly, could be applicable only to warfare beyond the frontiers of South Africa. By 1980, if not some years before, there was powerful evidence to suggest that the regime had achieved a capacity to make nuclear weapons and was in fact making them, once again with the collusion of European governments whose policies were opposed – on paper – to military support for the system.

In the short term, accordingly, all the signs by the middle of the 1980s pointed to widening aggression by the system as well as to still greater repression within its frontiers. That these trends could lead directly to disasters on a continental scale seemed now beyond dispute, and all the more because there was little in the immediate picture, whether local or international, to encourage any belief that the continuing slide into violence would be stopped or even contained. Only the optimists, and remarkably enough there were still some of those, held to a different view. They argued that this population of 4,500,000 whites, however embattled and besieged by its own ferocity, could never in the end conserve its domination or realize its plans. Their real strength came from powerful international backing. Sooner or later, this backing would be removed by the self-interest of those concerned. Then the regime would have to concede, compromise, retreat, and eventually disarm. This might indeed seem an optimistic view; but even optimists are sometimes right.

# Chapter 22

# The fruits of independence

Long and bitter struggles had been required to bring an end to foreign rule, and yet it seemed, in the aftermath, that repeated failure had derived from them. Good government grew hard to find; hunger remained widespread, or extended its miseries still further; everywhere problems appeared to multiply and to overwhelm solutions.

Yet the fruits of any great transition such as this were bound to be of various kinds, and not the least of these, quite irrespective of institutional failure, concerned men's inner hopes and satisfactions. Independence broadened the texture of daily life, promoted new opportunities and a renewed self-respect, and encouraged a constructive optimism seldom thinkable before.

Given everything that had happened in living memory, Africa's mood could scarcely be pessimistic, not even in the 1980s when prospects looked increasingly bleak. There were precious few people, now, who could regret the past, and these in any case were the old and the defeated, some of whom had never wanted independence. Nearly half the continent's entire population was under the age of 15 in 1980, and another quarter was under the age of 30: the future was theirs, offering a scope that their parents and grandparents did not and could not expect to possess.

The optimism of Africa in the 1980s, however apparently perverse in the circumstances, is partly the optimism of youth, but it is also more than that. It is the product of a new self-assurance that stems from the fact – not always obvious or easy to illustrate, but nonetheless central – that the history of the past is joined once more to what may be called the history of the present. These peoples have restored to themselves the sense of *possibility*. They had lost it for a long while, but now they have it back again. And it is infinitely precious: a source of initiative and self-confidence, even a source of joy. This is the creative truth that lies behind that much abused word freedom, a truth that exists and persists in spite of every degradation by demagogues or crooks.

Africa has gained enormously from its transition out of foreign rule. Its peoples are able once more to grow out of their own roots and nourish their new life from their old life. But how is one to demonstrate all this in everyday reality? How reveal this sense of possibility, even this sense of freedom? It is no small problem against all the background of grief and woe which the outside world tends to see in Africa to the exclusion of anything else.

One of the various ways in which Africa's transition can be measured occurred to me recently in the ancient city of Timbuktu, half-lost in the haze of a wind from across the Sahara desert that reaches to the city's doorstep. This venerable focus of the Golden Trade has long since lost its wealth, now that the Saharan caravans carry little more than cottons to the north and salt to the south. Timbuktu today seems principally to represent ruin and abandonment.

# The fruits of independence

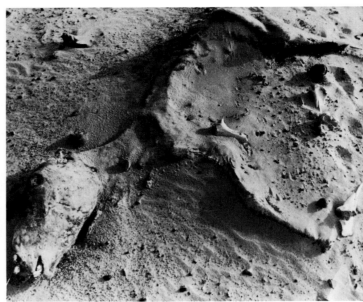

*Natural disasters such as the Sahelian drought (above and right), affecting six West African countries, compound the political problems of the continent. Yet hope for the future persists. A Cameroon street scene (right) with drums and dancing exemplifies the "sense of possibility" that pervades much of independent Africa today.*

Yet ruin and abandonment are not, in fact, any part of the essential truth of Timbuktu in the 1980s, for the city is as much alive today as it ever was, and more alive than in many past years, even if some of the commercial patterns have changed. The renown of Timbuktu literacy and learning may be less than when the great Ahmad Baba taught here in the early 1600s, at a time when the scholarly libraries of Timbuktu could vie with those of Cairo or Baghdad; but the traditions of that scholarship still hold firm. The chief Muslim judge of Timbuktu, Cadi Alhaji Issa, may teach no more than a dozen students in the higher reaches of *tafsir* and *fiqh* – theology and law – or so it was the other day while I sat listening at the door; and students may no longer come from distant

*At modern Timbuktu the chief* cadi *(Muslim judge) carries on the old tradition of scholarship and learning with classes in theology and law.*

lands. But nearby, in this city of the republic of Mali that was born in 1960, there stands a new institute and library devoted to the advancement of historical learning. Its distinguished director, Dr Mahmoud Abdu Zouber, has already collected, or rescued from the obscurity of private libraries, a remarkable range of volumes in manuscript, which prove not only that Timbuktu was once the greatest centre of learning in the Western Sudan, but that it reveres and enlivens, even today, the high traditions of its past.

New and often surprising cultural growths have been grafted onto this venerable heritage. For instance, the salt caravans still traipse northward 21 days with their camels on the outward stretch to Taodéni, and 21 days on the return journey. But the men who ply this ancient and apparently unchanging trade are liable to be thinking a whole manner of new thoughts. Lonely figures on a lost horizon, they will still croon songs to themselves as they go, but the melodies may well be new, for the present can rejoin the past in ways as up-to-date as unexpected. One star-lit night, not far from Cadi Alhaji Issa's house, I came upon a band of minstrels of a kind that have played here since time beyond memory, happily enlarging upon the dramas and romances of ancient Songhay to the accompaniment of drums and strings. But that night the music they were playing, to a numerous gathering of local enthusiasts, was not the sobbing rhythm of nostalgia – it was modern rock, possibly in a fashion unlike any in America or Europe, but nevertheless indubitably rock.

Somewhere between these two scenes of modern Timbuktu – Alhaji Issa's commentaries on Ahmad Baba or other ancient scholars, and the music of the city's avant-garde – there lies the large and elusive area of Africa's transition to a rediscovery of itself, a rejoining of the past with the present, a regained sense of possibility and reassurance. So it is natural and understandable that the gains of independence may most easily be perceived in terms of the gains, no less real for being subjective, of cultural development.

### Education for equality

Schools and schooling in colonial Africa were, as the records show, at best the product of a high-minded paternalism, and at worst the expression of a

# The fruits of independence

contempt for "raw natives". The prevailing attitude was likely to depend on the nature of the colony in question, as well as of the colonizing power. But no colonized people was ever endowed with a system of education based on attitudes and expectations comparable with those of Europe. Individual teachers from Europe might strive for that kind of equality of treatment and potential, but the colonial governments were universally and sometimes passionately unwilling to agree. Education for Africans was, for the most practical of colonialist reasons, an education for inferiority.

This was always obvious to educated Africans, and many of that small minority said as much. President Julius Nyerere of Tanzania, for example, was only saying what others thought but were seldom ready to state when he recalled in 1967:

> [Colonial education] was not designed to prepare young people for the service of their country. Instead, it was motivated by a desire to inculcate the values of the colonial society, and to train individuals for the service of the colonial state. This meant that colonial education induced attitudes of human inequality, and, in practice, underpinned the domination of the weak by the strong, especially in the economic field.

*President Nyerere of Tanzania: "Colonial education . . . underpinned the domination of the weak by the strong, especially in the economic field".*

Of course there were variations in this "underpinning of the domination of the weak by the strong". Some important educational advances were made in the 1930s in a few of the settler-free West African colonies, notably in the Gold Coast and Nigeria. Yet these were a minority of colonies, while at the other extreme there were many more in which the tenets of an all-embracing European racism governed whatever was attempted in the cultural field. Referring to the Portuguese colonies in 1960, the Patriarch of Lisbon, Cardinal Cerejeira, whose Church controlled most of the schools in Portuguese Africa, instructed the faithful:

> We need schools in Africa, but schools in which we show the native the way to the dignity of man and the glory of the nation [Portugal] which protects him. We want to teach the natives to write, to read, and to count, but not to make them *doutors* [university graduates].

Even in the more advanced of the British and French territories, educational systems were modelled on poor copies of the systems "at home", and were, as Nyerere explained, designed to produce convenient clerks even if, now and then, they were obliged to allow "insolent lawyers" to emerge as well.

The general principle was that all civilization in Africa had begun with the colonial invasions, and everything that had happened there before could be safely consigned to the savage annals of barbarous tribes inhabiting a moral and mental night. All progress must come from Europe, and all useful education must therefore inculcate the God-given superiority of European cultures. Anyone who argued to the contrary was bound to be a nuisance, and was probably a dangerous subversive.

Careful steps were taken, at the same time, to ensure that only a chosen few should receive this education. Large claims to the contrary were made after the anti-colonial agitations had got into their stride in the 1950s, but proved hard to support with facts. For the facts showed that the best of the colonial systems, in this respect, had provided primary school places for about 10 per cent of the 6–20 age group, while the worst (and more numerous) had provided for 3 per cent or fewer. Even in the most favoured colonies the number of primary students who stayed at school for more than one or two years was only a trickle. No more than a fraction of that emergent trickle could then go to secondary school, or, at best, to a secondary school capable of teaching to the level of university entrance or its equivalent.

As late as 1955 there was only one *lycée*, or secondary school preparing

Africans for higher education, in all the territories of French West and Equatorial Africa. Even in the relatively benevolent colonies of British West Africa there were only four such schools, while in British East and Central Africa there were none at all. Great wealth had been extracted from the mines or plantations of many of these colonies; too little had been left behind, in government revenues, for any administration in East and Central Africa to provide even a caricature of the kind of education that would be needed if these countries were to cope with an independent future.

These acute shortages of educational quantity and quality were tackled with vigour after independence, and sometimes with impressive results. Between 1960 and 1972 – before, that is, the world economic recession had begun to bite into revenues and realizations – the number of boys and girls attending school in the then 44 independent countries rose from 17,800,000 to 37,800,000. Upwards of a third of Africa's populations had meanwhile acquired, or been placed in a position to acquire, a practical grasp of literacy: still a low Third World percentage, but a great deal more than there had been 20 years earlier. Even the proportion of girls attending school in this continent of a traditional discrimination against women had advanced from about 33 per cent of all students in 1960 to about 37 per cent in 1972.

After 1972 expansion continued in countries with an appropriate revenue, especially an oil-produced revenue; and several of them, notably Nigeria, moved firmly in the direction of systems of universal national education. There were, not surprisingly, some large discrepancies within this particular transition. An impoverished Upper Volta could provide by the middle 1970s only enough school places for about 10 per cent of its relevant age group, whereas Ghana had achieved 70 per cent. The number of Angolan children in primary schools multiplied by about five times in the six years after independence, although from a very low starting-point, and comparable gains occurred in Mozambique. Several countries governed by militarist clowns could barely show any advance at all. Yet the overall picture was undoubtedly positive, both in terms of quantity and in the creation of non-racist or anti-racist syllabi.

Rapid expansion necessarily threatened the quality of teaching, not least because much of it had to be in French, English and Portuguese, none of which was widely spoken at an adequate level of understanding; but this disadvantage was consistently countered by a large improvement in the content of the lessons that were taught. The humanities were "decolonized", particularly in the area of history, while the teaching of the sciences was begun or enlarged. Fresh literacy campaigns were launched. Higher education, following a tendency throughout Africa for the already educated to assume power and privilege, not surprisingly did best of all: by 1972 there were three students in higher education for every two in 1965 (and the level of 1965 had been almost immeasurably higher than that of 1955), and most students were now in local universities or vocational colleges instead of having go to to Europe or America. Whatever disadvantages this might bring with it, the relatively high production of graduates could now provide a previously unknown sophistication.

**Breaching the barriers of racism**

As the literate population expanded, so did the arts and pleasures that could help to satisfy its needs. The old creativeness that had produced the decorative arts and sculpture of the past began to flourish in a new range of work that tried, at times with a vivid brilliance, to bridge the gap between tradition and modernity. The old arena of legend and folklore began to be filled with the art of poets, dramatists, novelists and singers who found an increasingly appreciative

# The fruits of independence

audience among their own peoples.

Even the newspaper press, although sorely beset by censorious governments or anxious officials, burgeoned in a previously unthinkable variety of prints and journals. And as the crisis of Africa's new political institutions deepened, no few writers and artists were prepared, despite persecution, to speak out against misrule – another sure sign that these cultures had begun to recapture, though now in modern guise, the self-assurance of pre-colonial times.

But that recapture derived above all from another of the gains of independence, something far more pervasive in its influence, though harder to define, than any of the gains in educational or artistic development. It may be too much to say that this central gain consisted of an end to colonial racism, for creatures of that kind seldom die so easily; but it certainly consisted of an end to the systematic applications of colonial racism. There was no longer any ground for supposing that "white rules black" by virtue of a superiority of talent that had to be taken for granted, and often was taken for granted, by blacks as well as whites. The mythologies of racism could be seen for what they really are – aids to alien domination.

The healing consequences were many and widely felt. Looking back to those heady and often hectic days when the imperial flags were taken down, or dragged down, one after another as political independence broadened, one can see this more clearly. What was really happening behind all that noise and scurry of departure and arrival, and somewhere in the subsoil of the consciousness of the times, was a large return to the white-black relationship that had existed in Antiquity and the Middle Ages. On each side of that divide, if with many doubts and hesitations, the consciousness of the times began to move from the familiar acceptance of a natural black inferiority to a new acceptance, which once had been a very old acceptance, of a natural black equality. Across the alienating centuries of the Atlantic slave trade and the dispossessions of colonial rule, people on both sides began to reach towards a common humanity. Whatever the backslidings, this enlightenment may come to be placed among the greatest achievements of the twentieth century.

This restoration of the ancient relationship of "different but equal" was helped along in those years by African participation in the forums of world opinion and discussion. The appointment of African-elected members of the National Assembly of the French Republic in 1946 certainly led the way, even if its significance was little noticed by the world outside. Those who were there at the time were in little doubt that the presence of African deputies in the sovereign parliament of France signalled one of the long-term gains of the anti-Nazi war which had become, by a natural progression, an anti-racist war. Here indeed was one of the real proofs that French civilization had retained its creative vigour through all the squalors of defeat.

Later, and on a wider scene, African participation in the forums of the world was extended by Kwame Nkrumah when, in 1957, newly independent Ghana acceded to membership of the British Commonwealth, and Nkrumah headed a long line of African leaders who would sit as equals with many other prime ministers in the sessions of that organization. For the British, at least, it was something of a crossing of the Rubicon when they were asked to applaud (and naturally did applaud) their monarch's invitation to Nkrumah to visit her castle in Scotland. Nothing, after that, could ever be quite the same again. The mythologies of British racism might still linger in a great many minds; they had ceased to be respectable.

The various agencies and assemblies of the United Nations Organization were a repeated help to the same enlightenment. African men, and even African women, as the years went by, were elected or appointed to international responsibilities such as the director-generalship of UNESCO, a position long occupied by the Senegalese educationist Amadou Makhtar M'Bow – and he was only one of a growing number of Africans who came to occupy comparable positions. A Liberian woman lawyer, Angie Brooks, chaired the general assembly of the United Nations in 1969; Dr Annie Jiagge, a Ghanian high court judge, became vice-president of the World Council of Churches; a Nigerian psychiatrist, Dr T.A. Lambo, was made deputy director-general of the World Health Organization; a leading anti-apartheid spokesman of South Africa, Chief Albert Luthuli, received the Nobel Prize for Peace; and no few others won a worldwide distinction. Any such appointments or conferments would have been impossible only a short time before, and a widespread white opinion would have thought them offensively perverse. Now they were accepted as natural and right.

*Chief Albert Luthuli was awarded the Nobel Peace Prize in 1960.*

Whatever else might derive from the struggles for independence, the barriers of racism were now well and truly breached, and on a wide front. It was an advance which many had looked for with ardent hope, even though rather few may have really believed that it would happen. As the Nigerian soldier Theo Ayoola, serving in India at the close of World War II, had written to the "father of Nigerian nationalism", Herbert Macaulay: "We have seen what we fought for. That is freedom. We want freedom, nothing but freedom." The veteran Macaulay, who had seen so much and waited so long, might have smiled in sceptical sympathy, but his archives, lodged in Lagos University library, contain no evidence of disagreement.

And freedom came. Just how far Private Ayoola will have judged the outcome as being commensurate with his expectations may be another matter. Or it may not: I have found that those of his fellow ex-servicemen with whom I have discussed the point are inclined to a positive view. They do not find the outcome very satisfactory, but have nothing to say against the euphorias of independence, because fervour and high hopes have their place at such a time. As survivors of a tough experience they did not expect Utopia: the argument,

# The fruits of independence

*Senegalese educationist, Amadou Makhtar M'Bow, Director-General of UNESCO.*

for them, was always about achieving the better rather than continuing to suffer the worse. These hard-headed men think that independence did most certainly achieve the better: they even consider it absurd to think the contrary. Their children have been able to live an entirely different sort of life from the one they had known in their youth, and on the whole they judge the change as being solidly to the good.

The gains of independence were real and many; and this is a fact, an absolutely central fact, that needs to be kept in mind when we turn to other sides of the picture.

# Chapter 23

# The legacy

If the Africa of the 1980s had no place for euphoria, this was because a crisis of collapse seemed to threaten on every side. Political troubles were rife, and solutions evidently far from found. Cities had grown out of all control and were increasingly the victims of corruption and worse. Africa was on the road to becoming a continental slum, and even, many feared, quite far along that road. What had gone wrong?

Much had gone wrong, or, more exactly, much had failed to be put right. That is the first point, I thnk, to be clear about: no matter how many of Africa's present miseries are the fault of human frailty, they derive essentially from the legacy that newly independent Africa was obliged to accept: not only from its own pre-colonial past, but, very much more, from its colonial past. The villains of post-independence times might be undeniably villainous, but they were nonetheless actors on a stage which they themselves had not constructed, and figures in a scenario that they themselves had not prepared.

**Factors of disruption**
Late in 1982 I asked the humane and thoughtful president of Tanzania, Julius Nyerere, why his country was in dire economic trouble, and his reply was sombre:

Here in Tanzania we have to spend 60 per cent of our foreign-exchange earnings on essential imports of oil. Another 15 per cent has to go in payment of interest on foreign money we have borrowed for development [in current African terms, as it happens, a rather low indebtedness]. And for all the rest of our needs we are left with a quarter of our foreign-exchange earnings.

Not far from Nyerere's modest house by the seashore stood the principal bus depot of Dar es Salaam, the country's capital. Row upon row of out-of-service vehicles, immobilized by lack of tyres or spare parts, all of which had to be imported, gave their silent comment on the president's reply. Some critics might blame Tanzania's economic troubles on bad state management, or too little state management, or too much, or other administrative failures. But no administration, no matter how skilled or careful, could have kept those buses on the road – save, of course, by immobilizing some other essential enterprise dependent on imports.

Dependence on imported oil, absorbing 60 per cent of foreign-exchange earnings in Tanzania's case, has been a part of the legacy that could be avoided only by the few countries which have found oil of their own: Algeria, Libya, Nigeria, Angola and several others. But dependence on imported food is a very different case.

In historical times Africa had always fed itself, apart from occasional periods of drought or human disaster; and modern Africa remains a largely agrarian

*An open drain runs through one of the many urban slums of modern Africa.*

continent with a predominantly farming population, well able to produce a wide range of cereals and other basic foodstuffs. Yet today Africa no longer feeds itself, nor even nearly so. It relies on ever larger imports of foreign food, including the wheat that African townspeople have come to prize above any of their home-grown cereals, but which Africa cannot grow except in pockets of land here and there. The result can only strike one as a kind of economic lunacy.

By the year 1990, according to Professor Adebayo Adedeji, executive secretary of the UN Economic Commission for Africa, the continent "will be spending as much on the import of wheat as it is now [April 1983], spending on the importation of oil", not to mention a host of other foreign foods now flowing in. Adedeji is no light-hearted prophet of woe, but his prognostications were grim. If many countries up and down Africa were now spending up to one third of all their foreign-exchange earnings on expensive foreign foods, this was clear proof of misgovernment and waste of public funds. Such countries were on the path to deeper ruin. Yet they were being just as surely pushed along it by another and far more stubbornly destructive pressure.

This pressure was an unavoidable part of the legacy of the past: specifically, of the colonial past. The Africa that the colonial invaders found was a land of slowly expanding food production in line with a slow but steady growth of population. At a pre-mechanical level, it possessed all the technologies and skills required to sustain that slow expansion.

But the colonial intrusions ended this productive balance. European demand for "colonial products" such as cocoa, coffee, cotton, or groundnuts, began to have its effects in reducing home-grown production of food – whether by diversion of land or of labour – as early as the 1900s in colonies such as Senegal and Gold Coast (Ghana). Food shortages were being officially noted in these territories, though without any remedial action, by the 1920s. The same trend continued through the 1930s and World War II, when rural food shortages became acute for the first time; and they continued again after that war was over until, by the 1960s, food imports had become a regular annual

*Washing hangs from derelict cars in Kano, Nigeria.*

need. In this way an agrarian continent had lost its most visible and useful means of support.

Another factor of disruption had meanwhile appeared on the scene. Whether to escape a worsening rural poverty or for other reasons linked to it – such as forced-labour exactions in a substantial number of colonies – rural people began flocking to the towns. By the 1970s the towns had grown enormously, and there seemed no way of preventing them from continuing to grow. Whatever the reasons, the rural exodus was now an irresistible flood, and vast numbers of former village people were enclosed in sprawling conurbations.

So it was increasingly the towns, after independence, that dictated the priorities of economic policy; and the new demands of the towns, pushing aside the needs of the countryside, increasingly called the tune. More and more exports had to go in paying for the imports demanded by the towns, whether in wheat or other foreign foods, cars, cosmetics and much else for which the rural peoples had no use. The towns and cities, in short, became the tail that wagged the economic dog, and the rural populations, still in most cases the great majority of all the people, had to suffer for it.

One should note that all the various factors of disruption – and I have sketched only two or three of the more important among them – would have had the same effect and conclusion without colonial withdrawal. There was absolutely nothing in the policies and actions of the colonial powers, down to the day of their political departure, to suggest that they would have averted the onset of crisis. On the contrary, it can be argued that the colonial powers, or at least the chief amongst them, merely handed on to Africans a crisis which they themselves could not resolve. They had unleashed a monster, but preferred that others should set about the killing of it.

Why then was the monster of oncoming crisis allowed to grow and flourish? Why was the legacy not rejected? One answer is that it took some time to discover the real contents of the legacy. By the middle of the 1970s there were several African governments or ruling systems strong and independent enough

# The legacy

*Rush hour in Lagos, Nigeria. The crowded towns of post-independence Africa have increasingly dictated the priorities of economic policy.*

to see the legacy for what it was, and to begin trying to reject it. But many remained far too weak or harassed to think of anything beyond a mere month-to-month survival. Others again – Kenya has been a good case in point – appeared to be doing well enough to suggest that their problems were simply those of early modernization and industrial development. Britain and France, after all, had gone through many troubled years before attaining levels of "high mass consumption" (not counting the unemployed): why should Africans be dismayed by their own troubles along the same road?

This seemed good sense, and foreign advice and expertise appeared to confirm it. Even if a few wise heads had inconveniently seen the realities of the colonial legacy when independence came, an army of foreign advisers, often with imposing academic qualifications, soon shouted them down. What the newly independent countries must do, it was almost universally advised, was to continue what the colonial governments had done before. Only they must do it "more and better". They must achieve "development" by maximizing their export of raw materials and cash crops – precisely the crops which had caused food shortage in the first place.

The advice was generally accepted because it looked so reasonable. If you wanted to "develop" you must accumulate foreign-exchange earnings to buy capital equipment, technological expertise, modern facilities of communication and so on. How could you expect to be able to do that other than by maximizing exports of raw materials and cash crops? Besides, wasn't it obvious that "developed" Europeans and Americans must know better than "undeveloped" Africans? And in any case, what practical alternatives existed? Any such alternative would call for united actions and struggles that might threaten revolution. The new leaders of Africa, when independence spread in the 1960s, were anything but revolutionaries.

Most of the new rulers were townsmen by origin or choice who assumed, fairly predictably, that economic progress must mean progress first and foremost for themselves and those like them: the "educated élite", the natural inheritors of European power, the men and women who understood the world of business. An extreme case, although not so extreme as to be untypical, has been that of Liberia. As early as 1966 a group of very highly qualified American economists, who had been asked to advise on Liberian policy, reached some very unorthodox conclusions.

These economists pointed out that Liberia was "growing, but not developing". The distinction was in fact a crucial one: mere growth of national production need by no means be the same thing as development of the national economy. As it happened, another country still under colonial rule, Angola, was handsomely proving this point in those same years of the 1960s. Through most of that decade the formal indicators of Angolan economic growth were sharply upward in their trend, even though the bulk of the country, much of it in the grip of an independence war, was in a state of ruin or hunger. Mineral exports could well increase while people starved, but it was the mineral exports that got into the statistics. Liberia, in less dramatic fashion, revealed the same contrast.

A continued growth of Liberian exports, these American experts found (and nobody has contradicted them), had gone together with social and economic stagnation for most of the country. This was because "the overriding goal of Liberian authority" was "to retain political control among a small group of families" of black American-settler origin, "and to share any material benefits of economic growth among its own members". So it came about that the colonial legacy of raw material and cash crop exports best suited the convenience of the country's rulers.

This might be called the human factor of disruption, the basic reason for the "mismanagement" that critics like Adedeji have denounced. Among the new ruling strata there increasingly developed a race for personal gain while the devil took the hindmost; and the gap between the few "haves" and the multiplying "have nots" became even wider and more socially destructive. This accompanied the era of what was generally called "corruption" (although the term is too restrictive, for "corruption", as often as not, was the necessary essence of a system and mentality which supposed that public progress could only come from private gain). The burgeoning wealth of the few was to be the guarantee, according to this view, of the welfare of the many.

This situation led to some astonishing scenes. At one point in the 1970s you could stand on the waterfront of the great city-port of Lagos, the federal capital of Nigeria (afterwards moved to Abuja), and see the lights of an altogether new and unknown city clustered on the skyline out to sea. Had some strange Atlantis risen from the waves? Not at all: they were the lights of an anchored armada of cargo ships, filled with European cement for Nigeria and waiting, often for months, for a chance to unload it. In the end much of it had to be sunk in the sea. Nigeria had needed cement, but not in such an avalanche. It had arrived for the simple reason that anyone who managed to bribe or hustle his way to an import permit could telephone Europe for cement, and could be sure, by reason of the import permit, of being able to sell it at a profit. The scandal was immense, but I could never discover that anything much came of it. The beneficiaries, after all, were not without their friends.

That was a situation easily recognized from European or American history; but the results in Africa were bound to be more serious if only because institutions of government were new and faulty. There were those who resented getting poorer while others got rich, and they happened to be far more numerous than the lucky few. Angry voices were heard. Politics grew violent. Regimes foundered or were kicked out of power. The barrel of the gun took over from the ballot box.

## The legacy

*A general view of Lagos, showing slums, skyscrapers, and the sea.*

*General Bedel Bokassa, self-proclaimed emperor of the Central African Empire.*

### A string of troubles

The problems of Africa's political legacy would have been extremely difficult to solve even if all its new leaders had been saints and men of genius. As they were rather seldom anything like that – although quite often they were persons of talent, honesty and courage – the problems were not solved. They merely decayed into upheaval and confusion. Wherever the civilians failed or were shoved aside, the military took over, sometimes labouring with patriotic zeal to bring order out of chaos, at other times bringing new and fearful disasters.

Much could illustrate this. Perhaps the saddest mockery of the hopes of Africa's old nationalist liberators was played out on a December day of 1977, in the capital of what was once Oubangui-Chari, one of the most obscure and poorest of the former French territories of the equatorial region. Oubangui-Chari, as it happened, had produced Barthélemy Boganda, one of the best of the early leaders of French African nationalism; and Oubangui-Chari had duly become the Central African Republic in 1960.

Boganda had died early in the story, and his successors found that the legacy of French rule fitted most happily with their own convenience, besides which they were tied to France by military and financial agreements and obligations. Decay set in and angry tumults duly followed. That was when a former sergeant of the French army, General Bedel Bokassa, installed himself. Possessing absolute power as well as the blessing of France, General Bokassa next decided that the blessing deserved an appropriate compliment. If the mother country could have a splendid emperor in history, why should her little child in the midst of Africa not follow suit?

Recalling Napoleon's glories to the best of his spending power – no small one, given his income from diamonds – Bokassa ordered all the necessary paraphernalia with crown and sceptre, ermine and attendant minstrels, and in scenes of grotesque magnificence had himself crowned Emperor of the Central African Empire, no less, even though its population barely topped 2,000,000 souls, most of them very hungry. It was reliably said that the whole thing cost a quarter of the country's annual earnings in foreign exchange, not counting substantial gifts from the mother country and her Central African diamond corporations. Africa might weep at the spectacle, but the rest of the world, being comfortably unsurprised, enjoyed its laugh. After all, the top hats and morning coats of dignitaries from America's black republic of Liberia had long prepared the scene.

This "Emperor Jones" of Central Africa met with disaster, as did other "imperial marshals" such as the catastrophic Idi Amin in Uganda, but not before some terrible damage was done. The era of corruption coincided with ruthless violence: and yet how could such things happen?

The root political problem was always the same: how to democratize, how to construct a national consensus or unity where none had existed before, how to build a system of self-rule in these new nations defined by colonial frontiers, whereby the majority of people could be involved in choosing and promoting policies, and the executive arm be protected from its own abuse of power?

Each of the colonial powers had governed by an outright and avowed dictatorship, allowing no authority to any of its African subjects save in very limited spheres of local government, and not always even in those. That was the political legacy; and the challenge to the nationalists was to convert colonial dictatorship into popular government. The British and the French, who took the matter seriously, in contrast with the Belgians and the Portuguese, thought that the only right and proper solution was to be found in a transfer of their own parliamentary systems. Let the sacred "models" of Paris and London be installed in Africa, along with useful symbols such as judicial wigs and Speaker's rules; and all would be well.

It was generally forgotten, however, that these "models" relied for successful operation not only on a capacity to use voting procedures – a capacity which Africans had long displayed in their own "models" – but more, and much more, on the nature and structures of French and British society. By 1960, these structures were the outcome of nearly two centuries of industrial capitalism, class differentiation, and huge internal upheavals, revisions, even revolutions, in a history entirely different from anything that had occurred in Africa. They might work well enough at home; but they were certainly not going to work in the former colonies.

The new parliaments fell more or less rapidly, and unavoidably, under the control of those relatively few persons who had the necessary skills and experience, mostly from a modern education. These beneficiaries of national-ism had then to operate in the circumstances that I have briefly sketched above. They failed repeatedly, and for a variety of reasons, some of which I have also outlined. Another of these reasons became known as "tribalism".

**Tribes and "tribalism"**
Wry commentators on colonial racism and its attitudes used to point out that "whereas Europeans have nations, Africans only have tribes". Yet the historical record indicates that if there were nations in Europe before the nationalism of the nineteenth century and its antecedents, there were just as surely nations in Africa before the colonial intrusion. Some of these were solidly conscious of their nationhood. Others were not, and among these were many hundreds of communities which each possessed their own language, sense of identity, and territorial limits recognized by neighbours as well as by themselves. Were these nations, or, if not, what were they?

Europeans found it convenient to call them tribes, and the label stuck. And then, as the colonial period unwound, it was often discovered that there were far too many of these tribes for cheap or easy administration. So quite a number of

# The legacy

*The Biafran war of 1967 (right) brought death and starvation before the Secessionist leader Colonel Ojukwu (far right) was finally forced by Federal victory to call a halt in January 1970.*

them were artificially clustered into new tribes, often with new names unknown to their own history. Over these new tribes were appointed new chiefs, often called "paramount chiefs", through whom colonial power could give its orders. Then tribalized or "re-tribalized" Africans soon enough saw that there could be gains in the process: a spokesman for many people could win a better hearing from colonial power against rival "tribes", than a spokesman for few.

Nigeria, always Africa's great microcosm, offers a clear example of the consequences. Adjusting to the politics of the colonial period, each ethnic community or "tribe" found its best defence in forming a "tribal union" or its equivalent, whose spokesmen could claim a wide support. The enterprising Igbo communities of eastern Nigeria had never been united in their own history, but now they formed an Igbo Union, and were soon followed in rivalry by the large Yoruba communities of western Nigeria. These formed the *Egbe Omo Oduduwa*, or union of the descendants of the Yoruba founding-ancestor Oduduwa. Other communities quickly caught on; and in due course these "tribal unions" or their like became the parents of as many political parties.

In this way the tribalism of the colonial systems of government, superimposed on the historical disunities of the pre-colonial past, was locked into the politics of independence. That being so, the various segments of the ruling groups who inherited Nigeria from British rule were likewise the spokesmen for as many ethnic unions or "tribes", but competing now against each other without the mediation of Britain. This was the rock of ethnic disunity on which the good ship Parliamentary Rule split hopelessly apart.

The shipwreck came in 1966, when the first military coup took place amidst scenes of growing disruption, and was followed by anti-Igbo massacres in the north of the country. This led to the self-defensive secession of eastern Nigeria, where Igbo communities formed a majority, under the name of the republic of Biafra. The resultant war lasted for 27 months, through 1967 to 1970, even though the armies of the Federal government of Nigeria had clearly won the upper hand by December 1968, as the forthright memoirs of the Biafran military commander, General Alexander Madiebo, convincingly show. Thereafter the war dragged on because the Biafran leadership, essentially Colonel Ojukwu, identified the survival of Biafra with its own continuing survival as a governing élite.

A final irony of this civil war, supposedly fought for the good of the Igbo people though increasingly to their cost and loss, was provided by the non-Igbo minorities inside Biafra. These were numerous, and were opposed to the secession because it brought them directly under Igbo majority rule. They sided with the Federal armies and opened the back door of the "Biafran redoubt". So there was no straightforward issue of "tribalism" at stake, but a complex network of local interests and calculations. And this was again confirmed by the way in which peace was made. With its eyes fixed on the needs of Nigerian unity rather than on sectional gains, the Federal leaders made a generous and tolerant settlement. Reconciliation followed. "Tribalism", no matter what snap judgments the outside world might make, was simply not in the picture.

That done, Nigeria set out once more on its search for a viable democracy under constructive military leaders, notably General Murtala Muhamad and General Obasonjo, who were determined to restore a civilian form of parliamentary government. Meanwhile other African countries were embarking on similar experiments, some with more success, others with less. But the legacy of the past has left them no sure and useful guides to democratic stability, and the search seems likely to continue.

Even this brief survey may be enough to show that the condition of Africa in the 1980s, with prospects for the 1990s threatening worse to follow, had a variety of origins, and that some of the most destructive trends have little to do with the frailties of human nature. Such frailties have often made things more difficult, as has the legacy of ethnic rivalry or "tribalism". But the core of the problem lies elsewhere. It consists in Africa's inherited relationship with the outside world, above all with the great industrial powers. If Africa is now in sore crisis, the fault is not only Africa's. It is also, in many ways decisively, the fault of external systems over which Africans have no control. One may therefore ask what these external systems are doing to alleviate or resolve this crisis?

## "North" *versus* "South": rich *versus* poor

The external systems of the "world outside" have continued to look after themselves.

In 1975 a tonne of African cocoa sold to foreign buyers was worth the cost of 148 barrels of oil imported into Africa. In 1980 the same tonne could buy only 63 barrels: in other words, even two tonnes of cocoa could no longer buy the same quantitity of oil that one tonne had bought five years earlier.

A tonne of African copper in 1975 could buy 115 barrels of oil: in 1980, only 58 barrels. A tonne of African cotton could buy 119 barrels in 1975, but only 60 barrels five years later. And so on down the line of Africa's exports.

Commodity prices go up and down, but the general trend of the terms of trade – the relationship between export prices and import prices – has continued to move to Africa's loss. Running harder to maximize its exports, Africa still falls behind.

But perhaps financial or other economic aid from the industrialized countries of "the North" has made up for this continued reduction in the value of the exports of "the South"? Not, certainly, in the case of Africa. Foreign aid to Africa fell steadily in the 1970s, and continued to fall in the 1980s, even though, at te same time, the terms of trade moved continuously to the North's profit and advantage.

Consider only the total value of all the rich countries' assessed and voluntary

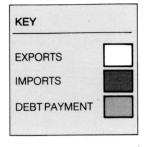

**KEY**

EXPORTS

IMPORTS

DEBT PAYMENT

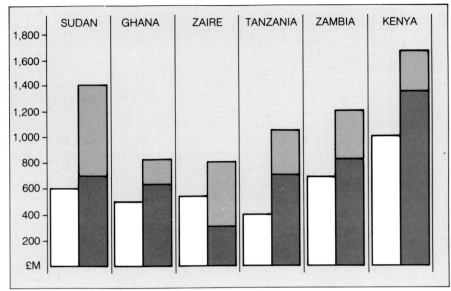

*The ever-growing burden of African indebtedness to the "developed" world.*

contributions to the aid system of the United Nations, in itself a fair indicator of the value of all other forms of aid. One careful estimate has shown that this total, or $3.9 billions shared across a continent, was equal in 1983 to no more than the education budget of one medium-sized European country, Sweden. Another comparison shows that this aid total was about half a billion dollars smaller than the value of dog and cat food sold through American super-markets in 1979. Such comparisons speak for themselves and apply across the whole developed world, whether "Eastern" or "Western".

In 1983 the US Secretary of State forecast that his country's Foreign Aid Bill in 1984 would propose a total of $8.3 billions (apart from another $6.2 billions of US military aid and armaments exported to the third World). This equalled an average of something around $43 per person in the countries towards which the money was directed. Yet it appears to be true that Americans in 1983 spent an average of $35 per person in barber shops and beauty saloons. Some Western countries did rather better than this, notably those of Scandinavia; but the rich world's "generosity", as it was often described, has remained largely verbal.

Seen in this realistic perspective, beyond the mythologies of African "incapacity" or "helplessness", the menacing crisis of poverty has derived, substantially, from a world economic system in which the North, with all its wealth and power, has stood ever more opposed in its policies and interests to the South, especially the newly independent countries with all their poverty and economic weakness. And this remains the toughest reality of all.

# What road ahead?

We have journeyed in this book among splendid monuments and through distant centuries. But what, at the end of it all, can this story of the past mean for people now? What value does it have, what help can it be?

Climb the broadcasting tower that spears into the sky above the bustling city of Lagos, and the view from its pinnacle will suggest that the answer is "no help at all". The vista extending dizzily below belongs entirely to the world of today. The whole horizon facing the sea is enclosed by city districts punctuated by skyscrapers and the full stops of traffic jams. Trucks and cars grapple and crowd the streets and freeways, trumpeting their rivalry and rush. The noise from down there promises no friendship.

If this is success in the modern world, then Lagos certainly has it. Yet what possible connexion can there be with the calm bronzes of Ife and Benin, the slow pageantry of ancient kingdoms, the enchanted walls of Meroe and Zimbabwe? Surely the past is an altogether different country, and therefore the telling of Africa's history can be of no more use than fairy stories from far away, an amusement or a means to an otherwise irrelevant university degree? So it may seem; and yet it appears that history does matter, and matter very much. For the facts indicate that people severed from their own roots are people deprived of the sap and vigour of self-confidence, orphans who must wear someone else's culture even though it fails to fit.

That is what black Americans have said about their plight: the slave trade and slavery severed them from their African roots, and the culture they had to accept proved to have no good place for them. It is what clairvoyant Africans said about themselves during a colonial period which taught them European history and European models, and left them, as one of them complained many years ago, "social hybrids, born into one race and brought up to live like members of another race", eternally in contradiction with themselves. The black peoples, it would seem, greatly need the conscious presence of their own history; and in needing this, they are no different from any other people.

### A lesson from Japan

I was discussing these matters with a colleague who has both lived in Africa and studied the history and culture of the Japanese. How, I asked him, did the development of Japan, the Japanese response to the modern world of industry and science, compare with the African experience?

He replied that the comparison was enormously to the advantage of the Japanese. They too had been very much a "Third World" country when first confronted by the ships and guns of the West. But they had not been colonized or dispossessed; they had not been cut off from their own roots, nor obliged to assume another people's culture. On the contrary, they had defended their own

# What road ahead?

*A shrine at Kaba Kangaba, Mali, built by the Kéita clan many centuries ago, and restored every seven years.*

beliefs and customs, traditions and independence, by a long closing of their frontiers. And so it came about in the 1880s, when the West's industrial skills and mechanical know-how arrived upon the scene, that the traditional culture of Japan proved strong enough to hold its own; and the Japanese were able to absorb industrial technology and science on their own terms. They could modernize, in short, while remaining themselves.

The Japanese today, he went on, stand economically at the head of the list of developed nations:

> But they've felt no need to renounce their past, much less despise it. Their traditions stay whole and healthy in their minds. If you visit the shrines and temples of Japan, you'll see lots of people finding comfort and reassurance there. But they're not just "old believers" lost in sentimental or superstitious awe of the gods of long ago. They're also very modern persons, electronic engineers, doctors, scientists, whatever, and they don't see any problem in reconciling the traditions of Japan with the Japan of now. That's one of their strengths.

The Africans, by contrast, have had no such luck. Colonialism has inserted a broad destructive wedge between them and their past. Over against the value of their own traditions there stretched in stifling discouragement the assumptions of white supremacy, the racism which taught black inferiority, the serried ranks of all those missionaries and masters who condemned African beliefs as "savage ju-ju", and wrote off Africa's achievements as nil or insignificant. And the effects go far.

A modern African equipped with half a dozen degrees and diplomas may still look for comfort and reassurance to the shrines and temples of the gods of long ago. But quite unlike his Japanese contemporary, he will be pretty sure to keep it from his foreign friends or employers. For wouldn't they laugh at him for indulging in "primitive superstition", and wonder if his mind was in good

order? I rather think they would. The African past is not only a different country: it is also, apparently, one to be disowned.

Now if the comparison with Japan has value, as certainly it does, then it follows that an important source of Africa's present confusion, perhaps in the end the most important source, is the loss of historical self-confidence and identity. The recovery of African history becomes essential to the solving of problems specifically African, just as that same recovery can help the rest of us to shed the blinkers of inherited prejudice.

*Women at a PAIGC (Guiné and Cape Verde) meeting during the struggle for independence. PAIGC leaders stressed the need for a mental as well as a material independence from foreign domination.*

Is this to say that Africa has to revert to the past? Some Africans have thought so, and have duly ended in disaster. Back in 1963, at the beginning of the liberation war in the Portuguese colony of Guiné (Guinea-Bissau), there were valiant guerrillas who thought that the Portuguese aircraft which bombed their forest shelters had been "called in by witches". They hunted for these "witches", and several "culprits" were even burned to death. Yet the aircraft kept on coming. Only when these guerrillas turned decisively to modern explanations of reality, as they did in 1964, could their struggle for independence begin to succeed.

The solution for the black continent, as the lesson from Japan confirms, has nothing to do with reversion to the past. It is to know and accept the past as the crucial soil that can nourish the present: in practice, to shape models of society, patterns of community, types of development, which are appropriate to African needs, and not to the needs of some other people in a different continent. It is to build the new on the foundations of the old: not to attempt any repetition of the old, which would be futile, but to develop from their own genius. It seems that this is what the Japanese have been able to do.

Certain African thinkers, grappling with the alienations of foreign teaching and example, have reached the same conclusion. Amílcar Cabral, for instance, talking in 1969 to members of the liberation movement that he had founded, the

# What road ahead?

PAIGC of Guiné and Cape Verde, spoke of the need for "cultural resistance" to foreign dispossession – the effort, that is, to win a mental and therefore eventually material independence. He said:

> We have to scrap colonial culture [the culture of white superiority and black inferiority]. We also have to scrap the negative aspects of our own culture [belief in witches, oppression of women, contempt for literacy] . . . We have to build a new culture that is based on our own traditions, but respecting everything that the world of today has conquered for the service of mankind.

True development therefore comes from mental liberation: and yet how can this unfold in a continent plagued by violence and confusion, as Africa is today? Is there any evidence, as our century nears its end, that can reveal an effort "to build the new from the foundations of the old", to restore and expand the self-development of Africa's past, to bring forth its human potentials? In this complex and continental transition from yesterday to tomorrow, where lies the useful road ahead?

The field for prophecy remains wide open, and there are numberless answers in the plans of experts or the intentions of governments. If these imply reform, then clearly the reform will have to be profound. If they call for revolution – and in many respects, of course, they must – then just as clearly the revolution has to be native born and no kind of import from outside Africa. And let me add in passing that while the "East-West" promotion of rival interests and ideologies has certainly impinged on Africa (though a good deal less than propagandists on either side have liked to suggest) it remains an external influence from which Africa can only be the loser.

Here and there, the effort and experience of Africans who have fruitfully embarked on solutions can already be discerned. It would be easy to look at these in detail, whether in their successes of their setbacks; but they are not yet history, and only the years ahead will reveal their full value. Even now, however, there are signs and indicators of renewal that call for notice, often small in scale but certainly instructive. A scene in Mozambique provides one example.

In Mozambique the colonial cut-off from the past had been especially severe because the Portuguese colonial system was persistently violent and repressive. If any good were to come from the independence won in 1975, a revolution against the means and models of colonial rule was more than desirable: it was altogether necessary. Here it was vital for development that Mozambicans should regain the confidence and self-respect that foreign rule had gone far to destroy. Yet for this kind of revolution, moral and mental in its substance, it was necessary to begin at the beginning: at the roots of society and daily life.

## "A handful of us women . . ."

The scene is a market garden on a peaceful noontime in 1982, near the modern city of Maputo, the capital of Mozambique. My friend Alphaeus Manghezi, who is a careful student of his own people, had proposed the visit. "There's nothing much to be seen," he offered in explanation, "and yet there's everything to be seen. Everything, I mean, that matters."

We stopped the car at a dilapidated wooden gateway set in a low wall of baked mud, got out and looked over the wall. Plots of vegetables covered a couple of acres within the wall. To one side there was a little cluster of cashew trees and a few huts for storage. This being noontime, workers were resting under the trees. They were, I noticed, all women.

"This garden," Alphaeus explained, "was the property of a Portuguese settler who fled back to Portugal when the country became independent seven years ago – one of tens of thousands of settlers who panicked themselves into

*Meeting of a women's farming cooperative in Mozambique: "We have formed a company. And this company works. Here are results."*

leaving at a moment's notice." They could have stayed, but the garden lay ownerless and produced nothing.

"The question was how to get it going again," Alphaeus continued. "In a nutshell, that was the whole and general problem of Mozambique when independence came." The country was at a standstill, producing nothing: how to get it going again? The new regime led by FRELIMO had no intention of attempting this by orders from above, for that would merely reproduce colonial dictatorship in a new form. Mozambicans had been the mere subjects of orders handed down to them: how to lead and help them, now, to shape their own lives, take their own decisions, find their own answers to the problems of production?

"Come and see how these women responded." Alphaeus led through the gate along a path to the cashew trees. As we drew near a worker rose to greet us, a strong peasant woman with a confident look of inquiry: who were we, and what did we want?

She spoke in Shangaan and Alphaeus replied in the same language, which is also his own, translating for me in his fluent English learned while working in neighbouring South Africa. "This woman is the leader of a cooperative, a women's cooperative, that owns and works this garden. She's the *responsável*, as we say here: you'd call her the elected chairperson." We sat down under the cashew trees and the chairperson agreed to tell me about their cooperative.

"A handful of us women began it," she said, "because we wanted to work and we knew how to do this work." She spread her hands and there were sympathetic murmurs from the other women. "But it was like beginning from nothing. Nothing at all. That was our first problem. The garden was ours, FRELIMO gave it to us, but what could we do with it? That Portuguese man left nothing behind him but the soil. God knows what he'd done with the tools, but there weren't any. No tools, no seed, no plants, no anything. So we decided that each of us had to get hold of some tools and seeds. And we brought enough to grow a crop of pumpkins, and we sold those pumpkins and we bought more tools and seeds."

She invited us to be comfortable and listen. The story of their early efforts grips them all: they want it told properly, as it was. There was much back-and-forth discussion in Shangaan, but the shade was cool and there was no need to hurry:

> So we started. Then we ran into our second problem. The men. Our husbands. They were against us having a cooperative of women. They were stuck in the old tradition of dividing work in the family: certain work to be done by men, certain work to be done by women. But we had our own idea.
>
> When we began our cooperative, our men saw that we were going to do things not usually done by women. Such as making decisions about work and money, for you can't run a cooperative without making decisions like that. Our men didn't like it, they didn't agree with it.

They solved this second problem by producing results. "For example, we began rearing chickens and we took home the eggs. The men were surprised: where did the eggs come from? We said we had formed an organization. Yes, we said, we have formed a company. And this company works. Here are results. They began to change their minds."

It was already, in the circumstances, a revolutionary beginning. It rested on the strong African tradition of collective field work, but it thrust hard against an equally strong tradition of female subjection, much reinforced through all the years of colonial rule.

Another woman took up the story: "Well, we thought we'd solved the problem of the men's opposition, but then we had a setback. Our water pump broke down, so our production fell. A man came here and told his wife to go home: you can't stay here, he told her, because you're not producing, you're not earning anything. So that woman pulled out of our cooperative. But we continued, we got our pump mended, and later she came back to us and left the man to go his own way." Sitting across from me, the woman in question nodded her strong assent.

Listening to these women in their cooperative, I decided that this was how I would end the book then forming in my mind. These women may be on the margin of all the big events in Africa now; but, however modestly, they do in fact represent the effort, down at the grass roots where it matters most, to open a way through the confusion of the times. This kind of effort wins no headlines, yet with patience you can track it down in other such scenes as this, often new and still quite rare in Africa today, all the way from Mozambique to Senegal and beyond. Sometimes it has official backing, and prospers; elsewhere it runs into official hostility, and struggles to survive. But it continues with the energy of conviction and confidence.

These women stand on their own ground that is also new ground. They are developing out of their own roots. They are beginning to knit new links between the past and the future.

**A different view**

A familiar view from the outside, well established by all the statistical indicators, is that Africa is steering blindly for the disasters of a vast excess of population beyond the means of its support. The view from the inside can also look like this. Most African populations in the 1980s were increasing at a rate that will just about double their size by the turn of the century, or very soon after. Home-grown food production altogether fails to match this increase, and imported food becomes ever more expensive. Meanwhile the cities continue to absorb new thousands, arriving often from a desolate or demoralized

countryside; and nothing seems able to reverse the flood.

It is possible to see a different view. Here is a half-empty continent which has barely begun to realize its possible resources, or, rather, its possible resources for its own benefit. Mozambique spreads across 16 degrees of latitude with soils and climate that could grow a vast range of tropical and sub-tropical crops, as well as possessing untapped mineral wealth. On any rational and effective system of self-organization, Mozambique could surely support 50,000,000 people; in 1980 it had fewer than 15,000,000.

The old Belgian Congo, now renamed Zaire, is about one-third of the physical size of the USA but with less than one-eighth of the population. Its potential resources could certainly give a good living to a far larger population, if only those potentials could be realized by good government instead of being destroyed by bad government. Its neighbour Angola is much more than twice the size of France but has less than one-seventh of France's population, while its natural wealth includes oil, diamonds, iron ore, manganese, coffee, cotton and much else. The problem for Angolans, again, is how to get it going, how to realize their abundant resources while ensuring that these are used for their own country's benefit.

The cooperative women in their garden outside Maputo may have achieved little beyond proving that they have found out how to realize their own potentials as well as those of the soil they cultivate together. Yet it is certainly a proof worth pondering. It may lie along a line of thought and action, an initiative "begun at the beginning", that will solve far greater problems. It stands, moreover, on the firm ground of the history we have travelled through.

Our journey through time has revealed no period without its miseries, but it has also revealed how Africans, century after century, have realized levels of self-development perfectly compatible with a stable life for a majority of people. The walls of Meroe endured for eight centuries, and were not built on poverty and confusion. The bronzes of Ife and Benin emerged from prosperity and comfort. The caravans of gold were links between well-ordered cities.

What Africa achieved in the past, Africa will in due course achieve again.

*Africa today: a scene at Jenne, Mali.*

275

# *Chronology*

**40,000BC**

Evolution of Homo Sapiens from early types of mankind whose earliest types had probably come from Africa

**8000**

Late Stone Age: origins of human (African) settlement of central Saharan regions and Nile

**5000/4000**

Transition in Saharan/Nile regions to early forms of farming

**4000/3000**

Egyptians begin using ploughs: further development of foundations of Egyptian civilization with emergence of kingships in Nubia and then Lower and Upper Egypt

**3200/2000**

Early period of Pharaonic power
*Minoan civilization in Crete; Hittite empire*

**2100/1000**

Late period of Pharaonic power

**900**

Decline of Pharaonic power

**800/700**

Rise of Kushite power south of 1st Nile cataract

**600/500**

Foundation of city of Meroe; Phoenician city of Carthage now a major Mediterranean power

**500BC**

Origins of iron-working in Nigeria, and nearby regions

Rise of Nok culture (500BC–AD200)

**400/300**

332BC  Alexander of Macedon invades Egypt; beginning of Greek dynasty

**200/100**

Romans greatly extend their settlements in North Africa

**BC 100**

Rise of Axum in Northern Ethiopia

**0–100AD**

Final decline of Egypt; Roman supremacy

**AD 100**

Earliest settlement at Great Zimbabwe: beginning of Iron Age in central & southern Africa

**200**

Further spread of iron-working through regions south and east of the Congo Basin, and south of Limpopo after AD 300

**200/300**

*Collapse of Western Roman Empire.*

**300/400**

End of the city of Meroe, and of Kushite power
*Rise of Eastern Roman Empire: Byzantium*

**600/700**

Conversion of Nubians to Christianity; Nubian kingdoms in area of old Kushite empire

622  Muhammed found Islam in Arabia. His followers soon embark on conquest of neighbouring countries. In 641 they drive the Byzantines (Greeks) out of Egypt, which becomes Muslim state under Arab Government

**700/800**

Rise of Caliphate of Cordoba under Arab and Berber rulers in Spain (al-Andalus)

**850/950**

Early Arab settlements along East African coast; origins of Swahili civilization

Fatimid line of rulers from Tunisia established (969) in Egypt. Foundation of city of Cairo (al-Kahira) on foundations of old city (Fustat)

**1000/1100**

Further development of Iron Age in West Africa; period of founding of new states in the coastal country and inland

Rise of Ife culture (12th–15thC)

First stone buildings at Great Zimbabwe by ancestors of Shona-speaking peoples

*Late Sung Dynasty in China*

Swahili towns begin to be built in stone, and to grow rich as trading intermediaries between inland Zimbabwe kingdoms and trans-ocean markets

## 1100/1200

Beginning of Christian crusades against the Muslims in Palestine and Egypt

1171  Ayubbid line of (Saracen) rulers take over power in Egypt from last of Fatimid sultans

1189  Third Crusade of Western Christians against the Saracens in the Holy Land (Palestine) (1189–92)

## 1200/1300

Crusades provoke war between Christian Nubia and Muslim Egypt

Mamluk, "slave kings" take over power in Egypt

Christian European slave trade in non-Christian Europeans, mainly from Italian city-states (Genoa, Venice) to Egypt and North Africa

Rise of Shona kingdoms in Zimbabwe

## 1300/1400

Decline and gradual disappearance of Christian Nubia under Muslim occupation and influence

Import of West African gold makes it possible for the more advanced of the European states to issue the first European gold currencies since Roman times (beginning with Florentine coins of 1252)

## 1400/1500

Zimbabwe culture at its height. Period of foundation of many kingdoms in central and southern regions

Portuguese sailors reach West African coastlands. English begin trading to West Africa in rivalry with the Portuguese; so do the French, then the Dutch

Benin, W. Africa, at height of power

Formation of new kingdoms in Angola and Congo Basin

1492  *Columbus crosses the Atlantic*

Rise of Luba kingdoms in Katanga (Congo Basin)

## 1400/1500 *continued*

1505  Portuguese raid and burn on East Coast (1505–15)

1515  Spanish planters send home their first cargo of sugar

1518  First cargo of slaves taken directly from West Africa to West Indies

1522  Major African slave revolts in Hispaniola trigger off revolts elsewhere which lead to harsh laws to control slaves

1562  First English cargo of African slaves shipped by Hawkins to Hispaniola

## 1600/1650

Rise of Oyo empire in Nigeria

Portuguese wars of invasion in Angola kingdoms

1602  States General of the Netherlands grants a charter to the Dutch East India Company

## 1650/1700

Origins of Asante Union in Ghana

*Dutch and then English dominate Indian Ocean, pushing aside the Portuguese*

1652  Small Dutch colony founded at the Cape of Good Hope

## 1700/1750

Beginning of Asante empire

Rise of Lunda kingdoms in Kasai region (Congo Basin)

1739  Treaty made in Jamaica in which the British give the rebel blacks their freedom

## 1750/1800

The Industrial Revolution in England begins, greatly helped by capital accumulated from slave trade and American plantation economy

1779  European settlers in South Africa begin a long series of wars of expansion to north and east of Cape Colony

1787  Sierra Leone founded as home for African men and women freed from slavery

## 1750/1800 *continued*

1789  French Revolution, promoting slave revolution in Haiti under Toussaint l'Ouverture

1791  Foundation of Freetown in Sierra Leone

1796  *Period of Napoleonic wars begins in Europe (1796–1815)*

1798  Mungo Park (Scots explorer) reaches Niger

Napoleon briefly invades Egypt

## 1800/1850

1804  Church Missionary Society begins educational work in Sierra Leone

Fulani conquest of Hausa kingdoms in northern Nigeria, completed in 1811; Muhamad Bello, Sokoto, becomes Amir al-Mumenim

1806  Cape Colony becomes a British possession (after defeat of French at Trafalgar in 1805)

1807  British outlaw the slave trade in British ships; British navy is used to stop the Portuguese and other slavers' ships and send their captives to freedom in Sierra Leone

1822  Freed blacks from USA found Liberia

1830  Rise of new slave trade in East Africa, chiefly by Zanzibar Arabs and Portuguese

French invade Algeria

1836  Afrikaners in Cape Colony trek north to escape British control

1837  *Queen Victoria succeeds to the throne of England*

1848  *Revolutions in Europe*

## 1850/1900

1859  Suez Canal opened

1861  British annex Lagos Island in Nigeria

1861  *American Civil War (1861–65)*

1867  Diamonds found in S. Africa

1874  First British invasion of Asante

1880  First Anglo-Boer War

1881  French occupy Tunisia

1884  South African goldfields opened

## 1850/1900 continued

| | |
|---|---|
| 1884 | Congress of Berlin between European powers leads to the colonial partition "Scramble for Africa" (1884–85) |
| 1890 | British take East Africa |
| | Germans take Tanganyika |
| 1896 | British occupy Kumasi in Asante and annex Asante in 1901 |
| 1896 | Ndebele and Shona resist British occupation (1896–97) |
| 1898 | British destroy the Sudanese power of the Mahdi at Omdurman, near Khartoum |
| 1899 | Second Anglo-Boer War (1899–1902) |

## 1900–1950

| | |
|---|---|
| 1908 | Belgians take Congo |
| 1910 | Union of S. Africa (Cape, Natal, Transvaal, Orange Free State) |
| 1912 | French take Morocco |
| 1913 | Africans debarred from owning land in almost all S. Africa |
| 1914 | First World War (1914–18) |
| 1917 | *Russian Revolution leads to establishment of USSR* |
| 1919 | British take over Tanganyika from Germany as a "mandated territory" |
| 1923 | Britain hands over power in Southern Rhodesia to local white settler community |
| 1931 | *Great Britain, Canada, Australia and New Zealand form the Commonwealth* |
| 1935 | Italian invasion and occupation of Ethiopian empire (1935–41) |
| 1939 | Second World War (1939–45) |
| 1940 | *Desegregation of Armed Forces in USA* |
| 1945 | *United Nations founded as successor to League of Nations* |
| 1948 | Afrikaner National Party forms Government in South Africa; gradual replacement of less rigid discrimination by full-scale apartheid |
| 1949 | *North Atlantic Treaty Organization (NATO) formed* |

## 1950/1980

| | |
|---|---|
| 1951 | Libya becomes independent under Sanussi King |
| 1952 | Rise of new nationalism in Egypt, and Gamal Abdal Nasser becomes president (1954) |
| 1953 | Settler-ruled Federation of Central Africa formed (S. and N. Rhodesia and Nyasaland) |
| 1956 | Morocco and Tunisia become independent |
| | Sudan becomes independent |
| 1957 | Ghana becomes independent under leadership of Kwame Nkrumah |
| 1958 | *European Economic Community founded* |
| | Guinea becomes independent |
| 1960 | Belgians withdraw from the Congo. Nigeria and many French colonies become independent |
| 1961 | Republic of South Africa formed, under Afrikaner Government, outside British Commonwealth |
| | Sierra Leone and Tanganyika become independent |
| 1961 | Angolan war of independence against Portugal (1961–74) |
| 1962 | Uganda and Algeria become Independent |
| 1963 | Federation of Central Africa dissolved |
| | Kenya becomes independent under leadership of Jomo Kenyatta |
| | Organization of African Unity formed (OAU) |
| | *President Kennedy assassinated* |
| | Guinea-Bissau War of independence against Portugal (1963–74) |
| 1964 | Zambia, Malawi and The Gambia independent (1964–65) |
| | Mozambique war of independence (1964–1975) |
| 1965 | Rhodesian settlers rebel against Britain and declare "unilateral independence (1965–1980) |
| 1966 | Basutoland becomes independent as Lesotho, Bechuanaland as Botswana |

## 1950/1980 continued

| | |
|---|---|
| 1967 | Nigerian Civil War, won by Federal armies against secession of Biafra (1967–1969) |
| 1968 | Swaziland becomes independent |
| 1969 | Disastrous drought in countries of Sahel (1969–1974) |
| 1971 | General Idi Amin Dada siezes power in Uganda |
| 1974 | PAIGC declares independence of Guinea-Bissau |
| | Revolution in Ethiopia; Haile Selassie dethroned |
| 1975 | End of Portuguese empire in Africa; Mozambique, Angola, Sao Tome and Cape Verde Island declare independence |
| | October 1975. South Africa invades Angola, but compelled to withdraw by Angolan resistance (March 1976) |
| 1976 | Internal resistance to apartheid in South Africa intensifies. Mass protests in large African towns |
| | Spain withdraws from its W. Saharan colony, and hands over territory for division between Morocco and Mauritania |
| 1976 | Hostilities between Somalia and Ethiopia; Somalia goes to military aid of Somali nationalists in Ethiopian-occupied Ogaden province of old Ethiopian empire; Ethiopians win with Soviet and Cuban military aid (1976–77) |
| 1978 | South Africa embarks on new invasions of Angola, and on subversive terrorism in Mozambique |
| 1980 | Nigeria returns to civilian rule under President Shehu Shagari |
| | New Republic of Zimbabwe emerges under nationalist government, with Robert Mugabe as prime minister |
| | Civil war in Chad as consequence of previous Tombalbaye dictatorship |

# *Bibliography*

The study of African history came of age, on a scientific basis, early in the 1960s, and the list of important books on the subject published since then is long and various in many languages. New readers of mine who may wish to enter deeply on their reading could begin by consulting the various volumes in the *Cambridge History of Africa*, published by Cambridge University Press, and the *Unesco General History of Africa*, published by Heinemann Educational Publishers and the University of California Press. For others who wish to extend their general knowledge without specialized study, the following list offers a brief preliminary guide to useful books in English, many of which have extensive bibliographies.

Ajayi, J.F.A. and Crowder, M., *History of West Africa*, 2 vols. London, 1971/1974.

Amin, S., *Neocolonialism in West Africa*. London, 1973.

Adamu, M., *The Hausa Factor in West African History*. Ibadan and Oxford, 1978.

Barbour, N.A., *A Survey of North West Africa*. London, 1959.

Bender, G.J., *Angola under the Portuguese*. London, 1978.

Brett, E.A., *Colonialism and Underdevelopment in East Africa*. London and New York, 1973.

Curtin, P.D., *The Atlantic Slave Trade*. Madison and London, 1969.

Curtin, P. D.; Feierman, S., Thompson, L. and Vansina, J., *African History*. Boston and London, 1978.

Davidson, B.D., *Africa in History: Themes and Outlines*. London, 1972/1984.

Davidson, B.D., *Africa in Modern History*. London, 1978.

Davidson, B.D., *Black Mother: Africa and the Atlantic Slave Trade*. London, 1980.

Fage, J.D.A., *A History of Africa.* London, 1978.

First R., Steele J., and Gurney C., *The South African Connection*. London, 1973.

Gardiner, A., *Egypt of the Pharaohs*. Oxford, 1961.

Iliffe, J.A., *Modern History of Tanganyika*. Cambridge, 1979.

Inikori, J.E. (ed.), *Forced Migration: Impact on Africa of the Slave Trade*. London, 1982.

Karugire, S.R., *History of Uganda*. Nairobi and London, 1980.

Mason, P., *The Birth of a Dilemma* (on the history of Rhodesia). London, 1961.

Munslow, B., *Mozambique: The Revolution and its Origins*. London, 1983.

Shinnie, P.L., *Meroe*. London, 1967.

Trigger, B., *Nubia under the Pharaohs*. London, 1976.

Troup, F., *South Africa: A Historical Introduction*. London, 1975.

*Unesco, Racism and Apartheid in South Africa*. Paris, 1974.

Willet, F., *Ife in the History of West African Sculpture*. London, 1967.

# Index

becomes independent of Portugal
(1975), 238
Probyn, Gen.
photographed with staff, Freetown
(c.1910), 206

# Q

Qustul, Nubia
excavation of royal cemetery, 26
finds from, *26, 27*

# R

Racism, 17–18, 208, 241
absent in Middle Ages, 45–6, 116
*apartheid*, see South Africa
breaching barriers of, 255–8
develops with slave trade, 142–4
European belief in negro's
inferiority, 15–17, 49, 205–6, 241
paternalism, 206
*Rassemblement Démocratique Africain*
(RDA), 227
Reubeni, David
visits Soba, Nubia (1525), 45
Rhapta, Tanzania, 118
Rhodes, Cecil, 175, 191
colonial career: gains control of S.
African mining concessions, 176;
wish to gain concessions in
Matabele territory, 176, 177;
secures charter for British S.
Africa Company, 178, 179;
threatens Matabele land with
armed column, 179–80; takes
possession of Mashonaland, 180;
invades Matabele territory, 181;
founds Rhodesia, 182
device of labour tax, 181–2
Rhodesia
foundation of, 182
Robinson, Kenneth, 66
Romans
and African trade, 90
Roosevelt, Pres. Franklin D., *218,* 219
Rorke's Drift, siege of (1875), 163
Ross, Capt., 186
Royal Geographical Society, 167, *168*
Ruiters, Dierick
reports on Benin (c.1600), 77

# S

Sabaean civilization, South Arabia, 37
St Maurice of Thebes, 45, *114*
black statue in Magdeburg, 45, *46*
St Philip
preaches to official of Queen of
Kush, 36
Saladin
recaptures Jerusalem, 44

Salazar, Oliveira, 237
Salisbury, Lord, 188
on "scramble for Africa", 183–4
Sahara
colonists from, 22–3
green land becomes dry, 22, 23
*harmattan* dust storms, *101*
Stone Age people of, 22
Tassili plateau, *24*
engravings of, 22, 23, *24, 25*
trans-Saharan trade, 90, 102, 108,
110, 134
map, *86*
staging posts, *88*
Sahel, 83, 118, 154
drought, *252*
tellers of history in, 83
Sandele, Mr
ill-treatment by Portuguese in
Angola (1940–3), 211
São Tomé island, 237
employment of slaves on sugar
plantations (16thC), 135
gains independence from Portugal
(1975), 238
Seele, Keith, 26
Ségou, R. Niger, 151, 153, *153*
Selous, Frederick, *180*
Senegal, 226
Senghor, Léopold Sedar, 227
Shaba, Congo
early kingship, 71
state in 19thC, 157
tries for independence (1960), 235
Shaka, King of the Zulus, 162, *162,*
176
military ability, 162–3
Sheba, Queen of, 13, *39,* 40
Shippard, Sir Sydney
on King Lobengula, 177
Shona people, Mashonaland, 69
importance of ancestors to, 46
invaded by British (1890), 180
lose land and cattle, 182
oral history, 69
"rebellion" of 1896, 181
Sierra Leone, 205, 221
freed slaves in, 170, *171*
gains independence of Britain (1961),
226
Sijilmasa, Morocco, 89
trade with Ghana, 90
Sindbad the Sailor, 119
Slave trade, 16, 17, 105–6
East African, (18th–19thC), 169, *170,*
170–2
European export to Africa, 113
loss of slaves' skills to Africa, 148
medieval E. African, 122
supplying New World, 137–42, 143–
auctioning, *147*
bill of sale (1835), *146*
branding of slaves, 144, *144*
consequences for Africa, 146–8
deaths on passage, 145–6

numbers of slaves, 147
transport, 144–6, *146*
unequal trading exchange for
Africa, 148–50
W. African, 135–6
Slavery, 105–8
cost of, 107–8
"king's men" slaves, 107
life of slaves, 106–7, 135
medieval, *106*
Smith, Ian, 240
Smuts, Jan, *164,* 165
Sofala, Mozambique, 120
gold of 122
map showing (16thC), *126*
Sokoto, Nigeria
market place (1853), *155*
Solomon, King, 13
"King Solomon's Mines", 11, 13, 66,
176
supposed connection with Queen of
Sheba and Ethiopia, *39,* 40
Somalia
banana plantations, 199
Italian campaigns in, 183, 191
Italians defeated in (1941), 217
Songhay, empire of, middle Niger, 91,
131, 154
decline of gold trade and (1575), 134
Soninke people, Ghana, 91, 100
Soromenho, Castro
*Camixilo,* 191
South Africa
*apartheid* in, 166, 242, *243,* 243–5,
248
"Bantu Homelands" (Native
Reserves), 166, 244, *244,* 245, 248
school (1920s), *165*
black protest in, 245–8
African National Congress (ANC),
246, 248
Black Consciousness movement,
247
Langa clash, 246
Pan-African Congress (PAC), 246
Sharpeville clash, 246
Soweto riot (1976), *249*
Dutch farmers (c.1801), *160*
historical events: arrival of Dutch
settlers (1652), 159; local black
inhabitants on Dutch arrival, 159;
"Kaffir wars", 159–60, 161; British
settlers (19thC), 160; banning of
slavery, 160; founding of Cape
Colony, 160; Dutch "Great Trek"
north (1836), 160, *161;* founding
of Boer republics, 160; Boer War,
160–1, 164–5; Act of Union
(1910), 165
Land Act (1919), 165–6, 202, 243
militarized system today, 248, 250
Ox wagon, *161*
Southern Rhodesia, 203
declares unilateral independence
(1965), 239